FORCED OUT AND FENCED IN

FORCED OUT AND FENCED IN:
IMMIGRATION TALES FROM THE FIELD

A Collection of Essays
Edited by Tanya Golash-Boza

New York Oxford
OXFORD UNIVERSITY PRESS

Oxford University Press is a department of the University of Oxford.
It furthers the University's objective of excellence in research,
scholarship, and education by publishing worldwide.
Oxford is a registered trademark of Oxford University Press in the UK
and certain other countries.

Published in the United States of America by Oxford University Press
198 Madison Avenue, New York, NY 10016, United States of America.

For titles covered by Section 112 of the US Higher Education
Opportunity Act, please visit www.oup.com/us/he for the
latest information about pricing and alternate formats.

Library of Congress Cataloging-in-Publication Data

Names: Golash-Boza, Tanya Maria.
Title: Forced out and fenced in : immigration tales from the field /
Tanya
Maria Golash-Boza.
Description: 1 | New York : Oxford University Press, 2017. | Includes
bibliographical references.
Identifiers: LCCN 2017007205 | ISBN 9780190633455 (paperback)
Subjects: LCSH: United States—Emigration and immigration—Government
policy.
| Emigration and immigration law—United States. | Immigration
enforcement—United States. | Deportation—United States. | Illegal
aliens—United States. | Illegal aliens—United States—Anecdotes. |
BISAC: SOCIAL SCIENCE / Sociology / General. | SOCIAL SCIENCE /
Emigration
& Immigration.
Classification: LCC JV6483 .G638 2017 | DDC 325.73—dc23 LC record
available at https://lccn.loc.gov/2017007205

9 8 7 6 5 4 3 2 1
Printed by LSC Communications Inc. Printed in the United States

Table of Contents

Foreword

Robert Lovato

A new age of US migration is upon us. Its colors and contours are abundantly clear: dark, shadowy, relentless, duplicitous. Amidst the darkness, only one light still shines: that of the migrant.

As a longtime former activist, as a journalist and writer and as a permanent student of immigration, I rank the work of Tanya Golash-Boza among the most consequential, in terms of mapping the darkness while also finding the Real Hope (as opposed to the multi-billion dollar "Hope" that deported 3 million, mostly non-criminals). Because of this, I responded immediately to the invitation to write the foreword for Tanya's next foray into the new world of US migration, *Forced Out and Fenced In: Immigration Tales from the Field.*

The book raises up the stories of the real people hidden behind layer upon layer of racist language and racist policies thrust upon migrants by both Democrats and Republicans in the immigration nightmare cynically described as a "bipartisan consensus": millions of deportations, hundreds of thousands of non-criminals jailed, thousands pushed to their deaths by the weaponized desert, jailing children and mothers fleeing rape, murder and other extreme violence, to name a few of the more salient contours of this new age in US migration.

I've spoken with Salvadoran and Honduran mothers and their children. Their twitching eyes, their involuntarily shaking arms and hints of hope are the most powerful testament to the dark moment in migration politics. *Forced Out and Fenced In: Immigration Tales from the Field* tells their story, deepens it and provides the kind of incisive analysis I have come to expect from Tanya Golash-Boza.

During my travels and reporting, I've also met and interviewed men, women and children fleeing the ongoing crisis in Mexico. Like Tanya, I've also traveled to Mexico and have watched as the Bush and Obama Administration's and their partners in the Mexican government turned Mexico, a country that had no military, into a country whose landscape is dotted with thousands of mass graves dug during the drug war by cartels and back-to-back Mexican governments, since 2006. I saw the US turn relatively peaceful Mexico into the wartime country of my parents, El Salvador. I've also watched as the victims of this violence and of the economic and cultural violence of NAFTA and other US policies are greeted by persecution, jailing, and record-breaking deportations like those of Barack Obama.

Golash-Boza, a tireless and prolific scholar, has spent a decade chasing shadows, finding people who have lived in the shadows for so long that they became shadows, immigrants in Bush and Obama's "America." *Forced Out and Fenced In: Immigration Tales from the Field* provides first-hand accounts of individuals and families torn apart by the cruel policies that began with Bill Clinton, continued with George Bush and were then expanded to record-breaking levels by Barack Obama—all of whom laid the foundation on which Donald Trump will build walls of continued and expanded death, exploitation and racism.

Golash Boza's ethnographic work is crucial at a time when the voice of the immigrant is the least-heard voice in the sea of Republican and Democrat talking heads, non-profit "leaders" and journalists whose reporting reads like they don't even read the immigration legislation proposals and policies they're talking about. In this context, *Forced Out and Fenced In: Immigration Tales from the Field* comes as a welcome dose of reality to an "immigration debate" that is largely devoid of reality.

Lost in the hyper-falsity of the immigration discourse is any sense of what the daily life of the human beings most impacted by the debate and the increasingly violent and punitive immigration policies that result; the children who wake up to violent raids only to watch heavily-armed men and women drag their parents off to jail; the immigrant worker exploited and living under the perpetual fear of deportation; asylum seekers who, under fair conditions would be treated as the victims they are, but are instead treated like liars and criminals. *Forced Out and Fenced In: Immigration Tales from the Field* tells these and other stories. And, in so doing, Tanya Golash-Boza provides us all not just a window into the lives of immigrants, but also a mirror into a country striking out at its immigrant self.

Introduction: Forced Out and Fenced In

Tanya Maria Golash-Boza

In 2013, over 400,000 people were deported from the United States. I can tell you this is the highest number of deportations ever recorded in a single year, but 400,000 is after all just a number. Who were these 400,000 people? What happened to them after they were deported? Who else was affected by their deportations? What happens if they return to the United States subsequent to a deportation?

Forced Out and Fenced In tells the stories of people who have been deported, whose families have been torn apart by deportation, and whose lives are regulated by the fear of deportation. These narratives help us to understand how laws structure our lives. Legal status is a textbook case of sociolegal construction: Whether a person lives in a country legally or illegally is a function of how the law is written. An undocumented person can become documented with the stroke of a bureaucratic pen, and vice versa. Without this pen stroke, however, undocumented people live in fear of deportation.

There are currently 11 million undocumented people residing in the United States. Although you do not have to be undocumented to be deported, undocumented people are at the highest risk for deportation. How have record-breaking deportations affected them and their families? How do immigrants and their families cope with "illegality" and the possibility of deportation?

Anthropologist Nicholas De Genova (2004, 161) argues that the "legal production of 'illegality' provides an apparatus for sustaining Mexican migrants' vulnerability and tractability—as workers—whose labor-power, inasmuch as it is deportable, becomes an eminently disposable commodity." There is a lot to unpack in this sentence that will be relevant for discussions in this book. First of all, De Genova mentions the "legal production of 'illegality,'" calling our attention to how legal status is produced by law. Being undocumented is not a natural state—it is a condition produced by laws. Secondly, De Genova speaks to the ways illegality is racialized by pointing out that people often conflate being Mexican with being undocumented. Even though US laws do not specify that only Mexicans should be policed for their immigration status, people from Mexico are the imagined (and real) targets of immigration law enforcement in the United States. Finally, De Genova contends that illegality produces deportability and hence disposability. By deportability, he means that not all potentially deportable immigrants are actually deported, yet that the possibility of deportation shapes the lives of all undocumented immigrants. Immigration laws work to make undocumented immigrants "disposable" insofar as they are easily replaced with new workers. This explanation of what illegality, deportability, and disposability are will be useful as you read the essays in this volume.

When we think of illegality, it is important to remember that this is a status people can move in and out of. If, for example, a person comes to the United States from India on a temporary work visa, they have entered the country legally and have the legal right to live and work here. If, however, they lose their job, or if their visa expires and they do not return to India, they become undocumented. Conversely, if a Dominican entered the United States without permission in 1980, yet married a US citizen in 1984, they could have attained legal status and be a US citizen today. The extent to which a person can move in or out of legal residency status is a function of US immigration laws.

Immigration laws in the United States are complex and it can be difficult for non-citizens to attain legal status. These laws, nevertheless, have no explicit race or gender provisions. In US immigration law, whether you are black or white, a man or a woman, has no legal bearing on your ability to attain legal status. Whereas people once could be barred from legal entry and citizenship based on their national origin (which were effectively racial bans), those laws have been struck down and replaced with racially neutral laws. Whereas immigration laws at one time had provisions that favored men and marginalized women, those provisions no longer exist. The current version of the Immigration and Nationality Act, which constitutes the body of immigration laws in the United States, does not include any provisions that explicitly discriminate based on gender or race. Nevertheless, its most draconian provisions tend to be applied more frequently to nonwhites and to men. Although all undocumented migrants are technically deportable, Mexican and Central American undocumented migrants have by far the highest rates of deportation (Golash-Boza 2012).

In the United States, 97 percent of deportees are sent to Latin America or the Caribbean and 90 percent of deportees are men (Golash-Boza and Hondagneu-Sotelo 2013). As Melvin Oliver and Thomas Shapiro (2006) explain, laws can create racial disparities in the absence of racially discriminatory language. Insofar as laws, policies, and institutions create inequitable outcomes in their implementation, they can be considered part of the institutional racism that has always been a core element of US society (Feagin 2000). As we will see in these essays, deportation laws are draconian. It is thus worth noting that they primarily target black and brown men.

As De Genova (2004) explains, deportability structures the lives of undocumented migrants in the United States, rendering them vulnerable to exploitation. Although all non-citizens are potentially deportable, most immigrants will never be deported. Although some politicians claim that, if elected, they will deport every single undocumented migrant, these claims are fantastical. A closer look at the numbers makes this clear. There were 400,000 deportations in 2013, yet this is the sum total of migrants removed in border regions (border removals) plus those removed from inside the United States (interior removals). A removal is a deportation that involves a court process, and an interior removal is a deportation involving a person who is arrested inside the United States and is not a recent border-crosser. The highest number of people ever deported from inside the United States in a given year is 237,941. That was the number of "interior removals" reported by the Department of Homeland Security's Immigration and Customs Enforcement (ICE) in 2009.[1] Keep in mind that those 237,941 undocumented immigrants expelled from the country represented a far higher number of interior removals than had ever previously been reported. Before 1995, there were never more than 50,000 total removals (including people caught crossing the border). At the record-high rate of 237,941 interior removals a year, it would take forty-six years to remove all 11 million undocumented migrants from the United States—and that's assuming no additional migrants enter the country. Mass deportation tears families apart and creates fear in migrant communities. It is not designed to remove all undocumented migrants. What purpose, then, does deportation serve? The stories in this volume will help us to answer this question.

It is worth noting that the patterns for interior removals are similar to broader deportation patterns. Ninety-four percent of interior removals involve men, even though women account for 47 percent of undocumented immigrants in the United States. And 88 percent of interior removals involve people from just four countries: Mexico, Guatemala, Honduras, and El Salvador, even though nationals from these countries only make up 66.3 percent of undocumented migrants (Passel and Cohn 2014; Rosenblum and McCabe 2014). Both border and interior removals primarily target black and brown men.

Deportations were a relatively rare phenomenon until the end of the twentieth century. According to annual reports produced by the Office of Immigration Statistics, the first year deportations were recorded was 1892, ten years after the passage of the Chinese Exclusion Act. In 1892, 2,801 people were deported from the United States. Over the next hundred years, deportations fluctuated, peaking around 35,000 in 1924 and again in 1954 and 1976, and then a marked increase from 70,000 in 1996 to 114,000 in 1997. Deportations have been on the rise ever since.

Peaks in deportation numbers also coincide with key moments in US legal and political history. The Immigration Act of 1924 greatly reduced immigration from Southern and Eastern Europe by introducing quotas, or limits, on the number of people from these countries allowed to enter the United States. In that same year, Congress passed the Oriental Exclusion Act and created the Border Patrol. The Border Patrol's massive roundups of Mexicans, a series of operations which would come to be known as Operation Wetback, culminated in 1954 and involved the return of about a million Mexicans to their home country (Hernández 2010). The 1965 immigration law set an annual quota for Mexican immigrants at 120,000—the first time there had ever been numerical restrictions on Mexican immigration. In 1976, the quota for Mexico was reduced to 20,000. This quota reduction did not affect the annual flow of Mexicans to the United States; it simply forced most Mexicans to enter the United States illegally (Massey, Durand, and Nolan 2002).

The year 1986 is critical because the Immigration Reform and Control Act (IRCA) was passed, which legalized more than 2 million undocumented immigrants, required employers to verify their workers' eligibility to work legally, and made it illegal for employers to knowingly hire undocumented immigrants. That year was also the last time a major legalization bill was passed. Since 1986, immigration laws have been largely punitive, especially the 1996 laws. Two laws implemented that year—the Anti-Terrorism and Effective Death Penalty Act (AEDPA) and the Illegal Immigration Reform and Immigrant Responsibility Act (IIRIRA)—fundamentally changed the rights of all foreign-born people in the United States. These laws were punitive for migrants in that they eliminated judicial review of some deportation orders, required mandatory detention for many non-citizens, and introduced the potential for the use of secret evidence in certain cases. The year 1996 marked the beginning of the era of mass deportation in the United States, where deportations rose each year until they hit a peak of 435,498 in 2013. In 2014, the number of annual removals began to slowly decline. As of this writing, the latest reports from the Office of Immigration Statistics show that there were 414,481 removals in 2014, 333,341 in 2015, and 408,870 in 2016. With Donald Trump in the Presidency, removals are widely expected to increase in 2017.[2]

While undocumented migrants must worry about being forced out, they also are fenced in. Undocumented migrants are prevented from returning to their countries of birth because of the very real fear that they may never be able to return to their homes in the United States. Since the last major legalization program was IRCA, passed in 1986, many people have been in the United States for twenty or thirty years and have never had the opportunity to legalize. The current historical moment is unique because we have a large population of settled migrants who have no option for legalization. In prior times, there were many more options for settled migrants to legalize. Unlike in times past, having US-born children or even a US-citizen spouse does not always mean that an undocumented migrant has a pathway to legalization. The passage of increasingly stricter laws since 1986 and the lack of an amnesty since that same year means that millions of settled undocumented migrants are fenced in and also must live with the fear of being forced out.

Acknowledgments

I decided to create *Forced Out and Fenced In* because I had an abundance of rich stories from my research with deportees that I wanted to share. As I thought about how to get these stories out to a broader audience, I asked myself if other researchers might also have stories that needed to be told. When I reached out to my colleagues, I received an enthusiastic response both regarding the desire to tell these stories and to hear the stories of others affected by immigration law enforcement. This enthusiasm then translated into what might be the most seamless production of an edited volume in the history of book publishing.

Edited volumes are notorious for being difficult to put together, so I am tremendously grateful to everyone who facilitated the production of *Forced Out and Fenced In*. The editorial team at Oxford, the contributors, and the reviewers have made this process smooth and I daresay enjoyable.

I cannot thank the contributors and the Oxford University Press editor, Sherith Pankratz, enough, not only for their enthusiasm but also for keeping this project moving forward without a single delay. This edited volume has come about in what must be record time due to their extraordinary efforts.

This volume took only a year to put together—practically lightning speed in academic publishing. In early September 2015, I sent a note to Oxford University Press editor Sherith Pankratz to ask if she might be interested in an edited book on immigration enforcement. She said she was. In mid-September, I sent a query out to twenty-five scholars. By mid-October, twenty-one of them responded and said they were willing to contribute essays. The other four politely declined. I wrote a full proposal and sent it to Sherith, along with a sample contribution. She got back to me with reviews in mid-December 2015. By January 2016, we signed a contract.

I then reached out to the contributors and asked them to send me their contributions by mid-March. If you have ever worked with academic authors, you will find the next sentence surprising. All of them sent in their chapter drafts on time. We sent the full manuscript out for review, asked the authors for revisions, and they consistently met every single deadline multiple times. This is practically unheard of in academia. By mid-October 2016, every single author had sent me the final version of their chapters and we were able to get this book into production by the end of November

2016. With an anticipated publication date of Fall 2017, that is about two years from idea to publication—which must break all kinds of records for edited volumes in academia. I feel fortunate to have secured contributors who are not only at the top of the field, but are also timely and responsive.

The project was also able to be completed in record time thanks to the sixteen reviewers who gave speedy and tremendously helpful feedback both on the proposal and on the full draft of the book manuscript. I am forever grateful to these esteemed and collegial reviewers: Aviva Chomsky, Salem State University; Louis DeSipio, University of California–Irvine; Aldo Garcia-Guevara, Worcester State University; Alfonso Gonzales, University of Texas–Austin; Josiah Heyman, University of Texas–El Paso; Michael Innis-Jiménez, University of Alabama; Nicole Lambert, University of Colorado–Boulder; Hans Leaman, Yale University; Alejandra Marchevsky, California State University–Los Angeles; Steven P. Miller, Webster University; Anna Ochoa O'Leary, University of Arizona; and five anonymous reviewers. Sarah Calabi's edits helped transform the manuscript into a cohesive work. I am also grateful to the production team who have shepherded this project through efficiently and effectively. I owe a special debt of gratitude to Roberto Lovato for agreeing to write a foreword for this volume, as well as for his insightful and critical work on immigration and foreign policy over the years.

I also need to thank my academic sisters who did not contribute essays to this volume, but helped to shape it through conversations and camaraderie. Zulema Valdez, Christina Lux, Jemima Pierre, Amani Nuru-Jeter, Ayu Saraswati, and Winddance Twine: I thank you for your camaraderie and friendship. I am humbled by your love and solidarity during these difficult times. Finally, I have to thank my amazing family: Fernando Boza for always being by my side; Raymi Boza for keeping a smile on my face; Soraya Boza for asking the right questions; and Tatiana Boza for being such a good kid.

Notes

1. *FY 2015 ICE Immigration Removals* https://www.ice.gov/removal-statistics
2. For the most recent data, please refer to: "Immigration Data and Statistics" https://www.dhs.gov/data-statistics

References

De Genova, Nicholas. 2004. "The Legal Production of Mexican/Migrant 'Illegality.'" *Latino Studies* 2 (2): 160–85.

Golash-Boza, Tanya. 2012. *Immigration Nation: Raids, Detentions, and Deportations in Post-9/11 America*. Boulder, CO: Paradigm Publishers.

Golash-Boza, Tanya and Pierrette Hondagneu-Sotelo. 2013. "Latino Immigrant Men and the Deportation Crisis: A Gendered Racial Removal Program." *Latino Studies* 11 (3): 271–92.

Oliver, Melvin, and Thomas Shapiro. 2006. *Black Wealth/White Wealth: A New Perspective on Racial Inequality*. New York: Routledge.

Feagin, Joe. 2000. *Racist America: Roots, Current Realities, and Future Reparations.* New York: Routledge.

Hernández, Kelly Lytle. 2010. *Migra!: A History of the U.S. Border Patrol.* American Crossroads series, vol. 29. Berkeley: University of California Press.

Massey, Douglas S., Jorge Durand, and Nolan J. Malone. 2002. *Beyond Smoke and Mirrors: Mexican Immigration in an Era of Economic Integration.* New York: Russell Sage Foundation.

Passel, Jeffrey S., and D'Vera Cohn. 2014. "Unauthorized Immigrant Totals Rise in 7 States, Fall in 14." *Pew Research Center's Hispanic Trends Project.* N.p., 18 Nov. 2014. Web. 25 Jan. 2017. http://www.pewhispanic.org/2014/11/18/unauthorized-immigrant-totals-rise-in-7-states-fall-in-14/

Rosenblum, Marc and Kristen McCabe. 2014. *Deportation and Discretion: Reviewing the Record and Options for Change.* Washington, DC: Migration Policy Institute. Online at http://www.migrationpolicy.org/research/deportation-and-discretion-reviewing-record-and-options-change

PART 1

MIGRATION HISTORIES

How Did We Get Here?

In the contemporary United States, it seems completely natural that we would enforce our borders and regulate the entry of people into this country. Many people believe that the failure to do so would result in complete chaos. It is thus remarkable that, for one hundred years after the founding of the United States, there were no laws governing who could enter into or remain in this country, even though large numbers of immigrants were entering the country during this time. In other words, illegal immigration did not exist because there were no restrictions on immigration. (As discussed above, illegal immigration only exists when there are laws that render some people undocumented.)

Discussions of immigration restriction only became prominent when large numbers of Chinese immigrants began to arrive in the United States after the 1848 Gold Rush. Even then, immigration restrictions were limited to the Chinese. This was the beginning of a trend that continues to the present day: Discussions of immigration are most heated when arriving immigrants are perceived to be nonwhite. In the 1850s, the arrival of thousands of Chinese immigrants into California provoked nativist sentiments among whites and these sentiments eventually translated into public policy.

In 1875, the Page Act was passed, which prohibited the entry of "undesirable" immigrants. This law was designed to prevent the entry of prostitutes and forced laborers from Asia, and effectively barred the entry of Asian women into the United States for the next few decades. The passage of the Page Law required the establishment of the first immigration inspectors. Prior to this law there was no need for immigration inspectors, and there were none.

The passage of Chinese Exclusion Act in 1882 expanded the duties of immigration inspectors in that they were required to police the entry of Chinese immigrants. The Chinese Exclusion Act "legalized and reinforced the need to restrict, exclude, and deport 'undesirable' and excludable immigrants" (Lee 2002, 37). The Chinese Exclusion Act was overtly racist because it targeted one specific group: Chinese laborers. As we will see in Elliott Young's essay in this section, the Chinese Exclusion Act applied even to people of Chinese descent who had naturalized as Mexican citizens. In specifically excluding a group because of race and class, the Chinese Exclusion Act set the stage for twentieth-century immigration policy, which had both overt and covert racial and class biases (Lee 2002). Historian Erika Lee (2002) explains that the Chinese Exclusion Act did far more than prevent the entry of Chinese immigrants: It marked the transformation of the United States from a nation of immigrants into a country of gatekeepers. Prior to the passage of this law, immigrants were welcomed into this country with very little or no inspection. Since the passage of this law, the proverbial gates to the United States have slowly but surely been shutting.

The Chinese Exclusion Act initially only governed entry policies, but worries over fraud and illegal entry gave rise to the 1892 Geary Act and the 1893 McCreary Amendment, which required Chinese people who resided in the United States to possess proof of their lawful right to be in the United States. These "certificates of residence" were the precursors to today's legal permanent resident cards. Only the Chinese were required to have these documents until 1928, when "immigrant identification cards" began to be issued to all arriving immigrants (Ngai 2004; Lee 2002). The requirement that immigrants have "documents" to remain in the United States is thus less than a century old. This is critical to keep in mind when people claim that their ancestors came to the United States the "right way." Not so long ago, there was no right or wrong way to come to this country and the concept of immigrants having "documents" to legitimize their presence did not exist.

Although the Chinese Exclusion Act was repealed in 1943, the court cases that stemmed from it continue to shape how we treat immigrants today. An 1893 landmark Supreme Court case, *Fong Yue Ting v. United States,* involved three Chinese nationals who claimed they deserved constitutional protections in their deportation cases. The court held that the power to deport non-citizens was inherent in the nature of sovereignty and that constitutional protections, including the right to a trial by jury, did not apply. This case defined deportation as an administrative procedure and not a punishment. According to the *Fong Yue Ting* decision, which still holds in court today, deportation is a procedure to ensure that people abide by the terms of their visas. When they do not, they face the possibility of being returned to their countries of birth with minimal court procedures or juridical protections. It is remarkable that this court decision, which was made in the context of strong anti-Chinese sentiment, continues to hold legal precedent today.

The importance of anti-Chinese sentiment in the formation of our immigration laws is made evident in the first two essays in this section—which deal with the ramifications of the Chinese Exclusion Act. In Elliott Young's essay, we meet Wong Foon Chuck, a man born in China who became a naturalized citizen of Mexico. Despite his Mexican passport, Wong was deported from the United States due to Chinese exclusion laws in 1892, even though he had lived in the country legally for decades.

The story of Wong Foon Chuck brings a human face to the impact of anti-Chinese laws and sentiments on both sides of the border, the value of transnational connections, and the resilience of immigrants who endeavor to establish themselves in a new country. Wong arrived in the United States from China in 1874, when he was twelve years old. Just eight years later, in 1882, the Chinese Exclusion Law was passed, meaning he would not have been able to enter the United States had he arrived a few years later. In 1892, Wong was arrested in San Antonio due to his alleged lack of papers, and he was deported to Mexico, where he had become a naturalized citizen. When Wong was deported from San Antonio, he had already become a prosperous businessman. In Mexico, his business empire flourished, despite rising anti-Chinese sentiment in the borderlands. Eventually, racially motivated violence as well as political and economic changes in Mexico led to him losing large sums of money and large quantities of land. Young's essay also makes clear how anti-Chinese sentiment was not restricted to the United States as Wong's properties were seized in Mexico during anti-Chinese pogroms.

Mae Ngai's contribution brings us into the early twentieth century through a discussion of Chinese American interpreters who helped immigration authorities apprehend and interrogate Chinese immigrants, providing us with a nuanced depiction of how the Chinese were both the targets and enforcers of immigration law. Although Chinese migration in the late nineteenth and early twentieth centuries is often imagined to primarily consist of low-wage workers, both Young and Ngai's essays render it evident that middle-class and wealthy Chinese immigrants also played an important role during this time period. Their essays also show how people of Chinese descent were racialized and excluded, despite their citizenship. Naturalizing as a US citizen or a Mexican citizen did not prevent Chinese immigrants from being viewed as outsiders. Nevertheless, their work shows that there was often room for some flexibility. Wong was able to make important connections with Mexican politicians. And, in 1923, Chinese interpreter Frank Tape was the first Chinese American called to jury service in San Francisco. He later was able to purchase a home in the Sunset district of San Francisco, despite the existence of racial covenants which restricted these areas to white homeowners. Whereas Wong was able to cross the borders of Mexico and the United States to conduct business, Tape and the other Chinese interpreters crossed language and cultural borders as they performed tasks in service to the United States government.

The second two essays deal primarily with Mexican immigrants, who became the target of restrictive immigration policies much later than the Chinese. The Chinese Exclusion Act was passed in response to the influx of Chinese immigrants. Ngai's essay shows how some Chinese immigrants were accepted during this time. The essay by Kelly Lytle Hernández reveals how these exclusion laws were eventually also applied to Mexicans. In the early twentieth century, Congress expanded the definition of who was deportable. By 1904, prostitutes, criminals, those liable to rely on the government for support, and all persons convicted of committing acts of "moral turpitude" prior to entering the United States were not eligible to enter the United States. If they were not Chinese, however, these grounds for exclusion became null and void if they had lived for at least three years in the United States. Hernández's essay introduces us to Anthony Villareal, a teacher and a rebel leader in the Mexican Revolution. Villareal traveled to the United States to organize with other rebels against the regime of Mexican President Porfirio Díaz. The Mexican government put pressure on the US government to deport Mexican dissidents back to Mexico where they would be tried for sedition. These political deportations in the early twentieth century were the very first wave of deportations of Mexicans from the United States.

Kelly Lytle Hernández explains that early-twentieth-century US immigration law prohibited all persons convicted of committing acts of "moral turpitude" in their home countries from entering the United States. However, there was a statute of limitations on deportation, and any person (except for the Chinese) who lived in the United States for three or more years was exempt from deportation, even if he or she should have been barred from entering the United States in the first place. These laws were used against Antonio Villarreal, when the Mexican government wanted to stop his attempts to foment revolution in Mexico from across the border in the United States.

The Border Patrol was not created until 1924. In that same year, the United States passed the Immigration Act of 1924 and the 1924 Oriental Exclusion Act, which expanded the Chinese Exclusion Act and prohibited most immigration from Asia. The 1924 immigration laws focused on preventing the entry of undesirable immigrants from Asia, Africa, and Southern and Eastern Europe, yet made no references to immigrants from Mexico or other parts of Latin America. Nevertheless, the creation of the Border Patrol and of immigration inspectors facilitated the deportation of Mexicans. In the early 1930s, the Immigration and Naturalization Service (INS) mounted a repatriation campaign in response to skyrocketing rates of unemployment during the Great Depression, and over 400,000 people of Mexican origin were returned to Mexico (Ngai 2004).

Just over a decade later, the United States began to experience labor shortages due to World War II. To meet the labor needs, the US government created the Bracero Program in 1942, an arrangement to bring in temporary workers from Mexico. Between 1942 and 1964, 4.6 million Mexicans, called *braceros* (after the Spanish term roughly translated as "farmhands"), came to work in agriculture in the United States under this program. As Adam Goodman explains in his essay, Mexicans also continued to immigrate to the United States illegally, because not all workers qualified for the Bracero Program, and the costs associated with immigrating as a bracero were prohibitive to some.

During the Bracero Program, men from Northern Mexico traveled frequently to the United States as temporary workers to supplement their income. When the program came to an end in 1964, Mexicans continued to travel to the United States to work, now nearly exclusively as unauthorized migrants. With the passage of the Immigration Reform and Control Act of 1986, many of these Mexican migrants were able to attain legalization and eventually citizenship. Goodman's essay renders it clear how the opportunity to legalize affected Mexicans both in the United States and in their hometown. We also can see the costs associated with the lack of any mass legalization programs since 1986, a theme explored in subsequent essays.

These four introductory essays take us on a tour of US immigration policy from 1882 to 1986, allowing us to see the wide variety of immigration laws passed during the first century of immigration legislation in the United States. The protagonists in these essays are Mexican and Chinese immigrants—the primary targets of deportation policies during this time.

References

Lee, Erika. 2002. "The Chinese Exclusion Example: Race, Immigration, and American Gatekeeping, 1882–1924." *Journal of American Ethnic History* 21, no. 3: 36–62.

Ngai, Mae M. 2004. *Impossible Subjects: Illegal Aliens and the Making of Modern America*. Princeton University Press.

1

Wong Foon Chuck

Making Home in the Borderlands between China, the United States, and Mexico

Elliott Young

The author, Elliott Young, is professor of history at Lewis & Clark College in Portland, Oregon. He is the author of several books including Catarino Garza's Revolution on the Texas-Mexico Border *and* Alien Nation: Chinese Migration in the Americas from the Coolie Era through WWII. *Young has written about immigration history and policy for the* Huffington Post, *the* Oregonian, *the* Portland Tribune, *and* Oregon Humanities. *His next book will focus on the intersection of immigration and criminal justice through a history of immigrant detention in the United States.*

Wong Foon Chuck was a typical Chinese migrant in many ways, but his transnational life between the United States, Mexico, and China and his intersection with the Mexican and Chinese revolutions make his story extraordinary. He managed to survive between nations and become a wealthy businessman with extensive landholdings in Mexico, but his prominence did not stop him from being deported from the United States in 1892, or from being the target of anti-Chinese pogroms during the Mexican Revolution, or having his properties raided during the anti-Chinese expulsion campaigns in northern Mexico in the 1930s. Wong Foon Chuck did not make it into the history books in China, Mexico, or the United States because he lived on the margins of all of these societies in spite of his wealth. He is a symbol of the transnational migrant that history forgot.[1]

The current talk of a "crisis" in global migration is based on the idea that countries cannot economically or socially absorb large numbers of new migrants from diverse cultures. Stories of migrants like Wong Foon Chuck suggest an alternative narrative, one that recognizes the transnational diasporic networks that such people form and their ability to adapt, adjust, and integrate without necessarily assimilating into culturally distinct and oftentimes hostile communities. That Wong Foon Chuck could be Chinese but also weave himself into the fabric of United States and Mexican society, points to a hybrid identity that immigration policymakers neither envision nor encourage. Over the past thirty years, scholars

Figure 1.1 Wong Foon Chuck, Nov. 1940, age 78.
Courtesy of Centro de Investigaciones Históricas de la Universidad Iberoamericana Torreón

have begun to identify and describe these transnational communities, but our policymakers continue to work within a very parochial view of the nation and supposed national interests.[2] More than just a novel academic approach, a transnational perspective can be the knife that allows us to cut the Gordian knot that is the "immigration problem."

Wong Foon Chuck's story challenges immigration historians' assumption that migrants will ultimately go through a process of assimilation and incorporation into their adopted nation. This view of inevitable inclusion is based on the idea that migrants move from point A (home country) to point B (adopted country), but Wong's trajectory like that of many of his compatriots was far more complex, involving long stays in more than one country and living a bi-national existence in the United States–Mexico borderlands region. Wong's story also provides a caution to historians who lump together the experience of all Chinese in the Americas, characterizing them as exploited laborers who were marginalized from mainstream society. Like the middle-class interpreters that Mai Ngai discusses in her chapter in this volume, Wong was both excluded *and* included just as he was both an exploited laborer in his youth and later a wealthy landowner in cahoots with the most powerful and anti-Chinese Mexican politicians of their day. His in-between status as a naturalized Mexican citizen who had lived in the United States and spoke English, Spanish, and Cantonese allowed him to take advantage of his fellow Chinese laborers to make himself wealthy. Although nationalism grew and borders hardened at the beginning of the twentieth century, Wong managed to profit from the rise in global trade among China, the United States, and Mexico during this period. In short, Wong represents the complexity of transborder migrant lives that resist the class, race, and national boxes that policymakers and scholars alike have created for them.

In February of 1863 Wong Foon Chuck (Huang Kuanzhuo) was born in Kaiping, Guandong province, about 145 kilometers away from Hong Kong.[3] We know nothing of his life in China, but Wong was part of a massive exodus of several million Chinese who left the Pearl River Delta in the mid-to-late nineteenth century for the Americas, Australia, and other points in Southeastern Asia. Of the hundreds of thousands who came to the Americas, most landed in Cuba, Peru, and the West coast of the United States and Canada. The rate of migration from Guandong rivals that of European countries at the same time.

At the time of his birth, China was at the tail end of a devastating civil war fought between the Manchu Qing dynasty and a Christian millenarian movement. By the end of this war, known as the Taiping Rebellion, between 20 and 30 million Chinese lay dead. The United States was in the midst of its own civil war that was tearing the country apart over the question of African slavery. It was in this context that President Abraham Lincoln, fearing the reintroduction of slavery in disguise, signed the Anti-Coolie Bill in 1862 to keep out low-paid Chinese workers. The term "coolie" was a derogatory label for Asian manual laborers, and although it had no legal definition, it was widely used throughout the world. In spite of the prohibition on coolies in the United States, Chinese kept coming to work on the railroads and in the mines along the Pacific Coast; they also came to toil on plantations in Cuba and Peru or to take advantage of the business opportunities selling goods and services to the growing Chinese community.

Setting off for California held the promise of a better life for Chinese who suffered famine, economic destruction, and political chaos at home. At just twelve years old, Wong Foon Chuck boarded a ship with his maternal uncle and sailed to San Francisco in 1874.[4] Although the Anti-Coolie Act prohibited Chinese contract workers from entering and the 1875 Page Act stopped single Chinese women, enforcement was weak and many Chinese laborers continued to enter unimpeded. A few years before Wong's arrival, the United States and China had even signed the Burlingame Treaty (1868) that reaffirmed the right of Chinese to voluntarily emigrate to the United States.

The young Wong arrived in San Francisco at a moment when the city was at the vortex of a struggle between the federal government, which wanted to encourage free trade and migration, and California politicians who advocated for an end to Chinese immigration. White trade unionists on the Pacific Coast decried the arrival of Chinese who they portrayed as diseased, sneaky, and dangerous competitors. It would only be a few more years before the restrictionists convinced Congress to pass the Chinese Exclusion Act, banning Chinese laborers from entering the country.

Wong was one of the lucky ones. Since he had entered before the exclusion law was passed, he could remain legally in the United States. Wong had studied in a mission school in China and learned English under the tutelage of a missionary family in San Francisco.[5] He found work as a servant in the missionary's home and as a waiter in the Hotel Jackson. Wong circulated in and out of various jobs as a domestic servant, waiter, and cook.

In 1881, Wong had been away from home for six long years. Missing his family, he returned home but only remained in China for five months before returning to the United States. Upon returning, Wong headed to Texas to work on the Southern Pacific Railroad line that was being built between Los Angeles and San Antonio.

In 1883, Wong moved to El Paso, Texas, and worked as a cook for six months. He then traveled again, first to Del Rio and finally to Eagle Pass, both small but growing border towns. Since Eagle Pass had sizeable Spanish-speaking population, Wong used the opportunity to learn Spanish. He soon bought the Hotel Central and established an adjacent restaurant, laundry, and curio shop where he sold souvenirs from China and Japan.

Wong was only in his early twenties, and had arrived in the United States fewer than ten years earlier, and yet he had worked his way up from domestic servant and cook to owner of a hotel and three other businesses. In 1886, Wong sold his hotel, laundry, and shop and crossed into Mexico, selling Chinese and Japanese souvenirs in small towns along the new Mexican International Railroad line between Eagle Pass and Torreón. When he reached Torreón in 1887, he set his sights on acquiring the Hotel Ferrocarril.

We don't know why Wong decided to head south from Texas, but his business instincts were right. Northern Mexico was going through an economic boom with the introduction of railroads. Under Mexico's President Porfirio Díaz, railroad construction exploded in the country, especially in northern Mexico where lines tied into the US system at places like Laredo, El Paso, and Eagle Pass. With railroads came increased mining activity and commercial agriculture. An enterprising young man stood to earn lots of money in this emerging market and Wong took full advantage, leveraging his multilingualism to sell to a growing clientele of Spanish-, English-, and Chinese-speaking customers.

In 1889, Wong again returned to China to visit his family, but ten months later he was back in Eagle Pass. This time Wong became a labor contractor in Eagle Pass for the Coahuila Coal Company from San Felipe, Coahuila. Within two years he had more than four hundred Chinese workers under his supervision.[6] Although the United States had banned Chinese contract labor in 1862 and prohibited all Chinese workers from entering in 1882, the modernizing Díaz regime welcomed Chinese as cheap labor. Wong took advantage of his position on the border and his multilingualism to recruit Chinese laborers for mining work in northern Mexico.

Wong had become a prominent figure in northern Mexico and in Eagle Pass, hobnobbing with powerful men like Miguel Cardenas, who would become governor of the state of Coahuila (1894–1909). However, when he left the immediate border zone he confronted the brutal Chinese exclusion laws head-on. On May 13, 1892, Wong was arrested in San Antonio for not having proper papers, even though, as one New York newspaper reported, Wong owned assets of more than $100,000.[7] The Mexican consul in Eagle Pass testified that Wong had a good reputation for "his conduct and honorability" and provided the US courts with documentation proving that he was a naturalized citizen of Mexico. Even though Wong had enough money to provide bond, US law prohibited Chinese from doing so, and thus he was forced to pay the salary of his jailer until he was able to appear before the commissioner.[8] The Western District Court of Texas ruled that Wong should be excluded because he was Chinese. The courts acknowledged that he was a businessman and had become a citizen of Mexico, both of which ostensibly should have allowed him to enter into the United States, even under the exclusion act. Nonetheless, the court sentenced him to one hour of forced work and then deported him to Mexico.[9]

The *New York Post* criticized the arrest of Wong, arguing that it violated the Treaty of Guadalupe Hidalgo that guaranteed Mexican citizens' rights in the United States. "Suppose Mexico were to pass a law putting a like stigma upon an Irish person or person of Irish descent, and ignore the fact that he might be an American citizen nevertheless," the *Post* argued. "We fancy there would be a good deal of foaming at Washington."[10] Although Anglo Americans constantly worried that Chinese could easily naturalize as Mexican citizens and cross into the United States, by the early 1890s there were very few who had done so. Mexican Foreign Minister Ignacio Mariscal wrote to the US ambassador about Wong Foon Chuck's case, noting that by July 1892, only five Chinese had naturalized as Mexicans, and that Wong was the only one of these who had crossed into the United States.[11] Given Wong's ties to Mexico, his naturalization seems to have been less an opportunistic strategy to gain entry to the United States than a legitimate desire to become part of Mexican society.

Almost certainly Wong faced discrimination as a Chinese person in California, but the 1892 arrest and deportation was the first time he was confronted by his status as an undesirable alien. This unpleasant experience might have been what led Wong to give up his lucrative job and move back to Torreón in 1893. Mexico, though not free from racism against Chinese, at least had no laws against their presence in the country. In Torreón, Wong became proprietor of the Hotel del Ferrocarril (Railroad Hotel).

By this time, Wong had established himself as a transnational businessman with connections across the northern Mexico–southwestern United States borderlands. In 1895, Wong married a young Mexican woman from Tampico, Cristina Vega Domínguez, after his Chinese village wife declined to join him in Mexico.[12] Although he had been deported in 1892, the couple was able to reside in Eagle Pass until the birth of their first daughter when they moved across the border to Piedras Negras. Border officials in Eagle Pass might have been more willing to recognize Wong's status as a Mexican citizen than those in San Antonio where Wong was just seen as Chinese.

Nonetheless, Wong chose to locate the headquarters for his extensive business empire in Piedras Negras (later renamed Ciudad Porfirio Díaz), on the Mexican side of the border. Wong and his wife had ten children: Elvira, Arturo, Lily, Santiago, Rosa, Margarita, Selina, Benjamín, Hortensia, and Rubén. It is noteworthy that all ten were given Hispanic names, reflecting the Wongs' decision to raise the children in Mexico and integrate into borderlands society.

Wong's reputation as a hotelier was respected by railway workers, passengers, and executives alike. By 1901, the Mexican International Railroad had leased to Wong six hotels at stops along their Eagle Pass-Torreón line. Wong was not merely a businessman out to make a profit, but was a civic-minded citizen eager to educate Chinese in Mexico and allow them to integrate into Mexican society. To this end, Wong established the Yue Mae school in Monclova, Coahuila, in 1904, not only for his own children but for the entire community. The curriculum included Chinese, English, Spanish, math, grammar, history, geography, music, and physical education.[13] Tuition was free in exchange for helping out in Wong's other businesses and upon graduation Wong helped to launch the students in their business careers.[14] The inclusion of Chinese language, along with Spanish and English instruction, suggests that Wong wanted Chinese Mexican children to maintain ties with Chinese culture, but also be versatile enough to maneuver in the bi-national borderlands region. In 1910, the school band was invited to play in Mexico City by Porfirio Díaz for the celebrations marking the hundredth anniversary of Mexico's independence.[15] Preserving Chinese culture and maintaining business ties to the United States was not antithetical but worked in tandem with Mexican patriotism.

In addition to his myriad legitimate businesses, it appears that Wong also helped smuggle Chinese across the border to the United States. In 1909, a former US deputy marshal identified Wong Foon Chuck, the "rich millionaire of Durango," as a leader of a smuggling ring. According to the former marshal, Wong used his many hotels along the Mexican International Railroad line as safe houses to lodge Chinese as they made their way north towards the United States.[16] Chinese merchants often acted as smugglers, using their contacts on both sides of the border and their links to the Chinese diasporic community to help their compatriots cross without detection, or obtain fraudulent papers. Given Wong's history as a labor recruiter and his ownership of several hotels, it seems plausible that he helped Chinese enter the United States clandestinely.

In addition to his business empire, Wong became involved with Chinese politics, and supported Kang Yu-Wei, leader and founder of *Baohuanghui*, or the Protect the Emperor Society. The elite Kang Yu-Wei, who was formerly a tutor to the emperor, led a constitutional monarchy reform movement in China in the late nineteenth century. After being exiled from China in 1898, the noted political thinker established hundreds of chapters of his association throughout the Americas. Kang piggy-backed on Chinese merchants' trading and migratory networks to form a political organization focused on change in China. Wong was just the guy for the job, becoming Kang's business partner and political supporter.

In the first decade of the twentieth century, Kang traveled up and down the Pacific Coast organizing chapters of Baohuanghui. In 1906, Kang visited Mexico City, staying at the home of Wong Foon Chuck, and then headed to Torreón, which was in the midst of a major agricultural and industrial boom. Wong supported Kang's political organization by helping to finance it. Kang invested in land in an undeveloped part of the city, earning huge profits by selling the land back to Chinese and other foreigners.[17] One of the Chinese who bought this land was Wong Foon Chuck. The value of land in the Lagunera region, adjacent to Torreón, was skyrocketing, but so much of it was dedicated to cotton fields that food was scarce. Wong acquired fourteen hectares of well-irrigated land in Torreón, renting parcels to other Chinese who produced food, and thereby taking advantage of rising rents for food-producing land. In 1907, the *San Antonio Express* noted all of Wong's business successes, describing him as "rich, highly educated, a financier of proved ability and a sound, common-sense business man to boot, who has built paying railroads and reaped heavy returns from agriculture."[18]

Wong's land was adjacent to the Metallurgic Company of Torreón, which was owned by the Madero family.[19] Francisco Madero would end up leading the 1910 Mexican Revolution and became the first revolutionary president of Mexico. The leaders of these two nationalist movements, Kang in China advocating a constitutional monarchy and Madero in Mexico plotting to overthrow Porfirio Díaz, were both profiting off of the agricultural and industrial boom on the outskirts of Torreón. It wouldn't be long before the two groups clashed.

Wong supported Kang's political movement financially by funneling money to the Baohuanghui through a commercial corporation Kang had established in Hong Kong, but he also advocated for Kang with the highest levels of the US government. When Kang sought to return to New York by way of Eagle Pass in 1906, it was Wong who sent a telegram to President Roosevelt asking that Kang be allowed to enter at Eagle Pass, which was not one of the five designated ports of entry for Chinese. Wong had himself been denied entry through Eagle Pass in 1905, reflecting a hardening of the border.[20] Even though Wong was unsuccessful in his petition, the fact that Kang relied on him and that he made overtures on Kang's behalf shows how important Wong had become to the overseas Chinese community in North America.

Kang had so much success in Torreón that he established a bank there in 1906 and formed a company to build a tramway in the city in 1907. These businesses were all subsidiaries of Kang's transnational commercial corporation. The joint company was named Compañía Bancaria y de Tranvías Wah Yick. Kang appointed Wong Foon Chuck as director of the bank. Building of the tram stalled after just seven miles had been constructed because Wong refused to extend a bank loan to continue the project. Wong's refusal may have been due to the precipitous fall in land values or to tensions with a rival who was building the tram line. In spite of the financial woes, by 1908, the bank had amassed close to $1 million in assets (almost $27 million in today's dollars). The financial collapse of Kang's commercial corporation was due to an economic crisis in the United States in 1907 which reverberated throughout the world. Although the bank Wong managed was a subsidiary of the commercial corporation, he managed to achieve some level of autonomy for himself and the bank, which led to conflict with Kang. This tension erupted into more open conflict when Wong refused to release funds for the completion of the tram line; one report indicated that Wong's refusal stemmed from his desire to seize control of the tram line for himself.[21]

The Chinese were hindered not only by infighting, but by the local Mexican elite, who feared a rising Chinese business class. Not only were the Madero family and Wong operating in the same vicinity, but the Chinese bank was direct competition to the Banco Mercantíl de Monterrey in Torreón, in which the Madero family held a majority stake. Furthermore, in addition to the successful bank, Wong owned large tracts of urban farmland, the Railroad Hotel, and boarding houses and grocery stores.[22] The emerging Chinese business elite in Torreón competed with Mexican capitalists like the Madero family, and thus were seen as a threat. Mexican antipathy, together with the populist racism against Chinese in Mexico, combined powerfully once the Mexican Revolution erupted in 1911.

The Chinese reversal of fortune was abrupt. In 1907, the governor of Coahuila, mayor of Torreón, and chair of the city's twenty-fifth anniversary celebration lauded Wong Foon Chuck as one of the city's "founding fathers" and "most favored sons."[23] By then, Wong had ingratiated himself with Porfirian politicians and emerged as one of the most successful businessmen in northern Mexico, but once the revolution broke out, his powerful protectors were on the run. The revolutionary forces of Francisco Madero were in the final stages of their battle against Díaz when they massed for an attack on Torreón.

As historian Leo M. Dambourges Jacques wrote, "Mexicans resented the presence of the prosperous alien colony in their midst, and this helped set the stage for violence."[24] When Madero's rebel army finally made its way into Torreón on May 15, they, along with mobs from nearby villages, set about pillaging businesses and private homes, particularly targeting Chinese homes and stores. Chinese found in the city were brutally murdered by the revolutionary army, resulting in 303 deaths, nearly half of the city's Chinese population. It was not only the number of deaths that is shocking, but also the brutality with which the Chinese were slaughtered. It was the worst massacre during the entire revolution and the deadliest one-day attack on Chinese in North America ever.

The Chinese community in Torreon suffered the brunt of the violence directly, but the shock waves reverberated through the entire Chinese community in Mexico. In the massacre that day, Wong lost forty-five employees: four in his laundry, nine in his railroad hotel, and thirty-two on his hacienda.[25] Kang's own relative was among those killed that day.[26] By this point Wong was living in Tamaulipas, and so he and his family escaped the violence. However, Wong was one of many Chinese who demanded monetary reparations from the Mexican government for damages done to his hotel, laundry, and other properties, including $150,000 for the Wah Yick bank, $59,000 for his farm, and another $18,000 for damages to his railway restaurant.[27] The claims, totaling $1.5 million dollars, were never paid.[28] In the aftermath of the massacre, Wong was appointed as special envoy by the Chinese minister in Mexico City to investigate the Chinese community's claims.[29]

The massacre was an omen of what the Chinese community in northwestern Mexico would face in the coming decades. In spite of the massacre, the Chinese community in northern Mexico continued to grow, reaching a high of 25,000 by the mid-1920s. The generalized violence of the Mexican Revolution mostly subsided by 1915 and Chinese may have hoped that they would become part of the new revolutionary Mexico. However, it turned out quite the opposite. Revolutionary nationalism sparked greater xenophobia particularly directed against the Chinese, but it also targeted Jews, Arabs, and others. The ideology of *mestizaje* (racial mixing) that emerged during the Porfiriato and flourished in the revolution glorified the mixing of whites and Indians, but condemned the Asians and blacks as unassimilable.[30] By the 1920s, activists formed anti-Chinese societies in the states of Sonora and Sinaloa and pushed for the passage of anti-miscegenation and labor legislation that targeted the Chinese. By the early 1930s, activists engaged in a full-scale effort to expel all Chinese from these states. Chinese were forced out of their shops at gunpoint and pushed across the border to the United States.[31]

Although Wong was not in Torreón during the massacre, having moved to the northeastern state of Tamaulipas, he suffered financially and personally. It is not clear if some Chinese fled the country in the wake of the massacre, but overall the population of Chinese continued growing. Wong might have believed that his ties to prominent government officials and tremendous personal wealth protected him. In either case, at this point in his life he was deeply embedded in Mexico, having a Mexican wife and children born in Mexico, as well as a vast business empire in the country. Wong was heavily invested in Mexico, financially and personally, and he decided to stay the course and seek to make a home in revolutionary Mexico.

Sometime between 1896 and 1908, Wong moved his family to Hacienda Cantón (Guangdong Yuan), which he established on 5,000 hectares of land he had purchased in Villa Júarez, in Tamaulipas. With reliable access to Chinese labor, Wong turned these remote haciendas, Cantón and Nuevo Canton, into successful enterprises producing sugar, rice, and sesame seed.[32] In 1919 Wong invited a group of governors and military generals from the northern states to his hacienda and, according to his own autobiography, "in spite of my bad Spanish and not being literally very eloquent," he convinced them to buy land to plant sugar. Forty percent of the irrigable land was in Wong's name, although much of it was in fact owned by Miguel Cárdenas. In 1926 Wong along with a few Mexican partners attempted to industrialize the production of sugar around the Mante River. Wong enlisted President Plutarco Elías Calles, who toured the region and ordered a damn and irrigation to be built in the area. In the next few years a railroad line and highway connected this region to Texas through Laredo.[33] The irrigation mostly benefitted fourteen families, including that of Miguel Cárdenas and president Calles himself. Wong and Calles were two of the largest landowners in the Mante complex, with 2,000 hectares each.[34]

In spite of Wong's connections to the most powerful politicians in Mexico, resentment at the success of the Chinese came to a head in 1930 when a Mexican thief was shot on one of the Chinese haciendas. Locals pressed the government to expel the Chinese, leading to a series of raids on the haciendas by government agents who searched for contraband and demanded to see the papers of the Chinese. Eighty-two Chinese were arrested and brought to Tampico where they languished in jail despite having legal papers to reside in Mexico. Reports suggested that the governor ordered the Chinese to leave the country. Rodolfo Elías Calles, son of Plutarco Elías Calles (the former president and Wong ally), orchestrated the raids through Gobernación, a federal government ministry. Rodolfo would become the virulently anti-Chinese governor of Sonora the following year and would lead the expulsion of Chinese from that state. Although Rodolfo directed the raids, he did not publicly acknowledge his role, while his father Plutarco confidentially told people in the government that he was pleased with the raids and asked that they be extended to Tampico. Whether the goal was to seize Wong Foon Chuck's considerable landholdings in the region or just displace the Chinese farmers, Plutarco Elías Calles had gone from business partner with Wong to enemy.[35]

After the eighty-two Chinese were released from jail some of them returned to Villa Júarez only to find themselves subject to another raid by local police a few months later, supposedly on the orders of Rodolfo Elías Calles. The Chinese were forced to sign a pledge to leave the area within ten days. Some returned to China while others moved to Tampico. The land that was taken from the Chinese was distributed to private landowners, many of whom were friends and cronies of former president Calles.[36]

Wong held on to a portion of his 2,000 hectares in the early 1930s, but El Mante Sugar Company faced a new expropriation in 1938 by President Lázaro Cárdenas who accelerated the pace of land reform throughout Mexico. On February 18, 1938, Cárdenas decreed the expropriation of El Mante sugar complex, accusing former president Calles of having used his office to benefit himself and his cronies.[37] The company protested the expropriation and the Supreme Court compelled the government to indemnify the owners. After their debts and lawyers had been paid, only half of the 22 million pesos remained to be divided among the owners. Fearing another expropriation, Wong sold his remaining 106 hectares and shut down his hacienda El Canton.[38]

Wong, who had tremendous success as a businessman and landowner in Mexico from the 1880s through the 1930s, had been reduced to owning just one small 124-acre hacienda in the mid 1940s. Wong lived out the rest of his days on his hacienda El Limón in Tamaulipas growing tropical fruits and vegetables.[39] Wong managed to hold on to some of his businesses in Torreón in the wake of the 1911 massacre, but within a couple of years his bank and streetcar company had failed. The Banco Chino and the Compañía Bancaria y de Tranvías Wah Yick were liquidated in 1913, but its assets were incorporated into a new company, the Fincas Urbanas de Torreón. Wong's creditors sued to gain control of a building that had been owned by the Banco Chino, but in a lengthy court battle the shareholders of Fincas Urbanas de Torreón claimed that Wong Foon Chuck was not actually the owner and they managed to hold on to the building until they sold it in 1941.[40] In 1947, a Torreón newspaper wrote a glowing biography of Wong's business accomplishments in Mexico, noting "as an Asian, he only had some of the peculiar characteristics of the yellow race."[41]

Wong Foon Chuck was a survivor. He survived deportation from Texas in 1892, the devastating massacre in Torreón that took the lives of scores of his employees, the failure of his bank, and finally seizures of his land in the early 1930s by anti-Chinese activists. Wong finally lost his vast landholdings when President Cardenas' expropriated El Mante sugar company, but he remained in Mexico. Wong, his wife, and his ten children lived in the Mexico-Texas borderlands even as thousands of other Chinese Mexicans were expelled and deported back to China. In the 1930s, Wong chaired Red Cross fundraising efforts in El Paso and in the 1940s he led the efforts in the Chinese community there to raise money for the war effort.[42] In 1946, a Chinese-language newspaper in San Francisco published a pamphlet commemorating Wong's seventy-three years in the United States and Mexico, lauding his accomplishments as a businessman.[43] In February 1950, at age eighty-seven, Wong died on his small hacienda in Limón, Tamaulipas.[44] According to one obituary, in spite of having been a wealthy businessman, Wong died a poor man, having had most of his properties and businesses seized during the anti-Chinese crusades in the 1930s.[45] A local chronicler noted that Wong's son Rubén turned Wong's small property into an unsuccessful trailer park, a sad coda to his father's illustrious career.[46]

In 2015, Wong's daughter Selina Chuck Vega was lauded in a Coahuilan newspaper as the oldest living person in Piedras Negras. She was 106. Selina Chuck Vega, born on the family hacienda El Cantón in 1908, had been a well-respected teacher in both Piedras Negras and San Antonio; she spoke perfect Spanish, English, and Cantonese.[47] Like her father, she continues

Figure 1.2 Wong Foon Chuck with his niece and her children. Feb. 1940.
Courtesy of Centro de Investigaciones Históricas de la Universidad Iberoamericana Torreón.

to lead a borderlands life straddling three nations and two continents, proudly representing her Chinese, Mexican, and American identities.

Wong Foon Chuck and his descendants lived transnational lives, stitching together communities torn apart by national borders, anti-Chinese laws, and deportations. Out of the borderlands riven with conflict and violence, they made a home. As politicians today face what they perceive as a "crisis" in immigration, they would do well to acknowledge that migrants can maintain complex multinational identities and also become successful citizens of their adopted countries.

Notes

1. A few historians have mentioned Wong Foon Chuck in their research on the Mexican Revolution or on Kang Yu-Wei. Historian Evelyn Hu-Dehart has written the most extensively researched history of his life in Mexico. Evelyn Hu-Dehart, "Kang Youwei and the Baohuanghui in Mexico (and Latin America)," (forthcoming), 8–9.
2. Roger Rouse, "Mexican Migration and the Social Space of Postmodernism," *Diaspora* 1, no. 1 (1991): 8–23. Michael Kearney, "Transnationalism in California and Mexico at the End of Empire," in *Border Identities: Nation and State at International Frontiers*, ed. Thomas M. Wilson and Hastings Donnan (Cambridge: Cambridge University Press, 1998), 117–141. Madeline Hsu, *Dreaming of Gold, Dreaming of Home: Transnationalism and Migration Between the United States and South China, 1882–1943* (Stanford, CA: Stanford University Press, 2000). Lynn Stephen, *Transborder Lives: Indigenous Oaxacans in Mexico, California, and Oregon* (Durham: Duke University Press, 2007), http://dx.doi.org/10.1215/9780822389965.

3. The basic outlines of Wong Foon Chuck's life in the United States and Mexico are described in an unpublished autobiographical essay written in English and translated into Spanish by Dr. César Méndez Osuna that was sent to the author by Lucas Martínez Sánchez. Basic information about Wong Foon Chuck can also be found in a footnote in a book about the Mexican Revolution, based on research done by Hortensia Chuck Vega, one of Wong Foon Chuck's daughters. Lucas Martínez Sánchez, *Monclova en la revolución hechos y personajes 1910–1920* (Monclova: np, 2005), note 159, p. 63. Online at http://ahc.sfpcoahuila.gob.mx/admin/uploads/Documentos/modulo11/LIBRO_REVOLUCION.pdf
4. Evelyn Hu-Dehart indicates that he was thirteen years old when he came to San Francisco, but if he was born in 1863, then he was most likely twelve as his daughter indicated in an unpublished biography she wrote. Hu-Dehart, "Kang Youwei," 8–9. Sánchez, *Moncolva en la revolución*, note 159, 63.
5. Hu-Dehart, "Kang Youwei and the Baohuanghui in Mexico (and Latin America)," 9.
6. Sánchez, *Moncolva en la revolución*, note 159, 63.
7. "Arrest of Chinese Mexican," *New York Tribune*, May 17, 1892, Archivo Historico de la Secretaria de Relaciones Exteriores de México (hereafter cited as AREM), 18-27-31, p. 2a.
8. "S. F. Maillefert, Consul in Eagle Pass, to Secretaria de Relaciones Exteriores," May 16, 1892, AREM, 18-27-31, p. 6–8.
9. "Los Estados Unidos Contra Foon Chuck," Eagle Pass, May 14, 1892, translation to Spanish, AREM, 18-27-31, p. 9–10.
10. *New York Post*, May 17, 1892, clipping in AREM, 18-27-31, p. 2a.
11. Ignacio Mariscal to US minister, AREM, 7-11-28, July 16, 1892, p. 31.
12. Hu-Dehart, "Kang Youwei," 9.
13. Information based on interview with Selina Chuck Vega, as cited in Orquídea López Allec, "Longevidad divina," *Zocalo Saltillo*, January 26, 2015.
14. "Old Capital of Texas Filled With Memories of Santa Anna and Texas Heroes: Slumber Across the Border; Monclova Picturesque Among Its Hills Once the Scene of History Making," *San Antonio Express*, April 2, 1911.
15. Hu-Dehart, "Kang Youwei," 13.
16. Richard Taylor to Commissioner General, October 5 1909, NARA, RG 85, entry 9, 52229/1E.
17. Robert Worden states that the Commercial Corporation was founded in 1904 in Hong Kong. Robert Leo Worden, *A Chinese Reformer in Exile: The North American Phase of the Travels of K'ang Yu-Wei, 1899–1909* (doctoral dissertation, Georgetown University, 1972), 189–90, 93–94.
18. "Old Capital of Texas Filled with Memories of Santa Anna and Texas Heroes: Slumber Across the Border: Monclova Picturesque Among Its Hills Once the Scene of History-Making," *San Antonio Express*, April 2, 1911.
19. Leo M. Dambourges Jacques, "The Chinese Massacre in Torreón (Coahuila) in 1911," *Arizona and the West* 16, no. 3 (1974): 234–46. Marco Antonio Pérez Jiménez, "Raza, nación y revolución: La matanza de chinos en Torreón, Coahuila, mayo de 1911" (Universidad de las Américas, 2006), ch. 5.
20. Worden, "A Chinese Reformer in Exile," 194–99.
21. Ibid., 191–94, 222–23.
22. Hu-Dehart, "Kang Youwei," 19.
23. Ibid., 18.

24. Dambourges Jacques, "The Chinese Massacre," 234–40, 245–46.
25. Ibid., 239–40.
26. Worden, "A Chinese Reformer in Exile," 224.
27. "Torreón Damage Claims Are Being Considered: The Total Will Reach the Enormous Sum of $1,500,000," *El Paso Morning Times*, June 29, 1911.
28. "Claims for Damages Heavy," *El Paso Herald*, June 28, 1911.
29. "Chinese in Torreón are Now Reassured," *El Paso Morning Times*, August 15, 1911.
30. Elliott Young, *Alien Nation: Chinese Migration in the Americas from the Coolie Era Through World War II* (Chapel Hill: University of North Carolina Press, 2014), 232–33.
31. Roberto Chao Romero, *The Chinese in Mexico, 1882–1940* (Tucson: University of Arizona Press, 2010), 56, ch. 6. Julia María Schiavone Camacho, *Chinese Mexicans: Transpacific Migration and the Search for a Homeland, 1910–1960* (Chapel Hill: University of North Carolina Press, 2012), ch. 3. Young, *Alien Nation*, ch. 6.
32. Fredy González, *Paisanos Chinos: Transpacific Politics Among Chinese Immigrants in Mexico* (Berkeley: University of California Press, forthcoming), 69.
33. Wong Foon Chuck, "Autobiografía de Wong Foon Chuck," translated by Dr. César Méndez Osuna.
34. Diana Lizbeth Méndez Medina, "En los bordes de la corrupción: análisis de la conformación, funcionamiento y expropiación de la Compañía Azucarera del Mante (1930–1939)," *Región y sociedad* 27, no. 16 (2015): 217–18.
35. González, *Paisanos Chinos*, 69–74.
36. Ibid., 75–76.
37. Evelyn Hu Dehart notes that he sold his holdings at El Mante and in Torreón, but it appears as if these were forced sales as part of an expropriation. Hu-Dehart, "Kang Youwei," 26. Méndez Medina, "En los bordes de la corrupción," 242.
38. Wong Foon Chuck, "Autobiografía de Wong Foon Chuck," translated by Dr. César Méndez Osuna.
39. Ibid.
40. "Amparo Contra el Embargo del'Banco Chino,'" *El Siglo de Torreón*, August 15, 1936. "Pidieron Amparo Contra un Embargo," *El Siglo de Torreón*, June 25, 1938. "Algo Sobre el Hotel Española: El Banco Chino—La Matanza—El Cambio de Propietarios," *El Siglo de Torreón*, February 17, 1945.
41. "La admirable empresa e iniciativa de Foon Chuck en favor de Torreón," *El Siglo de Torreón*, February 28, 1947.
42. "Open Red Cross Drive Monday: Kick-Off Luncheon Will Start Campaign for $10,000 Fund," *El Paso HeraldPost*, March 14, 1936. "Way Is Sought to Increase Chest Fund: Next Report Will Be Made Tomorrow at Luncheon," *El Paso HeraldPost*, October 11, 1943. "Start Gathering Red Cross Funds," *El Paso HeraldPost*, March 14, 1944.
43. "Huang gong Kuanzhuo lü wai qi shi san nian ji nian ce," (San Francisco: Jiujinshan, 1947).
44. Sánchez, *Monclova en la revolución*, note 159, 63.
45. "Falleció Ayer el Sr. Foon Chuck," *El Siglo de Torreón*, February 4, 1950.
46. Juan José Mata Bravo, Chronicler of El Mante, addendum to Wong Foon Chuck, "Autobiografía de Wong Foon Chuck," translated by Dr. César Méndez Osuna. Mata Bravo also questions whether the death certificate dated in 1950 is correct given the existence of a photograph of Wong dated in 1955.
47. Allec, "Longevidad divina."

2

Lost in Translation

Mae M. Ngai

The author, Mae M. Ngai, is Lung Family Professor of Asian American Studies and Professor of History at Columbia University. She is author of the award-winning Impossible Subjects: Illegal Aliens and the Making of Modern America (2004) and The Lucky Ones: One Family and the Extraordinary Invention of Chinese America (2010). Ngai has written on immigration history and policy for the Washington Post, New York Times, Los Angeles Times, the Nation, and the Boston Review. She is now working on The Chinese Question: The Gold Rushes and Global Politics *(under contract with WW Norton), a study of Chinese gold miners and racial politics in nineteenth-century California, the Australian colony of Victoria, and the South African Transvaal.*

When the Louisiana Purchase Exposition opened in St. Louis in 1904 it was the largest world's fair yet held in America. It covered 2 square miles and presented over 1,500 buildings and 75 miles of walks and roadways. All the states and territories and thirty-eight nations participated with pavilions that presented their civilizational achievements. Eighteen million people attended the fair over the course of eight months.[1]

The fair's honky-tonk entertainment zone, known as the Pike, featured thirty-six attractions, from the Tyrolean Alps to Jerusalem, including a "Chinese Village," a sprawling complex built in Orientalist style with pagoda-like towers. Although show businessmen and ethnologists organized most of the midway exhibits, Chinese American entrepreneurs sponsored the Chinese Village, which included a theater, a wedding performance, a joss house, eateries, and shops. The Hong Tai Company of San Francisco's Chinatown sent a group to staff the concessions. Among them were Herman and Mamie Lowe and their two young children, Harold and Emily; and Frank Tape, Mamie's brother. Herman worked as a clerk for Hong Tai, Frank as manager of one of the village's restaurants, the Dreamland Café.[2]

Herman and Mamie's children were among a dozen or so children who, dressed in Chinese costume, roamed the fairgrounds as little culture brokers, plying the Pike with flyers advertising the Chinese Village. Everyone adored Emily, the youngest child in the village. Guidebooks presented her photographed as an anthropological specimen: "Emily Lo, one of the many bright children in the 'Chinese Village.' This little girl is a full-blooded Mongolian 3 years old and measures only 2½ feet in height. The pride of the 'Chinese Village.'"[3] In fact, Emily was a third-generation Chinese American from Berkeley, California. The Lowe and Tape families had been in the United States since the 1860s.

Emily and her family's citizenship status and cultural identity were invisible to most observers, who simply assumed that "full blooded Mongolians" could not be Americans. In fact, the Lowes and Tapes occupied an in-between position. They were marginal to the mainstream of American society, but they were also uncommon figures in a predominantly immigrant community. From their in-between position they worked as culture brokers, language interpreters, and agents for companies that did business with immigrants (railroad and steamship companies, banks, etc.). The brokers were important figures who helped immigrants navigate the terrain of a new society and, at the same time, helped the institutions of the host country interact with and discipline the immigrants. This essay discusses the experience of the first cohort of Chinese interpreters who worked for the US Immigration Bureau in the early twentieth century. By virtue of their in-between position, interpreters were both marginal and powerful. They could use their position to help immigrants, but they could also exploit them. Either way, during the era of Chinese exclusion being an interpreter was one of the few ways that a Chinese American could gain access to the American middle class.

I.

It mattered greatly that the Lowes and the Tapes were Chinese Americans, indeed, United States citizens. Their status gave them a privileged position among the Chinese at the world's fair. Everyone coming to the fair from China had to contend with the Chinese exclusion law. Although the exclusion law formally excluded only laborers, all fair-bound Chinese, whether diplomats, merchants, exhibitors, actors, tourists, artisans, or workers, faced a nightmare of bureaucratic red tape, harassment, and worse.

The immigration bureau viewed all Chinese arriving to work at the fair with suspicion. It believed the fairs had created a giant loophole through which Chinese laborers could enter and remain in the United States in violation of the exclusion laws. Congress enacted in 1902 new provisions to admit Chinese to take part in the world's fair's exhibitions.[4] The Immigration Bureau imposed stringent inspection rules upon all world's fair–bound Chinese landing at San Francisco, especially Chinese actors and others engaged to work in the Chinese Village. The bureau considered them all to be "coolies" and "bogus merchants" who had no legitimate business at the fair and no intention of returning to China. Rumors that the head of the Chinese village, Lee Toy, was bringing upwards of fifty women for a "Chinese Court of Beauty" convinced immigration officials that they would all be sold into prostitution. The commissioner general of immigration considered the alleged plot afoot at St. Louis to be "the most daring and infamous attempt ever made to violate the Chinese exclusion laws."[5] The first group of two hundred Chinese to arrive at San Francisco in August 1904 landed under bond, traveled to St. Louis by train in locked railway cars, accompanied by over sixty US soldiers and customs officials, and put under virtual quarantine in the village with round-the-clock watch. No other group of foreign performers or workers was subject to such extraordinary restriction and surveillance.[6]

The immigration commissioner on site at the fair, James Dunn, added a piece to his strategy of containing the Chinese by hiring hire Frank Tape as an interpreter. Dunn believed Tape was "an intelligent Americanized Chinaman claiming to be able to obtain correct inside information." The job was a great opportunity for Frank; he quit his job managing the village's restaurant and was sworn in on August 17, 1904, as "Chinese Interpreter in the US Immigration Service at Large," at an annual salary of $1,200.[7] Tape did not really do interpreting work, at least not in the conventional sense. Dunn did not interview people, with Tape as interpreter. Rather, Tape acted as Dunn's undercover informant, the inspector's eyes and ears in the Chinese village. Frank hung around the village and picked up information, eavesdropping on conversations and reporting them to Dunn. He corroborated the bureau's belief that the women were to be imported—fifteen to fifty women, according to Frank—who would enter as laborers and post $500 bond each, and then be "spirited away, allowing the bonds to be forfeited, the amount of the bond being a mere bagatelle in estimating the value of a Chinese prostitute."[8]

Between September and November, the immigration bureau closed in on the Chinese village, arresting Lee Toy in San Francisco after he landed with twelve women alleged to be prostitutes; arresting other men and women at the Chinese village in St. Louis; and, finally, removing the remaining two hundred Chinese from the village on grounds that it was unsanitary and a firetrap. The Chinese Village was ruined, a month before the official closing of the fair. On November 18, Dunn's men handcuffed the deportees with rope, put them into patrol wagons, and drove them to the train station, where they were transferred to six locked railroad cars. The train left Wabash station at 8:15 that evening, carrying the deportees, watchmen, marshals, and interpreter Frank Tape.[9]

After delivering the deportees to the Bay Area, Frank returned to St. Louis, where he threw himself into the work of pursuing illegal Chinese immigrants. He raided Chinese laundries and arrested those without proper papers. He broke up a ring of merchants that sold counterfeit certificates of identity. He got write-ups in the newspapers for his work. His career, which had started by his eagerness to inform on the Chinese villagers, was now taking off.[10]

II.

Herman and Mamie Lowe and the children traveled back to California separately from Frank, avoiding the humiliation of the deportation spectacle. In April 1905, shortly after returning to the Bay Area, Herman was hired as an interpreter by the immigration bureau. He was the first ethnic Chinese hired as an immigration interpreter in San Francisco; his employment was remarked in the *Morning Call* with the headline, "Chinese Blood Goes into the Bureau." The *Chronicle* made its position clear with a headline linking Herman to the recent scandal at St. Louis: "Man Employed by Slave Importers during St. Louis Exposition is Presented with a Good Federal Position."[11]

Lowe's hire was a break in San Francisco's immigration bureau's longstanding policy of hiring only whites as Chinese interpreters, men who had spent time in China as members of missionary families. East Coast bureaus had hired Chinese as interpreters since the late 1890s. Terrence Powderly, who became Commissioner-General of Immigration in 1903, began to hire more Chinese as interpreters as a matter of practical necessity.

To be sure, the Chinese exclusion laws, first passed in 1882 after a long campaign of anti-Chinese agitation on the Pacific Coast, sharply curtailed Chinese immigration. But Chinese still ventured to America, often via San Francisco, where they attempted to gain legal admission as merchants or as sons of US citizens. In light of increasingly stringent entry procedures at San Francisco, Chinese also entered via other ports, where the chances of getting in were said to be better. Some sailed from China to Mazatlán and then traveled north to be smuggled over the United States-Mexico border. Others entered Vancouver (paying the hefty $50 Canadian head tax in order to do so legally), made their way east via the Canadian Pacific Railroad, and then slipped into the United States in upstate New York or Vermont.[12]

Between 1900 and 1907, the immigration service hired thirty-five Chinese as interpreters, in addition to a half-dozen white Chinese interpreters. San Francisco had five Chinese interpreters; other districts—Richford, Vermont; Toledo, Ohio; Portal, North Dakota; Tampa, Florida; El Paso, Tacoma, and San Diego, and others—had one each. Most interpreters were paid on a per-diem basis (usually $4 a day); Frank, in St. Louis, and Herman, in San Francisco, were among the seven interpreters to draw an annual salary of $1,200 a year. That was nearly as much as junior-grade inspectors, who were always white. Chinese who could speak even a modicum of English coveted these positions.[13]

While most Chinese interpreters secured their jobs—as often was the case with government work—through connections, some had unusual backgrounds and were well educated. William S. Lee was born in Auckland, New Zealand, to a Chinese merchant, was raised in Oregon and Wisconsin, and worked as a translator for banks in New York and Pittsburgh. Seid Gain (Xue Jing) was the son of a wealthy Portland, Oregon, merchant, labor contractor, and opium smuggler. Seid was educated at the Baptist Mission School and the Bishop Scott Academy in Portland, and received a LLB from the University of Oregon's law school in 1907; he was the only interpreter in the bureau who was well educated and fluent in both spoken and written Chinese and English. Most interpreters, though, were not well educated in either English or Chinese. Many immigrants had learned English in the Protestant mission churches and spoke with only a fair degree of facility. In some cases, they spoke a kind of pidgin, the simplified contact language of Hong Kong and other colonial-port cities in Asia. Only a few, like Seid Gain, Frank Tape, and Herman Lowe, were born and raised in the United States and hence fluent in English. Although some, like Frank, were barely proficient in Chinese, the American-born interpreters had the greatest advantage within the immigration bureau.

By 1906, three men of the Tape family were working as interpreters: Frank Tape and Herman Lowe for the immigration bureau, and Robert Park, the husband of Frank and Mamie's younger sister Emily, for Chinese defendants and witnesses in San Francisco's criminal court. Robert's younger brother Edward also secured a job as an immigration interpreter in San Francisco.[14] Save for Frank, who was in St. Louis, they all lived in Berkeley, where they owned homes in white neighborhoods. They were familiar figures in the Chinese mission churches of San Francisco and the East Bay. Their children went to white schools, unlike Chinese children in San Francisco, who had to attend a segregated "Oriental school." The Tapes, Lowes, and Parks were living the lifestyle of middle class Americans. But much more than economic status was at play: They were foundational members of something yet bigger, a new social class, the interpreter class.

To be an interpreter, whether for a government office like the immigration bureau, the police, or the courts, or for companies that did business with immigrants, such as the steamship lines and banks, was to occupy a very special position. For Chinese Americans, these were virtually the only employment opportunities outside the Chinese ethnic enclave economy. The interpreters not only earned relatively high wages. By working with mainstream American institutions, they had access to knowledge and officials with power and authority, which they often parlayed into authority and respect in Chinatown communities. But they also faced resentment and hostility. Since their hiring at the turn of the century, there had been charges of incompetence and corruption. An anonymous letter writer in St. Louis complained about Tape and Dunn to the Secretary of Commerce and Labor, "All our Chinese will have no life to see the sky and sun. O! Why our Chinese have so much misfortune happen to them and have such a cruel and corrupt officer; then what can we do?"[15]

The complaint against Tape was not unusual. For Chinese immigrants in America, the immigration bureau was an institution of state power that positively oppressed them: It held them for weeks upon arrival as though they were criminals, interrogated them in ways that created difficulty even for lawful applicants, and enforced laws that codified their racially-stereotyped status as "coolies" and "prostitutes." Government interpreters were quite literally mouthpieces for the coercive state. And, certainly, the state could not exercise its authority over the immigrants without such mouthpieces to make its authority intelligible, even as they mistrusted the mouthpieces. Yet the interpreters also made it possible for non-English-speaking immigrants to "speak" to the offices of power, to defend themselves or make claims in their own interests. These cross cutting interests created a complicated and unstable position for interpreters.

As in-betweens and go-betweens, interpreters thus occupied an interstitial space between social worlds that were otherwise mutually unintelligible. The interpreters' ingenious move was to turn this liminal position into social capital, to make themselves necessary by monopolizing access between parties seeking transaction over a desirable good. From this position they helped immigrants navigate the contours of life in a new country; but they also abetted the economic exploitation and social control of the immigrants. Herein lay the brokers' ambiguous yet powerful social position.

III.

In response to suspicions of corruption among the bureau's Chinese interpreters, Frank Sargent, the Commission General of Immigration, deployed Seid Gain in 1907 as an "interpreter-at-large" to investigate the linguistic and moral competency of the bureau's Chinese interpreters and to investigate charges of corruption.[16] Sargent also ordered agency-wide personnel transfers, hoping to sever Chinese interpreters' ties with their local communities.[17] Herman Lowe transferred to Detroit, then to Portland, Oregon. He and Mamie settled in a small wood-framed house in a white working class neighborhood in southeast Portland, across the river from Chinatown, where they raised Harold and Emily. Still, the family maintained some ties with local Chinese. Herman organized a Chinese children's music band, which played Western instruments and performed in the city's annual rose parade. Harold studied at Oregon State and became a dentist; Emily married the first Chinese American to graduate from the University of Oregon's medical school. Herman served as an interpreter for the Immigration Bureau for nearly thirty years, his integrity never questioned.[18]

Mamie and Frank's brother in law, Robert Park, interpreted for the San Francisco police court, also in a long career untainted by allegations of corruption. Park was well known, not just as the court interpreter, but as a civic leader in San Francisco's Chinatown. Park was both a founding member and leader of the Chinese American Citizens Alliance, which formed in 1893 to promote assimilation, civil rights, and American citizenship; and a leader of the Sam Yup Association (sanyi huiguan), the most powerful of Chinatown's traditional district associations. As an officer of the latter, Park negotiated with city officials after the 1906 earthquake and fire, defeating plans to relocate Chinese to the outer fringes of the city.[19]

Frank Tape, who survived an investigation into corruption charges in St. Louis, spent three months on detail in southern California in 1908, serving as interpreter to Richard Taylor, a special agent investigating Chinese alien smuggling from Mexico. In one case, Tape went undercover by spending three days in a Los Angeles jail cell with three alleged smugglers, befriending and soliciting confessions from them.[20] Frank then posted to Seattle, where he became the second Chinese interpreter in the district. Officials described the other interpreter, Quan Foy, as a quiet man who simply did his job and did not get involved in cases. Indeed, to many district officials, the interpreter who "sits there and asks the questions and gives back the answers" was the model worker. Notwithstanding the mistaken view of interpreting as a mechanical exercise these officials believed that getting interpreters involved in casework as informants and investigators was an invitation to corruption.[21]

Frank Tape exemplified that problem. Although an interpreter, Tape insinuated himself into the role of investigator, taking cases inspectors could not resolve and becoming involved in district efforts against smuggling. He presented himself to colleagues as a favored agent with connections in Washington and in Chinatown as the "big man" with "pull" inside the immigration bureau. He drove a Kissel, a fancy touring car; dated a white divorcee; and jingled gold coins in his pocket.[22] His flamboyant lifestyle, and not least his tendency to pass himself as a white man, stoked resentment among his colleagues. Rumors began to circulate that he was extorting immigrants for favorable immigration decisions. In 1913 and 1914 Tape was again investigated. A devastating report resulted, with eighty-one pages of testimony from Chinese witnesses, white lawyers, immigration inspectors, and a copy of Tape's bank account that showed that $9,000 had gone in and out in the past year. The report alleged that "Interpreter Tape extorted money from a large per cent of the Chinese passing through Seattle office irrespective of the merits of their cases. . . . It seems that in some instances where men stood upon their lawful rights and refused him tribute he so misinterpreted their testimony or threw such suspicion on them that meritorious cases were made to appear fraudulent and in some instances the applicant actually deported."[23]

In September 1914 Frank Tape was dismissed from the bureau and was then indicted on criminal charges of breach of duty, malfeasance, and extorting immigrants. A sensational trial ensued, during which time a witness was murdered in Chinatown and the prime suspect then found hanged, which police ruled as a suicide, conveniently closing both cases. With few witnesses to corroborate the bureau's charges against Tape, the jury acquitted him on all counts. Tape avoided conviction and jail, but his career as an immigration interpreter was finished.[24]

There is a certain pattern in Frank Tape's role as interpreter. In many instances, he was a zealous immigration agent who pursued smugglers and illegal aliens. But there is also considerable evidence that Frank engaged in extortion in Chinese admission cases. These practices—partnering with the government to pursue Chinese aliens and also bribing these aliens to ensure their entry—appear paradoxical, but both point to the interpreter's in-between position and the pursuit of his own interests above all.

IV.

In 1916–17 scandal rocked the San Francisco over widespread corruption at the Angel Island immigration station, where arriving Chinese were detained and inspected. A year-long investigation revealed extensive manipulation and theft of documents, extortion of immigrants, and fraud in the examination of applicants for admission. The practice involved clerks, stenographers, typists, watchmen, inspectors, and interpreters, as well as law firms, brokers and fixers, photographers, and counterfeiters working on the outside. In June of 1917, six employees were fired, including interpreter Edward Park, Frank Tape's brother-in-law. In October, fifteen people were indicted on charges of conspiring to mutilate government records and to land aliens unlawfully.[25]

People in Chinatown were overjoyed to learn of the dismissals and indictments. As one person wrote, "You have done a great justice to our Chinese peoples. (That is you have made a clean sweep oust all the crooks, and grafters, which is in Angel Island.)" Another stated, "If you go to Chinatown . . . [people] talk every day about the grafting—that you can't do anything without money. If you have money you can do anything." It was as though a double oppression, the exclusion laws and the bribes required to circumvent them, weighed upon the immigrants.[26]

In fact, Chinese had been writing complaints to the immigration bureau about corrupt officials for years. But it was not always clear if complaints about extortion and smuggling were grounded in fact, or spurred by angry people whose cases were not approved, or trumped up by the fixers involved in the illegal alien business in hopes of getting rid of the honest inspectors and interpreters. Investigations of corruption frequently exonerated those charged on grounds of the latter; although even here it was not always clear if the exonerations were actually cover-ups.

Indeed, how did one judge what was "honest" or "corrupt" when Chinese believed the exclusion law was unjust and immoral? Most

Chinese did not consider it to be morally wrong to effect unlawful entry into the country, even if they knew it was not legal. Arriving immigrants often expected Chinese interpreters to help them—perhaps they thought their relatives in the United States had paid off the right people or perhaps they simply assumed they could trust their co-ethnics—and could be sorely disappointed when they did not.

The scandals implicating Frank Tape, Edward Park, and scores of others in the early twentieth century reveal a dense web of practices and transactions that undermined the administration of the Chinese exclusion laws. Contrary to the racialized publicity surrounding these scandals, corruption had no color or racial signature. Ralph Bonham, the immigration inspector who investigated Tape in Seattle, understood this. When he testified before a Congressional commission on law enforcement, Bonham was asked if he believed the immigration bureau should employ only "American" (i.e., white) Chinese interpreters. He replied, "our past experience has been that . . . they need as much watching as anybody else."[27]

Chinese and white Americans, as well as blacks, Mexicans, and Native Americans, were lured into the business of illegal immigration by the potential for financial gain. Among Euro-Americans, brokers and lawyers profited substantially. For the smaller fry lower down in the chain—the interpreter or the clerk who stole records and stashed them in a barrel for someone else to pick up—the cut was modest, but on a steady basis corruption could make possible a more comfortable life. Yet, it is important to remember that while the temptation to take bribes was always present, not all brokers and interpreters—regardless of their ethnic background—were corrupt. Corruption requires more than opportunity. It requires a certain inclination, a certain lack of moral certitude. Most employees of the immigration bureau, whether Chinese or white, were not on the take.

V.

After his dismissal in Seattle Frank Tape returned to San Francisco, where he went to work for his father's bonding business in Chinatown and reinvented himself as a respectable middle class businessman. He married a Chinese American socialite and in 1923 was the first Chinese American called to jury service in San Francisco. The *Chronicle* lauded him as a "real American."[28] The Tapes purchased a home in the all-white Sunset District despite the neighborhood's use of racial covenants to exclude Orientals. Tape became known as a culture broker; one journalist described the Tapes' bonding business as a "link between Orient and the Occident," which served as an "informal information bureau where [immigrants'] problems are solved and questions are answered." Tape also promoted a mythology about his colorful past as a "government agent" along the Mexican border, although he never spoke of his years at Seattle.[29]

Seid Gain left the immigration bureau in 1909 after officials ignored his recommendations that three Chinese interpreters should be dismissed—two for incompetence and one for being an opium smoker. The commissioner of immigration found his judgments to be without grounds and believed that in making such recommendations Seid had "exceeded his authority." Angry and embittered, Seid quit the bureau and—like Tape—returned to tend his father's businesses and to play role of culture broker. In 1914 he gave an expansive interview to a Portland newspaper, in which he rehearsed his father's rags-to-riches story and his own experiences as an American citizen and lawyer, including a cryptic statement that the "extensive traveling" he had done for immigration bureau had opened his eyes and gave him "a real education in men and manners." The reporter noted the books in Seid's library—Shakespeare, Poe, Lincoln, and Chinese classics—but when he left, Seid gave him a copy of the "Maxims of Confucius." [30]

Other interpreters from the first cohort also did well, whether or not they remained in the employ of the INS. After Edward Park was dismissed from his job at Angel Island in 1917 for corruption he relocated to Los Angeles, where he became a court interpreter. His wife and two daughters worked in Hollywood, in a film-studio costume department and as studio actresses, respectively. Others went on to work for railway companies and banks.[31]

Quan Foy, the quiet interpreter from Seattle, also followed the path of upward mobility—he bought a home in Seattle, raised nine children as American citizens, and worked for the immigration bureau for thirty-two years. But his story ended differently. Quan was dismissed from his position in 1933, when the Immigration and Naturalization Service mandated the retirement of all persons with thirty years of service. Quan was sixty-seven years old and was put out without a pension. Hoping to conserve his resources, he departed to Hong Kong with his wife and children, save for his eldest son, who remained in Seattle. He left with a laborer's certificate—a stunning declaration of his legal status after three decades of government employment.[32]

Perhaps there was no other choice, for he was ineligible for a merchant's certificate, but being designated a "laborer" turned him into a legal undesirable. In 1939 Quan returned to the United States in order to visit his eldest son but as a "laborer" he was inadmissible under the Chinese exclusion laws. At inspection, he did not require an interpreter. He was deemed to be "afflicted with senility, Class B" (denoting a liability to become a public charge) but because he owned property and would be supported by his son, and in light of his career as a government interpreter, he was admitted as a temporary visitor for a period of one year.[33]

Aging and in declining health, Quan decided to remain in the United States. Every year he had to file for an extension, and every year his former supervisor at the Seattle immigration office wrote the San Francisco district (which supervised the visa) to reiterate Quan's faithful service and "bespeaking for him every consideration that the Government could render." In 1945 Quan's application for the extension was late and he was promptly notified that, as an "illegal resident," he was subject to deportation proceedings. But the application was made and the extension was granted for another year. In 1947 Quan Foy died in Seattle at the age of eighty.[34]

Reading through Quan Foy's file one would not know that Congress had repealed the Chinese exclusion laws in 1943. There was no change in the bureaucratic procedure that he was required to follow each year and he continued to remain in the United States at the sufferance of the INS. One wonders whether he felt humiliated each time he had to ask his old boss to vouch for his application. More broadly, several decades had passed since the 1910s, when interpreters were at the center of corruption controversies that wracked the immigration bureau. With a greater professionalization of the INS and with a larger Chinese American population, a job as Chinese interpreter in the 1940s carried more limited possibilities for graft, social status, and power. Quan Foy's experience suggests how little a career as a government interpreter had come to matter.

Historians have barely noticed the immigrant translator. Perhaps because the interpreter's mediation of language is taken for granted, thought to be seamless, the interpreter has been relegated to the sidelines of social interaction and history-making. But immigrants understood well that the interpreter's power was considerable, especially those interpreters who worked for the state. How the interpreter used that power—and one could not always be sure—could either assist or thwart the immigrants' chances for entry into the country, for justice, for survival. The officers of the immigration bureau and other state agencies knew, too, that legal and social control over the immigrants depended on the interpreters' linguistic ability and, more important, their sense of occupational, if not political, duty. If interpreters were simple word machines they would not have so confounded the parties they purported to serve, they would not have inspired such conflicting judgments of respect and doubt. That this liminal space at the boundary of two social worlds produced such power and affect should alert us that interpreters and interpreting are far from inconsequential in immigration history.

The history of the interpreters also complicates the conventional narrative of immigrant assimilation and ethnic middle-class formation—the idea that exclusion and racial discrimination are eventually displaced by inclusion and assimilation. The assumption that there is a normative path of inclusion in the country of immigration that *occurs over time* remains fixed in historical and social-science migration studies; it has not been dislodged by the so-called transnational turn, which focuses synchronically on the first generation.[35] The history of Chinese-immigrant interpreters suggests a different dynamic of middle-class formation that proceeded simultaneously along apposite vectors of immigrant experience, exclusion, *and* inclusion, a dynamic that was entwined and contingent. At one level, the social location of immigrant interpreters and other quotidian brokers allowed for some of the earliest occupational opportunities outside the ethnic-enclave economy for accumulating wealth and social connections and for testing the limits of racial exclusion. But Chinese interpreters also enabled and profited from exclusion in myriad ways: in its legal enforcement, by keeping Chinese immigrants within the social and economic boundaries that exclusion established, and in exclusion's illegal underground economy. Chinese interpreters incorporated themselves and their families into a new Chinese American middle class by managing and mediating the incorporation of immigrants into the margins of American society. Socioeconomic mobility was not, then, as stereotypically linear histories suggest, the result of studying and working hard to overcome obstacles of exclusion. Rather, social-class formation might be seen as a limit case, produced by practices of entrepreneurialism and self-fashioning that typify liminal figures, practices that might be understood too as acts of translation.

Notes

1. "Statistics, Facts and Trivia," in "The World's Fair and Exposition Information and Reference Guide: 1904 Louisiana Purchase Exposition–St. Louis World's Fair," Earth Station 9, http://www.earthstation9.com.
2. Advertisement, "On the Pike" (nd), scrapbooks of the Louisiana Purchase Exposition, vol. 16, p. 64, Special Collections, St. Louis Public Library; Frank Tape personnel folder, National Archives and Records Administration, National Personnel Records Center, St. Louis (hereafter "INS-PERS").
3. Edmund Philibert, "World's Fair Diary," Martha Clevenger, *Indescribably Grand: Diaries and Letters from the St. Louis World's Fair* (St. Louis: Missouri Historical Society, 1996), 87.
4. "In relation to the admission heretofore of Chinese persons to take part in exhibitions authorized by Act of Congress" (nd), file 11047/2, Records of the Immigration and Naturalization Service, RG 85, National Archives (Washington DC) (hereafter "INS").
5. F. P. Sargent, "Memorandum, in re regulations regarding Chinese coming to take part in the Louisiana Purchase Exposition," April 29, 1904, file 11047/2, INS; Dunn to Commissioner General, May 19, 1904, file 11047/25, INS; HH North to Commissioner General, June 23, 1904, file 11047/25, INS; Frank Sargent to FH Larned, Sept. 19, 1904, file 11047/37, INS; Frank Sargent to HH North, July 7, 1904, box 2, Henry Hart North papers, Bancroft Library (Berkeley).
6. "Uncle Sam Guards Chinese at Fair," *St. Louis Republic*, August 15, 1904; James Dunn to Commissioner General, May 19, 1904, file 11047/25, INS; "Uncle Sam Guards Chinese at Fair," *St. Louis Republic*, Aug. 18, 1904.
7. Dunn to Commissioner General, May 19, 1904, file 11047/25, INS; Frank Tape, personnel folder, INS-PERS.
8. Statement of Chinese Interpreter Frank Tape, Sept. 19, 1904, file 11047/37, INS.
9. "Second Arrest in Chinese Case," *SF Chronicle*, Sept. 24, 1904; sworn statements given to immigration inspector W. H. Webber by Yuen Choy Fong, Chan

Ho, Lee Kum Kew, and Leong Tuck, Aug. 12, 1904, file 11047/31, INS; James Dunn, letters to Commissioner General, Oct. 1, 24, and 26, and Nov. 2, 14, and 18, 1904, file 11047/37, INS; "Chinese Woman Under Arrest," *St. Louis Globe-Democrat*, Oct. 23, 1904; "Arrest Chinese Girls on Government Warrants," *St. Louis Republic*, Nov. 5, 1904; "Chinese Village Closely Guarded," *St. Louis Republic*, Nov. 17, 1904; "Could Not Secure Service of the Habeas Corpus Writ," *St. Louis Republic*, Nov. 18, 1904.

10. "Fan Tan Loser Mourns for Bride," *St. Louis Post-Dispatch*, Dec. 10, 1904; "Bogus Certificates are Sold to Chinese," *SF Call*, July 1, 1906.
11. "Chinese Blood Goes into the Bureau," SF *Morning Call*, April 5, 1905; "North Gives a Chinese a Job," *SF Chronicle*, April 4, 1905.
12. For the decade 1870–79, Chinese immigration was 123,201; for 1880–89, immigration dropped to 61,711; from 1890–1899, it was 14,799. Bill Ong Hing, *Making and Remaking Asian America Through Immigration Policy, 1850–1990* (Stanford, CA: Stanford University Press, 1993), table 3, 48; W. C. Witherbee to Commissioner General, August 20, 1900, file 1814, INS.
13. Rosters of Chinese inspectors, Chinese interpreters, and white Chinese interpreters, May 1907, file 52702/2, INS.
14. File 52127/1, INS; Joseph Caston, *Portland, Oregon, Its History and Builders*, Vol. I (Chicago-Portland, 1911), 347–48; US Industrial Commission, *Final Report, Vol. VII, Smuggling of Asiatics*, Senate doc. 415, 64th Congress, First Session (Washington, 1916), 6303–6312 (hereafter *Smuggling of Asiatics*).
15. Translation of anonymous letter "from St. Louis" to Charles Nagel, Secretary of Commerce/Labor, December 18, 1909, File 4, carton 21, Him Mark Lai Papers, Ethnic Studies Library, University of Berkeley (hereafter HML).
16. *Smuggling of Asiatics*, 6226; FP Sargent to Secretary of Commerce and Labor, October 24, 1907, file 53360/34, entry 9, INS. Seid gave separate evaluations for "ability to interpret [spoken translation]," "ability to translate [written documents]," "general bearing and personality," and "character and habits." Memorandum for the Assistant Secretary, March 13, 1908, file 53360.34, entry 9, INS.
17. "Chinese Interpreters Prefer to Remain Here; Order to Break Up Their Homes Causes Great Consternation," *SF Morning Call*, June 4, 1907.
18. Him Mark Lai and Philip Choy, interview with Mamie Lowe and Emily Lum, July 29, 1972, Portland Oregon (tape recording, in author's possession, courtesy Him Mark Lai).
19. Biographical sketch of Liang Guibo (Robert Park), *History of Sam Yup Benevolent Association in the U.S., 1850–2000* (San Francisco 2000), 214; "Chinese Natives. Organization of a Parlor of Sons," *SF Morning Call*, February 4, 1893; Immigration interview of Robert Leon Park, January 31, 1921, file 12016/1908, SF District case files, National Archives (San Francisco) (hereafter NARA-SF); "Chinese Make Strong Protest," *SF Chronicle*, April 30, 1906.
20. Richard Taylor to Commissioner General, October 3, 1908 (hereafter "Taylor Report"), INS microfilm, reel 8, pp. 27–28; *Smuggling of Asiatics*, 6257.
21. *Smuggling of Asiatics*, 6133, 6072; RP Bonham to District Director (San Francisco), August 10, 1940, 9600/10-3, copy in file 29, carton 23, HML; see also, "Personal History of 12 Chinese Interpreters Now Serving the Bureau of Immigration at Most Important Stations Who Are Without Right to Be in the United States," April 30, 1914, p. 1, file 151/121, box 154, General Records of the Department of Labor, 1907–1942, Record Group 174, National Archives (College Park).

22. *Smuggling of Asiatics*, 6186–87, 6123–33.
23. R. P. Bonham to Commissioner General, August 22, 1914, file 53000/910B, INS.
24. "Tape Arrested on Smuggling Charge," *Seattle Times*, September 16, 1914; "Important Government Witness Shot Down," *Seattle Times*, September 27, 1914; "Chinatown is Mum in Hunt for Assassin," *Seattle Star*, September 28, 1914; letter from Young Pin Chew to *Seattle Times*, September 28, 1914; "Asiatic's Death Suicidal," *Oregonian*, December 6, 1914; "Defendants Win in Tape Prosecution," *Seattle Times*, December 11, 1914; "Tape is Acquitted of Second Charge," *Seattle Times*, December 18, 1914; "Jury Finds Tape Took No Bribes," *Seattle Post-Intelligencer*, December 18, 1914.
25. Densmore to Secretary of Labor, January 11, 1916, INS microfilm, supp. reel 4, pp. 9, 19, 20–22; "15 Indicted in Angel Isle Graft Plots," *SF Examiner*, October 20, 1917; "Smuggling of Chinese Bared by Prisoner," *Examiner*, October 4, 1917.
26. Letter from "afraid to show his right name" to Densmore, October 30, 1917, file 12016/1076-3, entry 232, INS, NARA-SF; Lee Tin Yat, statement made to George Parson, April 20, 1917, file 54184/138 folder 3, ibid.
27. *Smuggling of Asiatics*, 6150.
28. "First Chinese Called on Jury Called a 'Real American,'" *SF Chronicle*, March 20, 1923.
29. "Former Policeman and US Investigator Takes Up New Post," [clipping fragment, c. 1923], copy in Frank Tape file, HML; John Bruce, "Skylines of the City, Frank Tape," *SF Call*, September 4, 1934; Hal Johnson, "Smuggler's Nemesis," *Berkeley Daily Gazette*, November 26, 1941.
30. DJ Keefe to Secretary of Commerce and Labor, March 13, 1909, 52129/1, entry 9, INS; "Seid Back, Jr., Discusses Chinese People—Their Manners and Customs," *Oregon Sunday Journal*, February 4, 1914, Section 3, 10.
31. 1928 voter registration list for City of Los Angeles, assembly district 75, precinct 586, microfilm roll 122, California Voter Registrations, 1900–1968, http://AncestryLibrary.com; Population Census of the U.S., 1930, California, Los Angeles County, Los Angeles district 64, series T626, roll 146, p. 16, ibid; *Chung Sai Yat Po*, February 21, 1916, October 2, 1919.
32. File 39600/10-3, INS, copy in file 29, carton 23, HML. Chinese interpreters were not civil service appointments and therefore were not entitled to a pension.
33. Board of Special Inquiry hearing, Angel Island station, October 14, 1939, "In the matter of Quan Foy," ibid.
34. Bonham to San Francisco District Director, August 2, 1944; Stan Olsen (Entry and Departure Section, San Francisco) to Quan Foy, December 13,1945; Bonham to Ugo Carusi, January 7, 1947, all file 39600/10-3, ibid.
35. Recent work on the second generation points to a gradual diminution of transnational practices and trends of adaptation and acculturation. See Robert C. Smith, *Mexican New York: Transnational Lives of New Immigrants* (Berkeley: University of California Press, 2005); Peggy Levitt and Mary Waters, ed. *The Changing Face of Home: The Transnational Lives of the Second Generation* (New York: Russell Sage Foundation, 2002); Philip Kasinitz, John H. Mollenkopf, Mary C. Waters, and Jennifer Holdaway, *Inheriting the City: Children of Immigrants Come of Age* (Cambridge, MA: Harvard University Press, 2008); Edward Telles and Vilma Ortiz, *Generations of Exclusion: Mexican Americans, Assimilation, and Race* (New York: Russell Sage Foundation, 2009).

3

Rebel, Deportee, Governor
The Life of Antonio I. Villarreal

Kelly Lytle Hernández

The author, Kelly Lytle Hernández, is an associate professor of history and African American studies at the University of California–Los Angeles, and is the author of *Migra!: A History of the U.S. Border Patrol* (University of California Press) and *City of Inmates: Conquest, Rebellion, and the Rise of Human Caging in Los Angeles* (University of North Carolina Press, 2017).

Deportation is a process of forcibly expelling a person from a country. But it can also be a process of forcibly repatriating a person to a country and, since the early-twentieth century, the Mexican government has repeatedly used US immigration law to force Mexican migrants to return south of the border. For example, during the Great Depression, the Mexican government supported efforts to force tens of thousands of Mexican immigrants out of the United States. At the time, the Mexican authorities imagined Mexicans who had lived and worked in the United States as potential leaders of agricultural modernization and technological modernization in Mexico. Therefore, Mexican authorities wanted Mexico's rural migrants to return home and help with the modernization of the Mexican countryside. And during the Bracero Era (1942–1964), the Mexican government demanded that US authorities conduct mass deportation campaigns to forcibly return to Mexico Mexican workers who had entered the United States with neither United States nor Mexican authorization. This time, they hoped to stem the loss of workers from Mexico.[1]

But Mexican authorities first began to use US deportation proceedings to repatriate Mexican nationals as early as the 1900s. In these years, Mexican authorities were not motivated by concerns regarding labor and modernization. They were motivated by fear and fury as they struggled to capture a band of cross-border rebels using the United States as a sanctuary from which to plan, organize, and launch a revolution in Mexico.[2] This essay tells the story of one of these rebels, Antonio Villarreal, who was targeted for deportation from the United States and repatriation to Mexico in years leading into the Mexican Revolution of 1910.

At the dawn of the twentieth century, a revolution brewed against Mexico's president, Porfirio Díaz. Díaz, who had ruled Mexico since 1876, had ushered in dramatic changes across Mexico. In particular, he courted foreign capitalists to invest in Mexican land and industries, triggering a massive dislocation of Mexico's rural population.[3] He also centralized and consolidated power in his office, leaving little room for opposition. In fact, Díaz routinely instructed the *rurales* (national police) to crush any whisper of dissent against his policies, practices, or rule.[4] By 1900, many Mexicans had begun to organize against the Díaz regime, holding study groups, organizing alternative political conferences, and publishing insurgent journals. Among them was a young teacher named Antonio Villarreal.

In 1901, Antonio was living in the industrial town of Monterrey in northern Mexico. By day, he was a teacher at a local school. By night, he organized political meetings to discuss the corrupt and antidemocratic tendencies of the Díaz regime. By 1903, Antonio had committed himself to more than meetings and critiques: He was publishing articles directly challenging the legitimacy of Porfirio Díaz's rule. But, after publishing a just few articles, Antonio was arrested and imprisoned.

When Antonio was released from prison (probably in late 1903), he fled Mexico and crossed into the United States with a band of hardscrabble Mexican rebels hell-bent on ousting Porfirio Díaz from office. Their plan was to organize a rebellion in Mexico from the sanctuary of the United States because from north of the border the rebels benefitted from escaping Díaz's *rurales* and prisons but were still able to live and work among Mexicans, especially the tens of thousands who had been displaced within Díaz's Mexico and, in turn, immigrated to the United States.[5]

By February 1904, Villarreal's rebel band was holding rallies in scores of Mexican immigrant communities north of the border.[6] They decried President Díaz as a tyrant and a butcher. They also published an incendiary newspaper, *Regeneracion,* which called for Díaz's immediate ouster. The rebels mailed *Regeneracion* deep into Mexico and, when Díaz denied them postal privileges south of the border, migrant workers carried the newspaper with them as they moved back and forth across the border in search of work. Díaz dispatched Mexico's "secret police" to crush the rebellion before it began. Throughout the United States and into Canada, Díaz's agents chased the rebels, spying on their activities and instigating their arrests on numerous charges. At first, Díaz's agents initiated extradition proceedings against the rebels to force the rebels back into Mexico for punishment—execution, most likely. When extradition failed (as explained below), they began to leverage the US deportation regime.

The United States Congress first invented deportation during the 1890s.[7] At the time, Congress was searching for ways to forcibly remove all Chinese laborers who entered the United States after the passage of the Chinese Exclusion Act. But, in the early years of the twentieth century, Congress significantly expanded the definition of who was deportable. By 1904, US immigration law prohibited Chinese laborers, prostitutes, criminals, and those liable to rely on the government for support from entering the United States. US immigration law also prohibited from entering the United States all persons convicted of committing acts of "moral turpitude" prior to entering the United States. But (with the exception of Chinese immigrants) all such exclusions became null, void, and unenforceable if excludable immigrants lived in the United States for three or more years without detection. In other words, deportation had a three-year limit, making deportability a short-term status for immigrants who, according to US immigration law, should have been excluded at the point of entering the United States.[8]

In 1906, Villarreal and his rebel crew had moved into El Paso, Texas. Their plan was to launch an armed raid on the city just across the border from El Paso in Ciudad Juárez, which was Mexico's most important land port with the United States. A joint team of US and Mexican authorities, as well as private detectives, heard rumors of the plan and poured into El Paso to stop the raid. On October 20, 1906, they caught one of the rebels in Juarez while he was trying to recruit fighters for the rebel army. In his pocket he carried a list of addresses for rebels living in the United States and Mexico.[9] Díaz's agents seized the list and began raiding homes and businesses across the borderlands. During the raids, they got a tip that Villarreal would be meeting with rebel leaders at the Legal Tender Saloon in El Paso on the evening of October 21, 1906. Mallen and his team rushed to the saloon, packed inside, and waited for the rebels to arrive. Villarreal arrived first. When he opened the bar door, Mallen's team tackled him and placed him under arrest.[10]

With Villarreal in custody, Mexican authorities first attempted to extradite him to Mexico. The US Secretary of State agreed to have Villarreal detained in the El Paso County Jail while Balbino Dávalos, the Mexican Ambassador to the United States, submitted formal extradition proceedings against Villarreal. But extradition required the government to produce, within forty days, evidence that the target of extradition had committed an extraditable, criminal offense. The Mexican government drummed up criminal charges against Villarreal, claiming he had stolen $7 in firewood in 1903. When the US Commissioner hearing the extradition case said that petty larceny was not an extraditable offense, Díaz's agents submitted a new charge. This time it was murder. But the Mexican authorities could not provide any evidence that Villarreal had committed murder in Mexico. As the forty day-mark neared, Ambassador Dávalos scrambled to find some way to force Villarreal back to Mexico. The US secretary of state recommended that he consider a relatively new practice in US law and life: deportation. Dávalos agreed and formally asked the US government to deport Villarreal as an unlawful immigrant. Villarreal had, he claimed, been convicted of murder and served time in prison in Mexico. Thus, as a former convict, he should have been excluded from entry into the United States. And since he had entered sometime after March 1905—less than three years earlier—he was eligible for deportation.

By triggering deportation, Mexican authorities found another way to force Villarreal's return to Mexico.

Then, as now, deportation occupies a peculiar place in American law and life. The US Constitution does not apply to the practices of US immigration control. As the Supreme Court ruled in 1893, "The provisions of the Constitution, securing the right of trial by jury and prohibiting unreasonable searches and seizures, and cruel and unusual punishments, have no application." In other words, the federal government has "unregulated" authority over immigration matters and the protections provided by the US Constitution and Bill of Rights do not apply to the laws and practices involved in identifying, apprehending, detaining, and removing immigrants.

Once swept into the US immigration regime, Villarreal would bear the burden of proving his lawful entry into the United States. That would prove nearly impossible with Mexican authorities testifying at his deportation hearing that he had committed a crime of "moral turpitude" in Mexico before entering the United States.

What follows is an excerpt from the transcript of Villarreal's deportation hearing. It was held in the El Paso County Jail where Villarreal was confined after his initial arrest in El Paso, Texas, on October 21, 1906. Consul Mallen not only attended the hearing, he testified against Villarreal, submitting evidence from a prison in Mexico indicating that a man named Antonio Villarreal had served time for murder in 1904. Throughout the hearing Villarreal disputed the Mexican government's evidence against him, arguing that Mexican authorities were orchestrating his deportation to get him back in Mexico for execution.

Deportation Hearing for Antonio Villarreal, 1906

Location: El Paso County Jail
Present: Antonio Villarreal (alien); Francisco Mallen (Mexican consul); T. F. Schmucker (immigration inspector), J. X. Strand (immigration inspector), C. G. Gatley (immigration inspector), George B. Oliver (secretary); Antonio Sierra (interpreter).

IMMIGRATION INSPECTOR: Have you anything to state to the Board at this time to show cause why you should not be deported from the United States in accordance with said warrant?

VILLARREAL: Yes, sir.

IMMIGRATION INSPECTOR: Then you may make your statement.

VILLARREAL: I am being prosecuted as a political refugee by the Mexican government. The Mexican government is endeavoring to get me back into the Republic of Mexico; Ambassador Thompson has asked that I be deported to Mexico as an anarchist; that charge has not been provided against me and I have not been deported.

IMMIGRATION INSPECTOR: Anything further?

VILLARREAL: Lately I have been accused of a violation of the neutrality laws of the United States. That charge has not been decided as yet. It seems that they have no proofs that I may be punished on that charge of which I am accused, and they have resorted to this new method of taking me back to Mexico as the Mexican government wants to get me back to Mexico and sacrifice me as it has done other newspaper men who have opposed the present government. They have tried to sacrifice all those who have done nothing more than fight the tyrant Díaz and have worked for a better government in Mexico.

. . .

INSPECTOR: Were you ever convicted of any crime in the Republic of Mexico?

VILLARREAL: No, sir.

INSPECTOR: Were you ever arrested by the Mexican authorities in the Republic of Mexico?

VILLARREAL: Yes, sir.

INSPECTOR: When and where?

VILLARREAL: I have been arrested in Lampasas. I don't remember when.

INSPECTOR: About when?

VILLARREAL: I do not remember.

INSPECTOR: On what charges were you arrested in Lampasas?

VILLARREAL: For political reasons.

INSPECTOR: What was the exact charge that was placed against you?

VILLARREAL: They did not have any charges. They simply took me because I wrote to the press.

INSPECTOR: Were you sentenced under that charge?

VILLARREAL: Only for two or three days.

INSPECTOR: Were you in confinement under that charge?

VILLARREAL: No, sir.

INSPECTOR: Were you ever charge[d] with any offense in the Republic of Mexico by the Mexican authorities?

VILLARREAL: Yes, sir.

INSPECTOR: When and where?

VILLARREAL: In Monterrey.

INSPECTOR: When?

VILLARREAL: In 1901, if I remember right.

INSPECTOR: What was the charge made against you in Monterrey in 1901?

VILLARREAL: Sedition and inciting revolution against the Mexican government.

Despite Villarreal's protests, the US immigration authorities ordered him deported from the United States. Mallen had given the US immigration inspector a copy of Villarreal's mug shot from his 1901 arrest and imprisonment in Monterrey, providing it as evidence that Villarreal had been convicted of a crime of moral turpitude before entering the United States. The US immigration inspector accepted the mug shot as proof that Villarreal was, as a former convict, prohibited from lawfully the United States and, thereby, ordered Villarreal deported from the United States. Two immigration officers promptly removed Villarreal from the El Paso County Jail and walked him toward the border. Along the way, Villarreal asked to stop and send a telegram to his family back home. The officers agreed, allowing him to enter a Western Union office while they waited on the street. Villarreal never returned.[11] He had jumped out a back window and disappeared, living on the run until arrested the following year in Los Angeles, California.

While Villarreal lived on the run, Mexican authorities and US officers on Díaz's payroll hunted him down. They also initiated more deportation cases against Mexican rebels living in the United States. For example, several dozen were arrested and deported in Arizona.[12] Therefore, Mexican authorities were applying what they had learned in the Villarreal case to many other Mexican nationals, triggering the first-ever wave of Mexican deportation from the United States.

Villarreal was finally arrested during a dramatic raid on a small home at the outskirts of Los Angeles, California, on August 24, 1907.[13] But, at this point, Mexican authorities did not seek Villarreal's deportation. Rather, they tried another tactic to silence Villarreal and his rebel cohort. This time, they worked with US authorities to charge Villarreal with violating the US Neutrality Act, which prohibited organizing invasions of foreign countries from US soil. It worked. A jury convicted Villarreal and two of his colleagues for organizing an armed raid in Mexico. A judge sentenced them to serve three years in prison.

When Antonio was released from prison in 1910, the Mexican government again tried to have him deported but, by then, Díaz's sway among US authorities had waned. A popular book published by a US journalist, *Barbarous Mexico*, had exposed the conditions of near enslavement in which many workers lived and the role that Díaz and his *rurales* had in protecting both Mexican employers and US investors in Mexican industries.[14] In 1910, the United States Congress held hearings on the issue. *Barbarous Mexico* and the hearings severely weakened US support for the Díaz government. With few reservoirs of support and rebellions mounting in Mexico, Díaz's reign was coming to an end by August 1910. In November, the Mexican Revolution began. By May 1911, Díaz fled Mexico and lived the rest of his days in France. Villarreal, on the other hand, voluntarily returned to Mexico and was later appointed governor of Nuevo León.

Villarreal's story provides an important reminder that the line between removal and repatriation is thin, unveiling how forced migrations are processes of going and coming, expulsion and arrival. For example, in the long history of Mexican migration to the United States, deportation has always involved US and Mexican authorities and the convergence of many interests across the United States-Mexico border. Therefore, to understand the impact of deportation on lives, economies, and societies it is crucial to look, study, and think beyond borders. Villarreal's story also shows that while deportation is a highly repressive realm of governance in the United States, immigrants quite often evade its reach and subvert its intentions. Antonio Villarreal, whom US authorities ordered out of the country in 1906, evaded deportation and continued to live within the United States without authorization. From the shadows of US law and life, he played a key role in the making of the Mexican Revolution, the first social revolution of the twentieth century. Deportees, therefore, are not always deported and despite the challenges of unauthorized status they hold the power to change history. In 1906, Antonio Villarreal, a Mexican deportee living on the run in the United States, stoked the rise of the Mexican Revolution of 1910. And across the United States today, hundreds of thousands of immigrants are defying US deportation orders. Many among them, especially undocumented youth and workers, are challenging and changing the US immigration regime. What will come of their rebellions is a story still brewing in the United States and beyond.

Notes

1. For more on the global context of deportation see Torrie Hester, *Deportation: Origins of US Policy* (University of Pennsylvania Press, forthcoming). For more on the role of Mexican authorities in US deportation campaigns, see Gilbert González, *Mexican Consuls and Labor Organizing: Imperial Politics in the American Southwest, 1920–1940* (Austin: University of Texas, 1999); Kelly Lytle Hernández, *Migra! A History of the U.S. Border Patrol* (Berkeley: University of California Press, 2010).

2. For more on Mexican efforts to stop Mexican rebels from organizing in the United States see, Ward S. Albro, *Always a Rebel: Ricardo Flores Magón and the Mexican Revolution* (Fort Worth: Texas Christian University Press, 1992); John Mason Hart, *Anarchism & the Mexican Working Class, 1860–1931* (Austin: University of Texas Press, 1978); and Dirk Raat, *Revoltosos: Mexico's Rebels in the United States, 1903–1923* (College Station: Texas A&M Press, 1981).
3. For more on Mexico during the era of Porfirio Díaz, see Friedrich Katz, "Labor Conditions on Haciendas in Porfirian Mexico: Some Trends and Tendencies," *Hispanic American Historical Review* 54, no. 1 (1974): 1–47; and Mauricio Tenorio-Trillo and Aurora Gómez Galvarriato, *El Porfiriato* (Centro de Investigación y Docencia Económicas, 2006). For more on the rise of Mexican evolution see, Adolfo Gilly, *The Mexican Revolution: A People's History* (New York: New Press, 2006); Emilio Kourí, *A Pueblo Divided: Business, Property, and Community in Papantla, Mexico* (Stanford, CA: Stanford University Press, 2004).
4. Paul Vanderwood, *Disorder and Progress: Bandits, Police, and Mexican Development* (Lincoln: University of Nebraska Press, 1981).
5. See note 2.
6. Letters from Consul Lomeli, January 25 and February 8, 1904, leg. 270, exp. 3, AEMEUA, Archivo Histórico Diplomático (AHD, Mexico City).
7. Daniel Kanstroom, *Deportation Nation: Outsiders in American History* (Cambridge, MA: Harvard University Press, 2007), 91–130; Torrie Hester, "'Protection, Not Punishment': Legislative and Judicial Formation of U.S. Deportation Policy, 1882–1904," *Journal of American Ethnic History* 30, no. 1 (2010): 11–36; Deirdre M. Moloney, *National Insecurities: Immigrants and U.S. Deportation Policy since 1882* (Chapel Hill: University of North Carolina Press, 2012); and Daniel Wilsher, *Immigration Detention: Law, History, Politics* (Cambridge, UK: Cambridge University Press, 2013).
8. Torrie Hester, "Deportability and the Carceral State," *Journal of American History* 102, no. 1 (2015): 141–51.
9. El Gob to Corral, October 23, 1906, folder 7A, box 26, Silvestre Terrazas Papers (STP), Bancroft Library, University of California, Berkeley.
10. Aaron Ortiz, "Exile and Utopia," available at http://www.magonista.net.
11. Night message (telegram) from Francisco Mallén (El Paso) to Enrique Creel, February 25, 1907, leg. 302, exp. 3, AEMEUA, AHD.
12. See Corral to Creel, October 9, 1906, folder 7A, box 26, STP; See also letters in leg. 285, exp. 6, AEMEUA, AHD.
13. "Nip Revolutionist in Los Angeles Den," *Los Angeles Times*, August 24, 1907.
14. John Kenneth Turner, *Barbarous Mexico* (Chicago: Charles H. Kerr & Company, 1910).

4

Mexican Migrants, Family Separation, and US Immigration Policy Since 1942

Adam Goodman

The author, Adam Goodman, is an assistant professor of history and Latin American and Latino studies at the University of Illinois at Chicago. He has written about United States and Mexican politics, migration, and deportation for academic venues like the *Journal of American Ethnic History* and popular outlets such as the *Nation*. Portions of this text first appeared in the *Pennsylvania Gazette*.

For a few nights each January, the palm-lined plaza of San Pedro,[1] a small town in the central Mexican state of Jalisco, fills with people. Men sporting cowboy hats and large belt buckles dance with their girlfriends or wives to the *ranchera* music of a regionally-known twelve-person band. Young men and women circle the plaza in opposite directions, seeking out

Figure 4.1 "San Pedro," Jalisco, plaza during the town's annual festival. Photo by Adam Goodman.

potential partners. A few blocks north of the plaza, a large multipurpose tent used for weddings and *quinceañeras* during the year is turned into a venue for *los gallos*—the nightly cockfights. The buoyant atmosphere makes it easy to understand why so many people would travel so far to attend.

San Pedro is largely an agricultural community, and most people make their living off the land. But many have left. The town, like so many others in traditional migrant-sending states such as Jalisco, Michoacán, and Guanajuato, has a long history of migration to the United States that dates back to the 1940s, if not before. Most residents who went north have had run-ins with immigration authorities, but, until recently, that hadn't stopped them from going—or coming back for the town's annual festival.

That's why Fernanda and Claudia Camacho and their husbands were there, home from the United States, to the delight of their younger sister Gabriela, who still lives in San Pedro. To celebrate the occasion, they slaughtered a 200-plus-pound pig for their extended family members and friends to enjoy during the week. Not all of the Camacho siblings could make it, however. Some, in fact, hadn't been back in years.

On August 4, 1942, the United States and Mexico signed the Emergency Mexican Farm Labor Agreement, marking the beginning of the Bracero Program—a series of bilateral agreements under which the two governments issued 4.6 million temporary labor contracts to Mexican men over the course of twenty-two years—and a new era of Mexican migration. Most of the contracted laborers worked in agriculture, although, in the early years, some worked on the railroads. During the same period, an equal, if not greater, number of Mexican men, women, and children migrated to the United States without authorization, and immigration officials carried out close to 6 million deportations (Calavita 1992; Ngai 2004).

Often times it was not easy to distinguish between the documented and undocumented migrants. As Mae Ngai has noted, "[b]raceros and 'wetbacks' (a derogatory name for unauthorized migrants) were sometimes members of the same family" and, in some cases, "illegal migrants were male relatives whom braceros recruited for their employers" (Ngai 2004, 150–1). It was common for men to migrate as braceros and then overstay or "skip out" on their contracts. Others decided to enter as undocumented workers, either due to the limited number of contracts (in the regions with heavy migration there were twenty interested men for every available contract) or in hopes of avoiding the long, costly, and humiliating formal contracting process (Fitzgerald 2009, 51).

In reality, many men migrated on multiple occasions, sometimes with contracts, sometimes without. Andrés Rodríguez was twenty years old the first time he left San Pedro for the United States in 1948. After traveling by bus to Empalme, Sonora, one of the main bracero contracting centers, he went by train to Mexicali, where US officials conducted a medical inspection and fumigated him before allowing him to enter. Rodríguez spent the next two decades traveling back and forth between San Pedro and different parts of California (Watsonville, Arroyo Grande, and Sacramento, among others), where he picked lettuce, celery, strawberries, apricots, and peaches.

Often times, Rodríguez was able to secure a bracero contract. When he couldn't, he went anyway, paying $80 (around $700 in today's dollars) to a *coyote* to take him across the border. As was so often the case, Rodríguez's connections to people from his hometown facilitated his migration and shaped his experience. On one of the farms where he worked, his immediate boss was a man nicknamed "El Manzano" (the apple tree), who was from San Pedro. El Manzano not only gave Rodríguez a job and a place to live, he also protected him from immigration raids. Each month, before *la migra* came to do a sweep of the farm, he warned the undocumented workers, "Tomorrow they're going to do a check, so be ready!" But immigration officials didn't always tip off growers and Rodríguez was apprehended and deported at least three times. That never discouraged him from returning the following year, though, whether or not he had a contract.

During the Bracero Program, the migration of millions of men like Rodríguez had a significant impact on Mexican communities. Mexican officials envisioned the program as an economic development plan. As historian Deborah Cohen has argued, while braceros went to the United States to provide for themselves and their families, the Mexican government saw them as idealized masculine subjects that would help modernize the nation. But modernization came at a cost. More than anything, the Bracero Program resulted in long-term family separation, the creation of transnational families, and shifting gender relations in Mexican families and towns (Cohen 2011; Rosas 2014).

After 1942, San Pedro's population skewed heavily female for much of the year, since so many men were working in the north. As in other parts of Mexico, the women and children left behind were forced to assume new responsibilities. According to Ana Rosas (2014, 4–5), the Bracero Program's impact on women was "a source of both stress *and* empowerment." On the one hand, it "enabled them to learn to act and function more independently"; on the other, it "cause[d] them emotional pain and labor exploitation." The impact on Mexican children was more one-sided. "The majority of [kids] here suffered because their fathers weren't around. . . . The majority were orphaned," Claudia Camacho recalled. Moreover, in their fathers' absence, many children toiled under exploitative conditions, sacrificing much of their childhoods in the process (Rosas 2014).

Regardless of the toll the Bracero Program took on men, women, and children, over time places like San Pedro came to depend on migration, just as employers in the United States continued to depend on Mexican migrant labor. This became increasingly true after December 31, 1964, when the program came to an end. The next two decades saw the dawning of a new era in the history of Mexican migration. From 1965 to 1985, the flow of migrants to the United States expanded to include many of the children of braceros, who followed in their fathers' footsteps in search of work, adventure, and a better life for themselves, their families, and their communities. But those who ventured north during these years did so under distinct political circumstances. The termination of the Bracero Program, combined with the first-ever cap on Western Hemisphere immigration under the 1965 Immigration Act (and subsequent 20,000-person country cap in 1976), resulted in a spike in undocumented Mexican migration (Ngai 2004). People from places like San Pedro, whose livelihoods had become intertwined with migration during the last twenty-two years, now had no choice but to go without a contract.

In the years following the Bracero Program, it was not uncommon for as many as half of San Pedro's three thousand inhabitants to be in the United States. The majority of people went to California and worked in agriculture, although, over time, a greater percentage found work in construction or the growing service industry. Today, it is not an exaggeration to say that the vast majority of men and a number of women older than forty have migrated from San Pedro to the United States—or at least attempted to do so—on one or more occasions.

Claudia Camacho first migrated to the United States in 1976, at the age of sixteen. She had recently married and went so that she could be with her nineteen-year-old husband, Manuel, who had spent much of the previous two years working in the central California fields. He had returned to San Pedro for the holidays and annual festival and, with no job prospects in Mexico, they decided to set out for the United States together in February, just a few weeks after they married and less than a week after her sister Fernanda and her husband Alejandro had done the same. When Claudia and Manuel told her mother that they also planned to leave, her mother responded, "Well, if you're going to kill me, better to do it all at once!"

The next day, Claudia and Manuel set out for Tijuana, by bus. When they arrived, they sought out a woman who helped people from San Pedro make arrangements to cross the border. Manuel paid a *coyote* to guide him through the desert at night and into the United States, just as he had in previous years. Manuel made it across without incident, but crossing was dangerous, particularly in the dark. The previous February, he and ten or fifteen other men had crossed the Tijuana-Chula Vista border by wading into the Pacific and enduring freezing cold water that went up to their chests, all while holding their possessions above their heads. Hoping to prevent something like this from happening to Claudia, they decided that she would cross in the morning, at a port of entry, with the aid of a passport of someone who resembled her. She did so, without any problems, and then traveled by car to Los Angeles before continuing on to her sister-in-law's house in an agricultural community outside of Santa

Barbara. When she finally arrived, at two or three in the morning, Manuel was waiting for her.

For the next decade, Claudia, Manuel, Fernanda, and Alejandro lived and worked in the United States. At first, they returned to San Pedro each winter, along with many others from the town who spent much of the year in "El Norte." Manuel estimated that one hundred to two hundred San Pedroans set out for the United States each February, after the town's annual festival, but doing so became more difficult once their families began to grow. Crossing with the aid of a *coyote* was expensive, and returning with small children complicated matters further. On one occasion, Claudia had to send her oldest daughter in a car with some of Manuel's relatives, before being reunited with her on the other side. It was a risky proposition, even if it was still relatively easy to re-enter the United States compared to how it would become in the decades ahead.

As undocumented migrations increased, deportations did as well. From 1976 to 1985, the INS deported close to 1 million people per year, nearly all of them Mexican. Manuel estimated that authorities apprehended him a handful of times over the course of a decade. Alejandro also had run-ins with the INS. On one occasion, after spending some time in San Pedro, *la migra* caught him near San Diego, soon after he had crossed, and held him in detention for three weeks. "They detained us there as witnesses to screw over the *coyote*," he remembered, "but in reality we didn't know him." Alejandro had a number of close calls, as well. Once, the INS raided the farm where he worked, forcing him to scale a 10-foot-tall tree and hide for a couple of hours as *la migra* circled below.

Between 1965 and 1985, enhanced enforcement at the border and in established ethnic Mexican communities in the US interior meant that the possibility of being apprehended at any moment became the norm for undocumented migrants. These tactics had a chilling effect on the lives of many Mexicans, some of whom stopped going to restaurants, stores, and even to church, out of fear that they'd be picked up. Mexican men may have represented the vast majority of all deportees during this period, but authorities also apprehended more than 2 million women and children, around 100,000 per year.

Everything changed in 1986, when Claudia, Manuel, Fernanda, and Alejandro became legal residents—and, later, US citizens—thanks to the Immigration Reform and Control Act (IRCA). More than 3 million Mexicans naturalized under IRCA, the last comprehensive immigration reform in the United States. Gaining legal status had a significant positive impact on Mexican migrants' lives. It not only meant that they could stay and work in the United States—it also meant that they could return to Mexico.

Since becoming legal permanent residents and eventually US citizens Claudia, Manuel, Fernanda, and Alejandro have returned to San Pedro at least once, and usually twice, each year. As a result, they are able to see their younger sister Gabriela, in addition to other friends and extended family. Gabriela is the only one of the family's eight siblings to have stayed in San Pedro. All the others live in California. Many of them, like Claudia and Fernanda, immigrated decades ago, when they were still teenagers. Although Gabriela gets to see her five US-citizen siblings once or more each year, her brother Tomás and her sister Conchita never naturalized. "It has been fifteen years since I last saw my sister Conchita. And my youngest brother, three years," Gabriela said as tears wetted her cheeks. "I want to see them."

In recent years, far fewer have made the journey to the United States, in part because of the heightened costs and danger of crossing without authorization. Since 1994, when the INS launched Operation Gatekeeper and adopted a strategy of "prevention through deterrence," border militarization has expanded at an alarming rate, with significant consequences for migrants. The construction of border walls and concentrated enforcement in populated parts of the US-Mexico divide have helped to create a thriving migrant smuggling industry, since crossing in more desolate areas requires the assistance of a guide. The current rate, in US dollars, to travel from San Pedro to California is around $6,000 to $7,000. Border crossing deaths have shot up, as well. Whereas known migrant deaths totaled 171 in 1994, they had reached 492 by 2005, and have averaged around 400 per year in the decade since, even though apprehensions fell during the same period (Nevins 2002; De León 2015).

In spite of these harsh realities, combined with the economic recession and a declining birth rate in Mexico, some San Pedroans have continued to migrate. Gabriela oldest son, Iván, is one of them. He first went when he was fifteen or sixteen, and tried his luck a handful of times or more between 2001 and 2011. Immigration officials apprehended and deported him on a few occasions, including one time in which he almost died in the desert after injuring his ankle. He only made it out alive thanks to a friend who insisted on staying with him until Border Patrol agents took them into custody. Gabriela and her husband Eliseo would prefer that Iván stay in the United States until he regularizes his status. Even though the fact that their eldest child lives thousands of miles away pains them, they don't want him to return to San Pedro and then risk crossing without authorization again. They're unequivocal on this point and yet, they remain somewhat optimistic. "We have this dream that one day our son will get his papers so that he can visit us," Eliseo said. "Come and go back, like the others who are documented."

The freedom of Gabriela's naturalized siblings and other San Pedroans to come and go has also made a remarkable difference to the town itself. When the Camachos migrated to the United States as teenagers, they were driven by need, and for more than three decades they have labored long hours doing physically taxing jobs on ranches, at wineries, and in the fields. The years of strenuous labor have exerted a physical toll; Fernanda is no longer able to work due to various ailments. Yet their hard work has paid off in the sense that they accumulated savings and property. Claudia and Manuel own two lunch trucks that they operate in the United States, and Fernanda and Alejandro own a house in California, and another in San Pedro—to which they recently added a second story.

Theirs is a familiar pattern. Walking around town during the day, it is hard not to be struck by the juxtaposition of cars bearing US license plates parked in the driveways of two-story California-style houses (remodeled using remittance dollars) next to one-room cement-wall houses that lack basic utilities: migration's impact on material well-being writ literally in bricks and mortar.

The impact of remittances has been uneven, but collectively there is little doubt that they have improved the overall material conditions of the town. Some of the money has been used for services, put into the church, and used to beautify the plaza and improve other public amenities. But this dynamic is not without drawbacks. There is a sense that the Mexican government does not feel the need to provide as much for remittance-dependent communities like San Pedro, which furthers its reliance on migration—and fractured families—as a means of economic development.

Comprehensive immigration reform would give the 11 million undocumented people living in the United States a chance to become citizens, in turn benefitting individuals, families, and communities on both sides of the border. Today, when the possibility of legislative action is discussed, the first thing people like the Camachos think about isn't the US economy, the potential long-term political impact, or border security. No. It's what a difference IRCA made for Claudia, Manuel, Fernanda, Alejandro, and San Pedro, and what a new comprehensive immigration reform that includes a path to citizenship would mean for Gabriela, Eliseo, Iván, Tomás, and Conchita. And so many other families.

Notes

1. I have changed the name of the town and the names of its residents, to protect their privacy. Most of the information in this chapter is drawn from oral histories I conducted in "San Pedro" in 2012–13. Statistical information is drawn from Immigration and Naturalization Service/Department of Homeland Security Annual Reports and the Office of Immigration Statistics Statistical Yearbooks.

References

Calavita, Kitty. 1992. *Inside the State: The Bracero Program, Immigration, and the I.N.S.* New York: Routledge.

Cohen, Deborah. 2011. *Braceros: Migrant Citizens and Transnational Subjects in the Postwar United States and Mexico.* Chapel Hill: University of North Carolina Press.

De León, Jason. 2015. *The Land of Open Graves: Living and Dying on the Migrant Trail.* Berkeley: University of California Press.

Fitzgerald, David. 2009. *A Nation of Emigrants: How Mexico Manages Its Migration.* Berkeley: University of California Press.
Nevins, Joseph. 2002. *Operation Gatekeeper and Beyond: The War on "Illegals" and the Remaking of the U.S.-Mexico Boundary.* New York: Routledge.
Ngai, Mae. 2004. *Impossible Subjects: Illegal Aliens and the Making of Modern America.* Princeton, NJ: Princeton University Press.
Rosas, Ana E. 2014. *Abrazando el Espíritu: Bracero Families Confront The US-Mexico Border.* Berkeley: University of California Press.

PART 2

FAMILIES TORN APART

How Do Deportation Laws Affect Families?

One of the most significant changes to US immigration law in the twentieth century was the 1965 Immigration and Nationality Act, also called the 1965 Hart-Celler Act. This act put an end to the racially biased quotas set forth in the 1924 Oriental Exclusion Act and the Immigration Act of 1924. In the spirit of the civil rights movement, the 1965 act set a universal quota of 20,000 immigrants for every country in the world. (Although as noted earlier, the quota did not go fully into effect for Mexico until 1976.) Each country could send up to 20,000 qualified immigrants a year, with no racial restrictions. Potential immigrants could now qualify for entry based on either family ties to the United States (relatives could petition for their entry) or their skills (employers could request immigrants based on their skills and education). The family reunification provisions in the Hart-Celler Act constituted an important recognition in immigration law that immigrants have families and should have the right to be reunited with them.

The 1965 act had two main consequences: (1) it increased immigration from Asia, Latin America, and the Caribbean due to the possibilities opened up for legal migration from these countries and (2) it increased undocumented immigration from Mexico due to unrealistic quotas placed on Mexican migration. The arrival of large numbers of nonwhite immigrants eventually led to new waves of anti-immigrant sentiment. The topic of illegal immigration first emerged on the national agenda in the 1980s when the tightening economy, combined with the settlement of increasing numbers of Latin Americans and Asians, generated waves of nativism and anti-immigrant sentiment. These sentiments eventually translated into legislation, and the Immigration Reform and Control Act (IRCA) was passed in 1986. IRCA contained both legalization and restrictive provisions. Specifically, it created a path to legalization for people who lived in the United States but did not have proper authorization to reside in the country, and it imposed sanctions on employers who hired people not authorized to work in the United States.

One of the major consequences of IRCA was to further encourage the permanent settlement of Mexican immigrants, who had formerly come primarily as temporary workers. Until the 1970s, over 80 percent of Mexican immigrants were temporary workers who came to the United States to work in the agricultural sector for a few months, and returned to Mexico with their savings. By 1997, only 40 percent of Mexican migration was for temporary work in the agricultural sector (Avila, Fuentes, and Tuirán 2000). The legalization of temporary workers encouraged more migrants to settle permanently in the United States, and to bring their families with them (Massey, Durand, and Nolan 2002). Once migrants obtained legal residence or citizenship, they were able to bring their family members to live in the United States, under the 1965 family reunification provisions. These provisions have meant that the face of immigration has changed since 1965—from primarily European to primarily Latin American and Asian.

Although no major legalization measures have made it through Congress since 1986, in 2012, President Obama signed an executive order called Deferred Action for Childhood Arrivals (DACA), which grants temporary reprieve from deportation as well as a work permit to youth who arrived in the United States prior to the age of fifteen and have completed high school. This executive order has opened up possibilities for hundreds of thousands of immigrant youth to come out of the shadows. In 2014, President Obama announced an expansion of DACA that would grant deferred action to the parents of DACA recipients. This program is called the Deferred Action for Parents of Americans and Lawful Permanent Residents (DAPA) program. However, a federal district court in Texas issued an order that blocked DAPA from being implemented. A subsequent Supreme Court decision upheld this injunction and DAPA has not become a reality. The consequence of this decision is that some undocumented youth have been granted temporary reprieve from deportation and a work permit, yet their parents and other family members still live with the threat of deportation. As we shall see in a chapter in this section, Rafael is one example of an immigrant youth who has been able to benefit from DACA while his parents and other family members are not.

US immigration law allows for family reunification yet various other provisions prevent families from being able to live together. For example, US immigration law often makes it difficult for married couples to stay together or to reunite even when one partner is a US citizen. A legal permanent resident, a temporary legal resident, or an undocumented migrant living in the United States has even fewer options in terms of family reunification. These laws often lead to people having to choose between their family and their country—an impossible choice. Gomberg-Muñoz describes a family that tried to legalize the status of the only undocumented member—the mother—which led to a cascade of heartbreaks.

The Brazilian twins discussed in Kara Cebulko's chapter never imagined they would be forced to live thousands of miles apart. Rafael's story, discussed in Lisa Martinez's chapter, renders evident what happens when the government fails to recognize the legitimacy of gay families, as well as the possibilities that open up when gay marriage is finally recognized.

The family reunification provisions in US immigration law allow for some families to be reunited yet deny this opportunity to other families. The provisions in US immigration law that tear families apart are in contravention to the human rights tradition, which upholds the right of all human beings, regardless of nationality, to have a family. The human rights tradition is based on the premise that all human beings share a fundamental right to live in dignity (Blau and Moncada 2005). Human rights, unlike citizenship rights, are applicable to all people, regardless of national origin or place of residence. The human rights tradition is particularly pertinent for international migrants, insofar as migrants live outside of their land of citizenship, and therefore are unable to exercise some of their citizenship-related rights and privileges (Basok and Carasco 2010). Human rights doctrine includes many rights that are relevant to migrants, including the fundamental human right to emigrate. Article 13 of the Universal Declaration on Human Rights (UDHR) sets out that "Every person has the right to leave any country, including his own, and to return to his country." The UDHR is not a legally binding doctrine yet can serve as a moral compass for people who believe that all human beings deserve rights and dignity, regardless of national origin.

The importance of families is also inscribed in the human rights doctrine. For example, Article 23 of the International Covenant on Civil and Political Rights (ICCPR)—which the United States has ratified—states, "[T]he family is the natural and fundamental group unit of society and is entitled to protection by society and the state" and that all men and women have the right "to marry and to found a family." Because the United States has ratified this covenant, we have a responsibility to uphold these principles. Immigration law, however, is often at odds with the human right to have a family.

These essays raise important questions about migration, human rights, and the family. If we accept that "the family is the natural and fundamental group unit of society and is entitled to protection by society and the state," where does that leave families separated by borders? They also raise questions about which families are deserving of protection. Does an immigration violation overrule one's right to be with one's family? What about siblings—is this a relationship worthy of protection? And what about same-sex marriage? The contributions in this section allow us to consider these and other tensions between immigration policy and human rights.

Rafael's story, told by Lisa Martinez, allows us to see how US immigration policy simultaneously allows for and denies the rights of people to be with their families. Rafael's family crossed the border without authorization from Mexico to the United States when he was just six years old. Like many undocumented youth, Rafael did not think much about his immigration status until he was making the transition to adulthood and sought to do things many teenagers do such as get a driver's license, find part-time work, and apply to college. He became more aware of his family's precarious status when his grandparents fell ill in Mexico and they struggled with the decision of whether or not to return to care for them. When his parents decided to return and then faced the brunt of immigration law enforcement, their status as undocumented migrants became even more salient. When DACA was announced, Rafael's life took another turn as he was finally able to secure employment in an area that matched his education and expertise. The ups and downs that Rafael and his family face due to immigration policies shed light on the contradictory nature of these policies as well as how immigration law both reunites and tears apart families.

Ramón and Lupita's story, narrated by Ruth Gomberg-Muñoz, also sheds light on the possibilities as well as the tragedies of immigration policy. Ramón came to the United States in the 1980s and thus was able to benefit from IRCA, similar to the migrants introduced by Adam Goodman. Ramón's wife, Lupita, however, came to the United States in 1992, and there have been no legalization laws passed that would apply to her. They thus waited until Ramón secured US citizenship and applied for legalization for Lupita on that basis. Despite their marriage and the fact that Lupita and Ramón had three US citizen children together, Lupita's application was denied due to the fact that she had returned to Mexico in 2002 to visit her ailing mother. Although family reunification provisions enabled Ramón to apply for legalization for his wife, other more punitive provisions prevented his wife from returning to Mexico to care for her mother and entering the United States illegally a second time. Now, Ramón and his children, all US citizens, have to face the impossible choice between living in their country of citizenship and being together as a family unit.

The twin sisters introduced by Kara Cebulko, Bianca and Roberta, have also faced heart-wrenching decisions and have had to choose between their families and two countries where they have strong ties. Roberta was granted DACA, which allows her to stay in the United States legally for now. This authorization, however, does not qualify her for any of the family reunification provisions of US immigration law. Bianca was denied re-entry to the United States after returning home to Brazil, and now the two sisters live separated by thousands of miles as well as strict border controls. With family members both in the United States and in Brazil, no matter which country they choose to spend their lives in, these twins are bound to live lives of forced separation from their family members.

Together, the essays in this section render evident the possibilities that open up when immigration laws recognize the importance of family unity and provide opportunities for legal residency for settled migrants. At the same time, they also render evident the heart-wrenching choices families must make when some family members are offered legalization while others are denied that opportunity.

References

Avila, José Luis, Carlos Fuentes, and Rodolfo Tuirán. 2000. "Tiempos de estancia de los trabajadores temporales en los Estados Unidos: Situación actual y perspectivas" ("Length of stay of temporary workers in the United States: Current Situation and Perspectives"). In *La situación demográfica de México, 2000. Mexico: Consejo Nacional de Población.* http://www.conapo.gob.mx/es/CONAPO/La_Situacion_Demografica_de_Mexico_2000

Massey, Douglas S., Jorge Durand, and Nolan J. Malone. 2002. *Beyond Smoke and Mirrors: Mexican Immigration in an Era of Economic Integration.* New York: Russell Sage Foundation.

Basok, Tanya, and Emily Carasco. 2010. "Advancing the Rights of Non-Citizens in Canada: A Human Rights Approach to Migrant Rights." *Human Rights Quarterly* 32 (2): 342–66.

Blau, Judith R., and Alberto Moncada. 2005. *Human Rights: Beyond the Liberal Vision.* Rowman & Littlefield.

5

Becoming American

Lisa M. Martinez

Lisa M. Martinez is associate professor and chair in the department of sociology and criminology at the University of Denver. Her current research examines the educational and occupational trajectories of undocumented Latina/o youth in Colorado pre- and post-DACA.[1]

The notion of the American dream was first popularized in poetry and books written in the 1930s, reflecting both the optimism and despair of immigrants arriving in a new land. The imagery and ethos of the United States as a beacon of hope remains popular today; yet, the dream eludes many who are unable to become American due to legal barriers, mainly, their undocumented status. Such was the case of Rafael, who was a sophomore in college when I met him. He was thriving in school, making the most of his college experience, participating in campus organizations and activities, and excelling academically despite attending under-resourced schools most of his life. He had been the first person in his family to graduate from high school and was well on his way to becoming the first in his family to graduate from a four-year college.

Rafael's path was a tumultuous one because of his legal status and that of his parents and older siblings. The family decided to migrate to the United States from a small town in Zacatecas, Mexico, as economic conditions there were deteriorating. Rafael's parents were in pursuit of the American dream, which they hoped would bring better opportunities for their children, if not themselves. After saying goodbye to parents, grandparents, and extended relatives, Rafael's family drove across the border, entering the United States through El Paso, Texas, on July 4, 1992. As families across the country commemorated Independence Day with picnics, baseball games, and fireworks, Rafael's family began their journey to Colorado where his parents had worked as migrant laborers in the 1980s and 1990s. They were on their way to a new life.

Like many 1.5-generation[2] children who are born in one country but spend most of their youth in an adopted country, Rafael was six years old when his family arrived in the United States. Initially, he faced many challenges as he was unfamiliar with the language, customs, and school system. Eventually, he would get a handle on things and go on to have a normal childhood, much like that of his neighborhood friends and peers at school. Although his family was poor and he attended schools that were majority Latina/o and African American, Rafael believed that his goal to be the first in his family to graduate from college was not insurmountable. The fact that he was undocumented did not deter him either, mostly because he "never knew what it meant. My parents always talked about papers, papers, papers, and when you are a kid, you are like, 'Papers? What is papers?' You think of a piece of paper or something like that." As is the case for most undocumented youth, the realization that his status would have consequences occurred when he was in high school, "When I first realized I was undocumented was when I first applied for my first job, when I was a sophomore in high school, because everybody in high school is like 'Oh, I'm turning 16, I'm getting my license' or 'Oh, I'm turning 16, I'm going to get my first job' . . . [A]nd when I really, really found out what being undocumented was, was when I applied to college, because I couldn't apply for any financial aid." Colorado did not offer in-state tuition for undocumented students when Rafael was applying to college, but he was hopeful private scholarships would be an option, prompting him to apply widely to colleges and universities throughout the state. He was accepted to his top school, which he attended on a full-tuition scholarship thanks to a benefactor who started a private fund in support of first-generation college students and those from lower income communities. The scholarship had come through at the last minute after another scholarship was rescinded because Rafael could not provide a social security number.

Once in college, Rafael took advantage of many opportunities and relished the chance to "give back" and work in support of other undocumented and first-generation students. Known throughout campus, Rafael took on leadership roles and soon amassed an impressive resume of awards and accolades in the hope that it would be enough to overcome his legal status. But reality began to set in once again as graduation approached. As his friends made plans for the future, Rafael became withdrawn and lost a bit of his spark. He tried to hide it from friends or attributed it to school-related stress but those closest to him knew what was really bothering him.

Following graduation, Rafael continued to work a job in retail, as he had throughout college, but it did not compare to his friends who were embarking on exciting careers or continuing their studies in graduate and professional schools. Rafael said, "I was very depressed. I wanted to give up. I was like, 'Why am I doing all this?' I felt like every time I have an opportunity to better myself, there is always something that brings me down. Coming to a private university, being undocumented, I was like,

'It's gonna open doors for me. I can work in a field, I can make a difference.' That didn't happen."

Circumstances deteriorated further for immigrant families like Rafael's in the years following the passage of SB 90, Colorado's "show me your papers" law, in 2006. SB 90 gave law enforcement the authority to report individuals suspected of being in the country without documents to Immigration and Customs Enforcement (ICE).[3] One of the many consequences of the law was an increase in the number of individuals apprehended, detained, and in many cases deported for traffic violations and misdemeanors.[4] These state-level efforts to detain and deport undocumented immigrants were accompanied by enhanced enforcement along the United States-Mexico border.

Rafael's first brush with border enforcement came in 2009 when his mother, Lucila, received news from Mexico that her father was ill. Unable to return to Mexico when her mother passed away years earlier, Lucila was determined to return to her father's bedside. Rafael's father, Humberto, decided to return as well after finding himself unemployed when his employer instituted the E-Verify system, which is used by employers to confirm the status of employees by electronically checking information on their I-9 forms against government records. If there is a mismatch in information, the employer is notified. Rafael's parents returned to Mexico and, to everyone's relief, his grandfather's health improved. It was at that point that Lucila decided to return to the United States. Humberto chose to stay in Mexico, knowing it would be difficult for him to find work. They also reasoned Lucila was more likely to find employment in the informal sector of the economy, such as domestic work,[5] where employers are less likely to use E-Verify. This demonstrates one of two ways in which female immigrants in the United States are advantaged relative to their male counterparts. The other is that they are less likely to be criminalized, detained, or deported than immigrant men.[6]

Rafael's mother set out to cross the Arizona desert with the help of a *coyote* (smuggler) they found through word-of-mouth. Two weeks passed and Rafael and his siblings began to worry as they did not hear from her:

> We didn't know anything about my mom for two weeks. Obviously, you start thinking the worst, but she was actually somewhere in Arizona, [and] we never knew exactly where specifically. But she was in Arizona for two weeks in the desert and she told us that she was never going to cross the desert again, it was too dangerous. She saw a lot of things . . . a lot of women getting raped, people were left behind because they were old . . . and she was

> old herself, she is fifty-six. She promised us she would never do that again because it was a lot for us to go through and a lot for her to go through.

Lucila eventually made it back to Colorado but, in 2011, returned to Mexico once again. When she and her husband then attempted to re-enter the United States, however, they encountered trouble. As before, they knew it would be impossible to cross the border by car and opted to hire a *coyote* once again to bring them across through Tijuana. After they settled on this plan, Rafael and his siblings pulled together $3,000 and wired the money to Los Angeles where the *coyote* was living. The *coyote* took the money but never picked up his parents in Tijuana as per their arrangement. Rafael's parents waited in Tijuana for a month before deciding to cross on their own through Ciudad Juárez, across the border from El Paso, Texas. Once there, Lucila and Humberto hired another *coyote* who told them he could get them across without going through the desert. Relieved they would not have to cross on foot, they agreed, but the journey was no less perilous. Rafael said:

> She hasn't told us exactly what happened but they were detained. My mom was detained at 3:00pm and my dad was detained at 3:10pm, so they were ten minutes apart. And when they got caught, we didn't know where they were. It was Friday, it was Saturday, [and] we didn't know where they were. We started calling hospitals. We started calling the emergency rooms and everything and we couldn't find my dad because he wasn't listed [as a detainee on the ICE website]. Because when you go onto the website, they tell you when the people have been caught. My dad wasn't listed, only my mom. Obviously, you start thinking the worst you know, but that is when they were actually detained.

As the only English-speaking sibling in the family other than his high school-age sister, Rafael took it upon himself to locate Humberto. At first, they wondered if he was not listed because he had successfully made it across. But as time passed without word from their father, fear set in:

> I guess we all go through different emotions and my idea was—the first thing that crossed my mind was—if my parents were to die, when am I gonna see them, since I am no longer able to go back to Mexico? So my biggest concern was if my parents died, or, . . . if something happened, will I be able to see [my dad] and if so, will he be alive when I see him?

Humberto was eventually located at a detention facility in El Paso. His parents were held there before being transferred to another facility in New Mexico. They were detained for a total of six weeks before being deported to Mexico. Around the same time, Rafael decided to quit his job when his employer began using E-Verify as well. Losing a job he enjoyed and was good at, coupled with his parents' detention, resulted in another bout of depression. "I made really close friends at my job and when I had to quit, everybody asked me, 'Why did you quit? Why are you leaving? Why are you not here anymore?' And I never told anyone. I made up a lie." Rafael eventually found work at a call center for a debt collector. Although he was grateful to have found another job, it was not the type of work he envisioned doing with a college degree. He also learned that his new coworkers were not sympathetic when it came to undocumented immigrants. Months after he had been hired, Rafael's employer began using E-Verify as well, which flagged an applicant whose information did not match their Social Security number. When everyone found out, Rafael's coworker commented, "He wasn't legit. He's a liar, he is a criminal. They should deport him." Hearing the coworker's comments hurt Rafael as he considered her a friend but it also made him hesitant to share his status with other people because "you never know who to tell and who not to tell. That is why when I work, I don't build close friendships or try to get close to anyone because, at the end of the day, you don't know how they feel about immigration."

That Rafael felt guarded was understandable. His coworker's comments about immigrants affected him deeply and, even though they were hurtful, he offered that she was not ignorant per se and entitled to her opinion. Consequently, Rafael became more guarded and was careful about sharing information about himself, despite the fact that he played a leadership role in a local civic organization where people sometimes asked questions about his line of work:

> When people ask me, "What do you do for a living?" Well, I do collections. "Well, don't you have a bachelor's degree [in field]?" "Well I do, but I can't really work in my field because everything that is in my field requires a background check and requires some type of traveling or something I am not able to do." So I feel like sometimes people look down on me because I do collections. And they are like "Why are you the president [of the civic organization]?" and "Why do you do this?"

The toll of being undocumented, coupled with their parents being detained, adversely affected Rafael's siblings as well. Having always been close to their parents, his younger sister, who was the only citizen in the family, struggled the most. Rafael explained, "It probably affected her the most because just being the youngest and so attached to my parents . . . she gets really angry at everyone and she didn't understand why she couldn't do anything because she was born here." Despite her citizenship, Rafael's sister felt helpless as she could not do anything to prevent her parents' deportation. Rafael viewed things a bit differently but understood his sister's point of view:

> I am undocumented. . . . I know we broke the law. I know to come here illegally is against the law but she doesn't understand that because she is a citizen. And she was in high school. The immigration policies, they don't make a lot of sense and she was like, "Why?" And you just tell them, that is just the way it is and sometimes it is a good enough answer and sometimes it is not.

In 2012, the Obama administration announced the Deferred Action for Childhood Arrivals (DACA) program which granted undocumented students who came to the United States as children relief from deportation and work authorization provided they meet eligibility criteria. As a result, nearly three-quarters of a million undocumented youth have been able to attend institutions of higher education, find employment following graduation, and earn higher wages than they would have without DACA.[7] Rafael is one of the beneficiaries of the program, which has provided new opportunities including a job where his skills, education, and training are better utilized while also preparing him for a career in his chosen field. A few months after landing the new job, Rafael and I met to discuss how things were going for him. He beamed as he described how much he loved his new colleagues, the work they were doing, and the fact that he had his "own office and health benefits!"

Rafael had other reasons to be excited. After dating for nearly ten years, Rafael and his partner, Alonso, a US citizen, became engaged. He had come out in high school, but very few people outside his closest circle of friends and a few allies knew he was gay. Even though he suspected Lucila and Humberto knew, it had always been a difficult subject to broach with them and he struggled to "find the right time to tell them." He also faced pressure from people who told him to get married as a way to gain residency but the implication was always that he should marry a woman. Rafael disclosed, "I am gonna be honest, my sisters were like, 'Well, just marry a US citizen, apply for your residency and that is the end of that.' At the time they didn't know I was with my partner, so I would always make up excuses. I was like, 'Oh, well, I am in school, it will mess up her financial aid' or some really dumb excuse."

In July 2013, the US Supreme Court ruled that Section 3 of the Defense of Marriage Act (DOMA) was unconstitutional, allowing US citizens to sponsor their same-sex spouses or partners for permanent residency for the first time.[8] The following year, gay marriage became legal in Colorado, prompting Rafael and Alonso to get married. Rafael decided it was time to tell his parents he was gay and wanted to do so in person. Toward that end, he took advantage of Advance Parole, an immigration document that allows DACA recipients to travel outside the United States for humanitarian, educational, or employment purposes. Upon return, recipients get their passports stamped showing legal re-entry, which allows them to begin the process of obtaining a green card. It was a gamble, but one Rafael was willing to take. Upon his return, Rafael shared his experience crossing the United States–Mexico border:

> After over twenty hours from my home town to the border, we decided to purchase tickets to cross the border from Ciudad Juárez to El Paso on a Transborde bus. As we were approaching the border, I became very nervous. After waiting in traffic for about an hour to reach the checkpoint, we were told to get off the Transborde at the customs checkpoint and make our way across the border on foot. I entered the line for people crossing on the Transborde. The line seemed to move fast and after about fifteen minutes I was waiting in front of a customs officer and handed him my passport and my I-512L [authorization for parole]. The officer seemed confused and didn't recognize the document and told me he had to speak to his supervisor. After a few minutes, the officer came back and told me I needed to proceed to secondary inspection. I followed him through several doors before finally entering a waiting room with several chairs with handcuffs. I was told to sit down and wait until my name was called.

Rafael continued:

> As I was sitting in the waiting area, I tried to stay calm but the overwhelming feelings and doubts of not being able to cross back continued to cross my mind. I thought, "What if I'm not allowed back to the United States? Where will I go? How will I get home? How will I notify my family?" I tried calling Alonso but couldn't reach him. After a while, I finally heard my name and an officer approached me. He spoke to me in Spanish, but I decided to respond in English. He asked me where I was going and why I had been in Mexico. He took my picture and my fingerprints. At this point, I was still very nervous. The officer then took me to his desk and began asking me more questions.

Rafael was questioned for two hours before being told he was free to go.

Rafael and Alonso eventually returned to Colorado and, because Rafael's passport was stamped, it was a legal entry and he was able to begin the process of applying for a green card on the basis of his marriage to a US citizen. When it came time to submit his green card application, he approached the application with the care, thoroughness, and level of detail he had used for writing papers or studying for exams in college. The packet included a personal narrative, bills, rental leases, schoolwork, pictures, and awards he had amassed as well as affidavits in support of his application. Although most of the materials were not required, he had pulled it together as part of the process and noted how funny it was he kept these documents over the years without knowing how important they would be. Asked how he felt, Rafael commented that he was hopeful things would move forward smoothly and was excited at the prospect of no longer having to live in fear of being pulled over without a driver's license or getting deported. He knew, however, his parents would likely never leave Mexico again and his opportunities to see them would be limited as well. Rafael concluded by saying, "I feel very privileged because I know a lot of people didn't have the opportunities I've had. If it weren't for DACA, I wouldn't be here today. It's not everything, but it's something." In some ways, Rafael's narrative parallels those of the other individuals highlighted in this volume. Like Roberta,[9] his family members were removed and, much like Maria Inez,[10] he experienced adverse mental health effects, including depression, as a result of the uncertainty in his life and deportation of his father. Rafael could also have ended up like Ezequiel,[11] deported following his high school graduation. However, a serendipitous turn of events, including the repeal of DOMA, and Advance Parole, provided a different avenue for him than the ones available to Roberta, Maria Inez, and Ezequiel.

Hundreds of thousands of families like Rafael's have experienced the firsthand effects of family separation due to shifts in immigration policies that center on border enforcement, detention, and deportation, which have resulted in an all-time record number of removals in 2012.[12] The Obama administration has promised to prioritize the removal of individuals with criminal violations, yet thousands of individuals without criminal violations continue to be deported every year.[13] Experiences such as Rafael's highlight the contradictions inherent in our nation's immigration policies, providing small glimmers of hope on the one hand and immeasurable obstacles on the other.

In August 2016, Rafael sent his contacts an email with the subject line "Green Card!" His message read, "After so many years, I can finally live without fear! My green card application was approved a few minutes ago!" Despite the challenges he has faced, Rafael believes he is one of the lucky ones as he was able to navigate the rocky terrain on what he hopes is an eventual path to citizenship. Ironically, it was a shift in same-sex marriage policy rather than comprehensive immigration reform that facilitated Rafael's ability to obtain a green card. His parents, however, are ineligible to receive Deferred Action for Parents of Americans (DAPA) and his older siblings are ineligible for relief through DACA because they did not graduate from high school. In many ways, Rafael's family exemplifies how immigration policies result in family separation by physically separating them and structurally privileging those deemed more deserving than others.[14] Countless challenges therefore remain for millions of immigrants waiting to become American.

Notes

1. I am grateful to Rafael for allowing me share his narrative. This chapter is dedicated to his father who passed away in November 2016.
2. The 1.5 generation are children who migrated to the U.S. as children and have spent their formative years, including schooling, here. See Ruben Rumbaut. "Ages, Life Stages, and Generational Cohorts: Decomposing the Immigrant First and Second Generation in the United States. *International Migration Review*, no. 3 (2004):1160–1205.
3. http://www.leg.state.co.us/clics2006a/csl.nsf/fsbillcont3/D44C4D655410B398872570CB005DB438?Open&file=090_enr.pdf
4. http://www.coloradofiscal.org/wp-content/uploads/2013/05/2013-3-1-v.2-SB90-Misplaced-Priorities-Ed.pdf http://www.coloradofiscal.org/wp-content/uploads/2013/05/2013-3-1-v.2-SB90-Misplaced-Priorities-Ed.pdf,
5. Hondagneu-Sotelo, Pierrette, *Doméstica: Immigrant Workers Cleaning and Caring in the Shadows of Affluence* (Berkeley: University of California Press, 2007).
6. Golash-Boza, Tanya, *Deported: Immigrant Policing, Disposable Labor, and Global Capitalism* (New York: NYU Press, 2015).
7. http://www.americanimmigrationcouncil.org/special-reports/DACA-at-Year-Three-Challenges-and-Opportunities
8. https://www.uscis.gov/family/same-sex-marriages
9. Cebulko (this volume).
10. Garcia (this volume).
11. Silver (this volume).
12. https://www.ice.gov/removal-statistics
13. https://www.ice.gov/removal-statistics#wcm-survey-target-id
14. Katie Dingeman-Cerda, Edelina M. Burciaga, and Lisa M. Martinez. "Neither Sinners nor Saints: Complicating the Discourse of Noncitizen Deservingness," *Association of Mexican American Educators Journal* 9, no. 3 (2015): 62–73.

6

'Til Law Do Us Part

Immigration Policy and Mixed-Status Family Separation

Ruth Gomberg-Muñoz

Ruth Gomberg-Muñoz is an assistant professor in the department of anthropology at Loyola University Chicago and the author of Labor and Legality: An Ethnography of a Mexican Immigrant Network *(Oxford University Press, 2011) and* Becoming Legal: Immigration Law and Mixed-Status Families *(Oxford University Press, 2017).*

NINETY-NINE YEARS

Ramón and Lupita met in California in 1995. They were both originally from Mexico City, and both had migrated to California as young adults in search of work. Ramón arrived in California in the early 1980s as an undocumented immigrant, and in 1986, he applied to become a lawful permanent US resident through the IRCA amnesty program. Lupita came to the United States without papers in 1992, after the amnesty program had ended.

When Ramón and Lupita got married in the late 1990s, Ramón could have filed a petition for Lupita's lawful residency then. But the wait for such a process was long—about four years at the time—and a new law, the Illegal Immigration Reform and Immigrant Responsibility Act (IIRIRA) of 1996, had made the process more difficult. Lupita and Ramón were afraid they might be separated if they filed, and they decided to wait and hope for another change in law, maybe even another amnesty program, that would allow Lupita to change her status without risking separation from Ramón.

Over the course of the next ten years, Ramón and Lupita lived in California as a mixed-status family, and they had three US citizen children together—all boys. In 2005, they moved to Chicago and bought a house on the city's south side. Then, in 2008, Ramón became a US citizen. Because he was now a US citizen, the process for getting Lupita's residency would be much shorter. And with no immigration reform on the horizon, they decided to stop waiting and apply to change Lupita's immigration status.

Ramón and Lupita consulted with an attorney and began filing the paperwork and paying the fees they would need for Lupita's application for a "green card," or immigrant visa that confers lawful residency. First, Ramón filed a "family petition," which would make Lupita eligible to apply for a green card based on their marriage. After that petition was approved, Lupita received a notice in the mail with the date and time of an interview with a US Department of State official. Because Lupita is a Mexican citizen and she had never legally entered the United States, her interview was scheduled at the US consulate in Ciudad Juárez, Mexico.

The week before Lupita's interview, on a warm June day in 2011, Ramón, Lupita, and their three sons drove to O'Hare airport, where Lupita boarded a plane headed for Ciudad Juárez. Lupita had to get a physical examination in Juárez, and then have her fingerprints taken before the day of the interview. On the morning of her interview, Lupita arrived at the US consulate in Juárez early. There were hundreds of people already lined up outside, most of them clutching thick files of paperwork. Lupita entered the consulate with her own thick file, was handed a number, and then sat down to wait for her turn to speak with an agent.

When Lupita's number was called, she walked up to a long countertop, where an official was seated behind a thick pane of glass. Lupita slid her file under the glass and explained that she had come to the United States nearly twenty years earlier. Now that she had a US citizen husband and three US citizen children, she told him, she hoped she could change her status. The agent reviewed Lupita's paperwork, then informed her that her application for a green card was denied; in fact, he said, she would not be able to return to the United States at all. "For how long?" she asked him. "Ninety-nine," answered the officer. "Ninety-nine what?" Lupita asked. "Ninety-nine years." Stunned, Lupita left the consulate to call Ramón and break the news.

When I met Ramón and the three boys at their Chicago home a month later, they were still in shock—reeling from the blow of Lupita's unexpected banishment and unsure how to move forward. In 2011, Lupita was one of more than 20,000 undocumented people who left their US homes and families in an attempt to legalize their status; she was one of thousands who were then barred from returning. Ramón and Lupita's story illustrates the ramifications of a US immigration system that claims to prioritize family reunification but tears mixed-status families like theirs apart.

FAMILY IN TWO PLACES

Like many undocumented people in the United States, Lupita had left her parents behind in her home country when she migrated. And because a militarized United States–Mexico border prevented her from traveling back and forth freely, Lupita was unable to visit her parents in Mexico without risking a permanent separation from her husband and children in the United States. So Lupita did not see her parents for nearly a decade, until her mom got sick in 2002.

With her mother ailing in Mexico City, Lupita decided to take the risk and return to Mexico to take care of her. Over four months, Lupita cared for her mother at her parents' home. When her mother recovered, Lupita and Ramón began to make plans for Lupita to come back to the United States. Like many undocumented travelers, Lupita hired a *coyote*, or guide, to bring her across the desert on foot. As a "plan B," Lupita also carried the driver's license of a US citizen in her pocket—a document that Ramón had procured for her just in case.

Lupita was caught by US Border Patrol agents as she and her fellow migrants crossed into California. The agents loaded Lupita and the other migrants onto a bus and drove them back over the United States–Mexico border and into the Mexican border city of Tijuana. Perhaps moved by Lupita's distress, one of the agents whispered in her ear as Lupita disembarked from the bus: *"No están checando las cajuelas hoy."* "They are not checking trunks today." Lupita left the bus and checked into a room at a nearby hotel, and then she called Ramón.

Ramón had been waiting for Lupita just across the border in California. He knew that something was wrong when she did not arrive at their appointed rendezvous on time, and he had already begun driving toward Tijuana when Lupita called to tell him that she did not make it across. Ramón found Lupita at the hotel in Tijuana, where she recounted her interaction with the Border Patrol agent. "That's it, then," Ramón told her, "You can cross in the trunk." Lupita climbed into the trunk of their car, and Ramón drove through the border checkpoint and back into the United States.

THE FAMILY-BASED IMMIGRATION SYSTEM

Like many US citizens, Ramón had thought that his marriage to Lupita would ensure her ability to legalize her status. This assumption is based on the US immigration system's stated emphasis on family: About two-thirds of all immigrant visas issued each year are allotted to the family members of US citizens or lawful permanent residents. Visas for family members can be roughly divided into two groups. The first are for "immediate relatives" of adult US citizens, which includes spouses, unmarried children under the age of twenty-one, and parents. These immediate relatives are not subject to numerical restriction, so they can immigrate as soon as their paperwork is processed. The second group of visas is allotted to other qualifying relatives, including adult children and siblings of US citizens, and spouses and minor children of lawful permanent residents. Visas for family members in this second group are subject to annual quotas, and qualifying family relationships are ordered into a "preference system" that prioritizes some relationships over others. For these relatives, immigrating to the United States involves waiting "in line" for a visa to become available.

All countries are allotted the same number of visas for "preference" relatives, and wait times for these visas range from a few months to more than two decades, depending on where a person is from and how many of their co-countrymen are awaiting a visa already. For example, in February of 2016, the US Department of State (DOS) was processing visa applications for adult unmarried children of US citizens that had been filed in July of 2008—an average worldwide wait time of eight years. But for adult unmarried Filipino children of US citizens, the DOS was processing applications that had been filed in November of 2003—longer than a twelve-year wait. Visa applications for adult unmarried Mexican children of US citizens were being processed from January of 1995—a whopping twenty-one-year wait time for them. Paradoxically, the stronger the family ties between the citizens of any particular country and those of the United States, the more demand there is for these visas and the longer people in those places will have to wait to be reunited with their US family members. People from Mexico, India, China, and the Philippines face especially long wait times, and it should not be surprising that many people from these nations have abandoned the wait and attempted reunification with their US families without the benefit of visas.

The visa "line" is the primary reason why Lupita and Ramón did not file for Lupita's residency while Ramón was still a legal resident: Lupita would have been subject to a long wait. But even after Ramón became a US citizen, Lupita encountered insurmountable barriers to becoming legal because the family-based visa system is not designed for undocumented people like Lupita. For her, attaining residency involved the additional step of leaving the United States and being barred from coming back.

BARS ON REENTRY

Nearly ten years after she visited her mother, when Lupita became eligible to apply for lawful permanent residency through her marriage to Ramón, she encountered several legal obstacles. First, because Lupita had never been lawfully admitted to the United States, she had to leave the country and apply for lawful residency at a US consulate in Mexico. Second, when she left and applied to come back, an automatic ten-year bar on her return was triggered. This ten-year bar was established by the 1996 law IIRIRA and applies to anyone who has lived in the US without authorization for a year or more. The bar is only triggered when a person leaves the United States, and thus the requirement that people like Lupita apply for admission abroad means that the process of legalization routes them into a ten-year separation from their US families.

Between 1996 and 2001, the US Congress would periodically suspend the requirement that undocumented applicants must leave the United States to apply for a green card, thus allowing them to change their status without triggering the bar. But ever since the attacks on the World Trade Center and Pentagon on September 11, 2001, that opportunity has remained closed, compelling applicants like Lupita to separate from their families and get barred from returning to the United States in order to apply for residency.

In select cases, US citizens like Ramón can petition to have the bars on their family members waived if they would cause the US citizen "extreme hardship," such as the loss of medical care, a career, or a home. Thus, when Lupita left the United States to attend her immigration interview, she and Ramón knew that she would be barred from returning for ten years. But they were confident that they could put together a compelling case for Ramón's extreme hardship, since Lupita is the primary caretaker of their three children and Ramón relies heavily on her. What they did not know is that Lupita was subject to a third obstacle known as the "permanent bar." The permanent bar is applied to anyone who lives in the United States for a year or more without authorization, then leaves, then re-enters the United States unlawfully. The permanent bar is waivable, but only after a ten-year period.

The ten-year bar for unlawful presence and permanent bar for unlawful re-entry are only two of dozens of bars that applicants face when they try to become legal. People can be barred from the United States for past drug and alcohol use, helping someone cross the border unlawfully, criminal and immigration violations, making a "false claim" to US citizenship, and even having a "suspicious" tattoo. This legal minefield makes it extraordinarily difficult for undocumented people to change their immigration status, even for those who qualify for a visa because of their family relations with US citizens.

Bars on re-entry are not the only hurdles that undocumented applicants must overcome. Applying for immigration benefits is also expensive. Filing fees for immigration forms can cost hundreds of dollars, and the application process is so complicated that many people find that they also need the assistance of an experienced attorney. For undocumented applicants like Lupita, the costs of filing and attorney fees rise dramatically with the complexity involved in leaving, triggering a bar on re-entry, and petitioning to have the bar waived with a claim to extreme hardship. In Chicago in 2011, such an application process could cost upward of $10,000. Legal expenses are further compounded by travel costs and lost income. The high cost of the application process alone pushes it out of reach for many working-poor families.

While the financial costs of immigration processing are steep, the emotional costs are even higher. Undertaking this process requires families to separate and send one member abroad in the hope that he or she will able to return lawfully. But nothing is guaranteed, and families separate unsure of when they will be together again. The uncertainty and anxiety can wear on a family, causing prolonged stress to everyone involved, especially children.

When applications are successful, families are able to reunite and live together with some protection from deportation. When applications are unsuccessful, families must make difficult decisions about whether to live apart or relocate outside of the United States. In Lupita's case, the permanent bar was unexpected, and when I met with Ramón they were only beginning to come to terms with its implications. "When I talk with her, I don't even want to bring it up," Ramón told me, "[Lupita] tells me that she wants to come running to us, but she knows she can't." Unable to face the prospect of a lifetime without Lupita, Ramón began to make desperate plans.

THE AFTERMATH

The immediate effects of Lupita's banishment on her family were sudden and vicious. When their oldest son learned that his mom would not be returning, he left the house and began walking aimlessly down the street. Five hours later, he returned complaining of stomach pains, and he went to his room to lie down. He stayed in bed for four days before Ramón took him to the emergency room. And though he is now recovering physically, the emotional trauma suffered by him and his younger brothers will not heal so easily. The youngest boy, only three, cannot comprehend why his mother is not with him. Ramón says that every night the boy asks, "Is my mommy coming back soon? When is my mommy coming?" He is too young to understand that his government keeps his mother away from him.

Ramón says that he prays that God will help him figure out a way to put his family back together. "Everything I have here, photos of her, I can't look at them, I feel so desperate because my heart starts to vibrate like it's telling me that my need for her is here [inside my body]," he explained. The family is also now struggling financially. When Ramón went to Mexico City to visit Lupita, he was robbed and beaten. His shoulder was hurt in the attack, and Ramón has been unable to return to his job in a meatpacking plant. And Lupita has so far been unable to find work in Mexico. "We are running out of money," Ramón explained, "and she needs money [in Mexico], too."

To make matters worse, cancerous cells were found during a routine check of Ramón's prostate, and he has been too busy caring for the three boys to follow up with a biopsy. "The cleaning needs to be done, the kids can't do it all, the laundry needs to be done, the dishes, mopping. The oldest boy helps me, but he has a lot of homework," Ramón told me.

He feels utterly overwhelmed. "[Lupita's absence] has affected all of us," he said, "and none of us feel like doing anything."

Now, Ramón and Lupita must weigh their limited options. In ten years, they will be able to apply for a waiver of the remainder of Lupita's permanent bar, but Ramón says that they cannot wait ten years for her to come back. And they have decided that moving the children to Mexico would be unfair to them. "I've told the kids, let's go to Mexico, but they say they don't know anyone there. Anyway, in the capital, [there's so much pollution] you can hardly breathe." With no legal avenues to bring Lupita home, Ramón is now considering other possibilities. Perhaps Lupita could apply for a tourist visa to visit Canada, he proposed, and then enter the United States from the North. "But if that doesn't work," he said, "ultimately, I will go get her. [If] she tells me to, I will go get her. I don't know how I'll do it, but I will go get her." For now, Lupita has asked him to wait; she does not want to risk going to jail if she is caught entering the United States again, or, worse, dying in an attempt to cross the desert. But neither can she face a lifetime away from her husband and children. She and Ramón are in an impossible situation. "It's disgusting what Immigration does to people," Ramón said, ruefully considering his broken family.

TIL LAW DO US PART

Many people are aware that deportation rips families apart, often separating US citizen children from their undocumented parents. Fewer people understand that the legal immigration system also separates families, sometimes forever, when they try to stay together lawfully.

Indeed, changes in US immigration law since the 1990s have made it nearly impossible for millions of people like Lupita to ever become legal—even when they have lived in the United States for decades and have US citizen family members. Between border policies that prevent undocumented people from leaving and immigration policies that prevent them from changing their status, there are now more undocumented people settled in the United States as members of mixed-status families than ever before. According to research from the Pew Hispanic Center, by 2012 more than 60 percent of the undocumented population had lived in the United States for a decade or longer. Nearly 40 percent, or 4 million people, were parents of US citizen children.

These numbers, and the stories of mixed-status families like Lupita and Ramón and their children, demonstrate that the fates of undocumented people and US citizens are often bound together: Policies that target the undocumented also devastate US citizens (García this volume). Moreover, they show why the US immigration system's claim to prioritize family unification rings hollow for millions of mixed-status families subject to separation by prolonged bars on legal re-entry. For Ramón and Lupita, trying to "do the right thing" by legalizing Lupita's status has resulted in her banishment. With no possibility for lawful reunion, they will seek to reunite however they can. At best, Lupita will remain undocumented and subject to deportation; at worst, she will be imprisoned or dead. "The law makes people break it," Ramón explained tearfully as his three boys stood protectively around him in the kitchen of their Chicago home. "We need her here. My children need her here."

More broadly, this family's story highlights the absurdity of immigration policies that reduce people to an individualized status and cannot account for their deep social and familial ties with others (Barak, this volume; García, this volume; Sarabia, this volume). The result is a gross mismatch between social inclusion and legal exclusion, in which undocumented people and their family members become trapped. And potential immigrants are not all equally likely to encounter this mismatch: rather, as US policies disproportionately hinder the lawful immigration of Mexicans, Chinese, Indians, and Filipinos who face especially long visa lines, as well as people who entered the country unlawfully and the working-poor, they face even greater barriers to reuniting with US family members safely. No mere failures of a broken immigration system, these obstacles reproduce long-standing inequities in US immigration laws (see Ngai, this volume; Young, this volume) that make certain people especially vulnerable to separation and deportation. For Lupita, Ramón, and their three children, their separation is experienced as acute physical and emotional pain, wrought by the devastating effects of US immigration laws on their broken family.

7

Double Jeopardy

Deportation and the Life-Course Rituals of Twin Sisters

Kara Cebulko

Kara Cebulko is an associate professor of sociology and global studies at Providence College. Her recent work focuses on legal status as a form of stratification, deconstructing legality/illegality, and the transition to adulthood for unauthorized youth and has appeared in the Sociological Quarterly, Sociological Perspectives, *and* American Behavioral Scientist.

In the summer of 2013, Roberta d'Antona, twenty-six, and I met for an interview for the second time in six years.[1] In 2007, she and her twin sister, Bianca, were nineteen and living with their parents and younger brother in their family's home in Silver, Massachusetts, a small city south of Boston. During those interviews, both sisters had expressed cautious optimism for their futures despite the barriers they faced as unauthorized young adults. Specifically, they were confident that they would fulfill their college dreams. But as happens in life, especially when one lacks legal status, plans often change.

Six years later, in 2013, Roberta was the only one in her family who remained in the United States. She worked as a nurse, finally able to reap the benefits of her investment in education because of the Obama administration's 2012 Deferred Action for Childhood Arrivals (DACA), a policy that provided temporary relief from deportation *and* work permits to certain eligible unauthorized immigrants who migrated as children. But Bianca and the rest of Roberta's family had returned to Brazil. Bianca, who taught English and continued to follow her beloved New England Patriots each Sunday during American football season, said she became "emotional" when I contacted her for another interview, saying it "brought me back to the day we talked and my high hopes for my future in the United States." Meanwhile, Roberta choked back tears and cried during most of our second interview, especially as she described being separated from her twin.

As of spring 2016, the twins, who had done almost everything together for the first twenty years of their lives, had not seen each other in seven years. While both sisters have made the best of their circumstances, there are deep holes in their hearts as they miss out on everyday interactions and important life-course rituals, including engagements, weddings, and childbirths. Both dream of the possibility of raising their families near each other.

But how did this happen? How did these twins, who did nearly everything together for twenty years, come to be living nearly 5,000 miles apart, uncertain of when they would see each other again? The answer to understanding their separation lies in an analysis of the harsh, far-reaching US immigration policies and the intersection of these policies with the twins' generation status (as so-called 1.5-generation immigrants—immigrants born abroad, but raised in the United States) and life-course stage (as young adults).

In 2008, the twins' lives took a dramatic turn when their younger brother was deported, setting in motion a series of heart-wrenching decisions for each family member over the next few years, decisions that ultimately led to every family member but Roberta returning to Brazil. While the twins' mother decided to return to Brazil to support her son following his deportation, the choice to leave or stay was much more difficult for the American-raised twins who were now young adults hoping to pursue college educations. Both initially stayed. Yet other life-course milestones—including becoming a parent and falling in love—ultimately led the twins down different paths. For Bianca, motherhood shaped her decision to join her own mother in Brazil. For Roberta, the pursuit of higher education and a potential engagement to her boyfriend, an unauthorized Brazilian, led her to stay in the United States.

While Bianca is now "forced out" of the United States, Roberta is "fenced in" a country that she considers home. DACA was a welcome movement toward inclusion for Roberta, but the temporary status does not guarantee safe international travel. Thus, even as she feels less constrained in her daily life, DACA has not ameliorated the pain of family separation.

Bianca and Roberta d'Antona were two of the forty-two 1.5-generation Brazilian young adults I first interviewed between 2006 and 2008. They came to the United States in 1999 at age twelve with their family. They were part of the large number of Brazilians who migrated on tourist visas during the 1980s and 1990s and then violated the terms of the visa, becoming "unauthorized." Many of these visa over-stayers were middle-class Brazilians who left during and following an economic crisis in Brazil, which brought massive hyperinflation (Goza 1994; Margolis 1994). While some Brazilians who migrated prior to April 2001 were able to successfully adjust their statuses in the United States under Section 245(i) of the Immigration and Nationality Act (Cebulko 2014), many were not, including the d'Antonas.

Of course, experiences of illegality are shaped by other forms of stratification, including race. While Roberta and Bianca are considered "white" in Brazil (where the racial logic of whiteness is more expansive than in the United States) and are not officially classified as Hispanic in the

United States (because they speak Portuguese, not Spanish), the twins have often been racialized as Hispanic in the United States. Indeed, despite the fact that they have some physical features that "fit" certain Eurocentric standards of beauty, including their straight hair and fair skin, Roberta believes that most people in the United States perceive she and her sister as Hispanic. Like many of their 1.5-generation Brazilian peers, however, how others perceive their "race" is situational, depending on how tan they are, what they are wearing, who they are interacting with, and what language they are speaking (Cebulko 2013).

During the interviews in 2007, Roberta and Bianca described their initial adjustment in the United States as difficult. They struggled to learn a new language and culture. Yet, with family support they started doing well in school, formed a Brazilian cultural club at their high school, and got jobs at a local grocery store, contributing some of their money toward rent at home. It was not until it came time to apply to college that the weight of their legal status hit them hard. Without a Social Security number, neither sister knew how to fill out the applications. Fearful of disclosing their statuses to teachers or advisors, they had no mentors to help them navigate the process.

Bianca and Roberta's education struggles are not unique. Unauthorized students, depending on the communities and states in which they live, face a constellation of legal, financial, and/or other barriers to higher education (Abrego 2006; Cebulko 2014; Gonzales 2011; Rincón 2008; Silver 2012). In all fifty states, unauthorized youth are ineligible for federal grants and loans to pay for college. While the Supreme Court's *Plyler v. Doe* (1982) decision guaranteed K–12 public school education for all children, the court never ruled on access to higher education. Thus, individual states have set their own policies. Massachusetts, unlike California, Texas, and some other immigrant destination states, charged out-of-state rates for unauthorized immigrants. Thus, the cost of higher education was prohibitive for Roberta and Bianca, even if they had known how to fill out the applications.

Not going to college immediately after high school was deeply frustrating for the twins. While their American peers were living out their college dreams, they were stuck working in low-wage jobs. In 2007, Roberta explained how frustrating it was to watch her peers go to college while she faced a "huge wall."

> I felt like my life had come to a stop and I wasn't allowed to move forward, to reach my dreams, 'cause there was this huge wall in front of me. And my future now didn't depend on me, but on the government, and whether or not they allowed me to go to school. Even though that's the one thing I had always had on my mind to do. I've always been a good student and college was never out of my future.

Frustrated and uncertain of their futures, the twins decided to vacation in Brazil, feeling as if they had, in Bianca's words, "nothing to lose." As unauthorized immigrants, however, the trip was extremely risky. Indeed, it's a vacation most would not dare try. Their tourist visas were technically valid for "ten years," but for tourism purposes only. The twins had violated the terms of their visas and had started accruing "illegal time" when they turned eighteen. While Bianca and Roberta would likely have no trouble reaching Brazil, returning to the United States was not guaranteed. Yet, the twins were young, frustrated that they could not figure out how to apply to college, and willing to take a gamble together.

They got lucky. Aided by being light-skinned, English-speaking young women, they re-entered the United States without hassle. They returned to Massachusetts, started working, and figured out that they did not need Social Security numbers to apply to college. Although they would be charged out-of-state tuition, both sisters, in 2007, were determined to save money for college and hopeful about their futures in the United States. Less than one year later, however, the twins' lives were turned upside-down when their younger brother, Miguel, turned eighteen, and his drug-related arrests led to his detention and eventual deportation.

Miguel, who was more consistently racialized as nonwhite than his sisters due to his physical features, dress, and peer groups, is one of the many Latino and Caribbean men who have been deported over the past few decades. Ninety percent of deportees are men and 97 percent are from the Americas (Golash-Boza 2015), creating a system of "gendered and racialized removal" (Golash-Boza and Hondagneu-Sotelo 2013). The War on Drugs has notoriously targeted men of color (Alexander 2010). Meanwhile, harsher immigration laws have expanded the grounds of deportability. The Immigration Act of 1990 made many immigrants deportable for having committed "aggravated felonies" (Fragomen and Bell 2007). Six years later, the Illegal Immigration Reform and Immigrant Responsibility Act (IIRIRA) expanded the definition of an aggravated felony, an expansion that included many more drug-related offenses. Thus, Miguel's deportation was not only the result of what Bianca described as his "poor life choices," but also the convergence of changes in immigration and criminal law and the racial and gendered system of removal.

Deportation, however, did not just impact Miguel; it impacted his entire family. The twins' mother, worried for her son's well-being in a country he barely remembered, decided she must return to Brazil with him, even though she might never be able to re-enter the United States. Initially, however, the twins and their father stayed in the United States.

Their father was recording an album and his economic prospects in Brazil were less certain. The twins, who were largely raised in the United States, were not ready to give up on their American Dreams. They knew they had been fortunate to re-enter the United States once and did not want to risk their luck again.

The twins planned to stay in the United States and enroll in college, but their plans diverged when Bianca found out she was pregnant. While Roberta pursued a nursing degree at a local community college, Bianca decided to work full-time at a local store. No longer together with the child's father, she felt pressure to support her child. Less than a year after Bianca's son was born, however, she decided to go to Brazil after speaking with her mother. She explained:

> I was working ten-hour shifts and (my son) was at the day care the whole day. As much as I liked working at the store, I knew I wasn't happy with the lifestyle I was leading. I couldn't have a driver's license, couldn't go to school while working full-time and having to look after a baby.

Bianca does not directly attribute her return to Brazil to her brother's deportation, yet she likely would have stayed in the United States had circumstances been different. As an unauthorized, single mother, she felt that she needed the support of her mother to raise her son. Had her mother stayed in the United States, Bianca would have stayed too. Furthermore, had she not given birth to her son, she also would have stayed, pursuing her education.

Indeed, when Bianca returned to Brazil, she did not see it as a permanent move. She wanted more for herself and her son—and she believed that would happen with a US college degree. She ultimately intended to return to the United States and apply for a student visa. Roberta told Bianca that her plan to return to Brazil and then re-enter the United States was too risky; Roberta was unwilling to take that risk. But unlike her sister, Roberta did not have a young son, was already enrolled in school, and was deeply committed to her boyfriend.

Thus Bianca left on her own, with her son and without her sister. However, she booked a return flight for September 2009, leaving her son with her mother in Brazil. As she went through customs in Miami, her luck ran out. The officer flipped through her passport and questioned her about why she had lived so long in the United States. After eleven long hours of questioning, she was deported back to Brazil and barred from re-entry. Bianca was now "forced out" of the United States, unable to return to her home and sister in Massachusetts, the place she had been raised since she was twelve years old.

Bianca's deportation was devastating for her. She explained:

> When I first returned (to Brazil) for vacation with my sister in 2006, it was great. . . . It was a whole different story when I went back after being deported. Knowing that I wouldn't step a foot in the United States or see my sister, friends, and everything I left behind again was really difficult. I was pretty devastated the first few months. I didn't know where to begin. I felt like the US Immigration System was completely unfair. They took a huge part of my identity. I was completely lost. . . . There were days that I would just cry and just want to go anywhere else.

As Bianca so painfully expressed, deportation took "a huge part of (her) identity." She had gone to middle and high school in Massachusetts. She had her first job there. Her son was born there. Her twin sister still lived there. And now, under IIRIRA, she faced a ten-year bar to reentry because she had accrued more than a year of "illegal time" in the United States.

Yet devastation has given way to resilience. Over time, she translated her American upbringing and English skills into job opportunities. She also discovered that she values the more laid-back lifestyle in Brazil. Reflecting on her life in 2013, Bianca stated:

> After a long while, I decided to accept that I had to make the best of the situation. I started to look for a job and it was nice to be close to family and friends. The fact that I spoke English and had lived in the United States for ten years helped me a lot in regard to finding a job. My first job was as an English instructor on offshore oil vessels, which paid pretty well. I got my first teaching experience there and that is when I decided I wanted to become a teacher. I started working as a teacher assistant at a renowned American International School. I began studying pedagogy, which is the teaching credentials you need here in Brazil and I am now finishing my second year. As with any change, I think we all need time to adapt. For me, it took about three years to fully adapt and accept what I couldn't change. I love my job. I work with great people and the best thing about Brazil is that you still manage to have a social life. It's a different culture, but it seemed that in the United States everyone is spending their time chasing after money, and not having enough time to enjoy life. I work Monday through Friday, I get out while the sun is still out. I am able to travel on the weekends, I have time to be with my son and partner.

Bianca did not choose this life, but she has made the most of opportunities. Yet, as she also expressed to me, she misses her sister very much. She actually tried to return to the United States five years after being deported, but her visa request was denied.

Back in Massachusetts, Bianca's deportation exacerbated Roberta's sense of loss. She hated being separated from her mother—and now her sister was gone. Eventually, in 2013, her father left too, leaving her as the last d'Antona in the United States. But at least her father was at her wedding in 2010; no other immediate family member could attend. During our interview in 2013, Roberta cried as she recalled how Bianca and her mother, two of the most important people in her life, missed her special day. It was the first of many milestones the twins would miss in each other's lives.

But like Bianca, Roberta has been resilient, despite the barriers she has faced. She finished her nursing program and was finally able to work as a nurse after becoming "DACAmented" in 2012. Like other DACA recipients I have interviewed in Massachusetts, DACA provided her with a sense of legitimacy and was a significant policy in her life. Yet Roberta also spoke of DACA's limitations. Her husband, who migrated at age sixteen, was ineligible. DACA was also not a permanent solution, leaving her in legal limbo. Moreover, DACA did not provide her with a guaranteed secure way of traveling to Brazil to see her family. While she could apply for Advanced Parole to travel to Brazil (because of DACA), at the time of our interview in 2013, she perceived it as too risky. Furthermore, there was no guarantee that she would be granted travel allowances.

Thus, Roberta felt in a constant state of personal and legal limbo due to her "liminal legality" (Cebulko 2013, 2014; Menjívar, 2006). On the one hand, she did not want to leave the United States, her home since age twelve. She was fearful of "restarting" in Brazil. On the other hand, she missed her family and wanted to live close to them.

> [My husband and I are] more used to living here [in the United States] already. I mean, we both grew up here. And I know it's tougher in Brazil. Especially for us to now go back. And all of our schooling was done here. And then to go back and kind of restart all over again. . . . So I think we would both rather live here, but I do want to be closer to my family. I don't want to grow up [*sniffling*], you know, have my nephew [Bianca's son] grow up, when I have my kids, and they can't be together. So, I don't want that either. So . . . [*sniffling*] I want to somehow be close to our families, you know?

Thinking about her future was extremely painful for Roberta, especially when she thought about being separated from Bianca. During the interview in 2013, she said she was hesitant to "settle down" by having kids and buying a home because "you don't know what tomorrow is going to bring." Roberta eventually did have a daughter, but it was another milestone she was unable to share with her sister. As of spring 2016, Bianca had never met her niece.

Roberta longed for a pathway to citizenship—and for her sister to join her in the United States. In 2013, she said:

> I hope that my sister would somehow be able to come back and live with us. And that would . . . I don't know. [*sniffling*] I would hope to be here [in the United States], but only if this more permanent immigration law does pass. . . . We just can't live like this, you know?

The pain in Roberta's voice underscores the need for policies that provide access to citizenship. Had the d'Antona family been offered paths to citizenship, they would have been able to travel between Brazil and the United States freely. Without them, Miguel's deportation caused painful decisions for each family member about whether to stay in the United States or to return to Brazil, decisions that were shaped by generation status and life-course milestones. Thus, just as generation status and the life-course shape the experiences of illegality (Abrego 2006; Cebulko 2014; Gonzales 2011; Silver 2012), they also shape the experiences of deportation and family separation.

The twins' and their family's story also complicates strict demarcations between "voluntary" and "involuntary" returns. Indeed, the decisions to return for Bianca, her mother, and father were highly constrained. For example, to what extent was Bianca's return and/or continued presence in Brazil truly "voluntary?" Moreover, their story, like the stories described by Gomberg-Muñoz and Martinez (in this section), forces us to think about our commitment to human rights and the rights of families, including which families, if any, we are committed to keeping together. While some might argue we should keep together married couples and parents with young children, that commitment would not have helped the d'Antonas. Yet, their story underscores the importance of other familial relationships—sibling relationships, adult children and parent relationships, and grandparent/grandchildren relationships—all of which provide crucial emotional and material support. Individuals do not live in isolation and when we deport one family member, it hurts not only that individual, but many others.

Notes

1. Pseudonyms are used for all names and most cities.

References

Abrego, Leisy Janet. 2006. "'I Can't Go to College Because I Don't Have Papers': Incorporation Patterns of Latino Undocumented Youth." *Latino Studies* 4 (3): 212–31.

Alexander, Michelle. 2010. *The New Jim Crow: Mass Incarceration in the Age of Color Blindness.* New York: New Press.

Cebulko, Kara B. 2013. *Documented, Undocumented, and Something Else: The Incorporation of Children of Brazilian Immigrants.* El Paso: LFB Scholarly Publishing.

Cebulko, Kara B. 2014. "Documented, Undocumented, and Liminally Legal: Legal Status During the Transition to Adulthood for 1.5-Generation Brazilian Immigrants." *Sociological Quarterly* 55 (1): 143–67.

Fragomen, Austin T. and Steven Bell. 2007. *Immigration Fundamentals: A Guide to Law and Practices.* New York: Practicing Law Institute.

Golash-Boza, Tanya. 2015. *Deported: Immigrant Policing, Disposable Labor, and Global Capitalism.* New York: New York University Press.

Golash-Boza, Tanya and Pierette Hondagneu-Sotelo. 2013. "Latino Immigrant Men and the Deportation Crisis: A Gendered Racial Removal Program." *Latino Studies* 11 (3): 271–92.

Gonzales, Roberto. 2011. "Learning to be Illegal: Undocumented Youth and Shifting Legal Contexts in the Transition to Adulthood." *American Sociological Review* 76 (4): 602–19.

Goza, Franklin. 1994. "Brazilian Immigration to North America." *International Migration Review* 28: 136–52.

Margolis, Maxine. 1993. *Little Brazil: An Ethnography of Brazilian Immigrants in New York City.* Princeton, NJ: Princeton University Press.

Menjívar, Cecilia. 2006. "Liminal Legality: Salvadoran and Guatemalan Immigrants' Lives in the United States." *American Journal of Sociology* 111 (4): 999–1037.

Rincón, Alejandra. 2008. *Undocumented Immigrants and Higher Education: Sí se Puede!* New York: LFB Scholarly Publishing.

Silver, Alexis. 2012. "Aging into Exclusion and Social Transparency: Transitions to Adulthood for Undocumented Immigrant Youth. *Latino Studies* 10 (4): 499–522.

PART 3

LIVING WITHOUT PAPERS:
How Do Undocumented People Navigate the Challenges They Face?

Eleven million people live in the United States without legal status. Any one of them could be subject to deportation if apprehended by immigration law enforcement agents. At the same time, the likelihood of any individual undocumented migrant being apprehended is relatively small—less than 2 percent of undocumented migrants are apprehended every year. Thus, undocumented immigrants often choose to remain in the United States, even though their lives are circumscribed by local, state, and federal laws.

The essays in this section render it clear that there is considerable variation in the experiences of undocumented people. Undocumented immigrants face both inclusion and exclusion. In a 1982 court case, *Plyler v. Doe*, the Supreme Court held that states cannot constitutionally deny students a free public education on account of their immigration status. Thus, undocumented children attend public K–12 school alongside their documented peers. The same rules do not apply for tertiary education, and the ability of undocumented youth to access college is much less certain. Insofar as undocumented people live and work in the United States, they also have access to hospitals, at least in life-threatening situations. However, their undocumented status may prevent them from getting routine medical care insofar as they often do not have medical insurance. Roberto Gonzalez (2015) has described being undocumented as living in limbo due to the simultaneous inclusion and exclusion that undocumented migrants face. Growing up in the United States, many undocumented youths become integrated into society and feel as if they belong in their communities. At the same time, they are denied full membership due to their immigration status (Gonzalez 2015).

The status of being undocumented is determined by federal law. However, as Angela García's chapter helps us to see, local laws and policies are important. Any undocumented migrant can be put into deportation proceedings if they are apprehended by either a Customs and Border Patrol (CBP) or an Immigration and Customs Enforcement (ICE) agent. The likelihood of being apprehended is a lot higher in border regions because CBP agents are authorized to operate up to 100 miles from the border. Thus, in a town like Escondido, which is 40 miles from the United States–Mexico border, residents have to worry about CBP checkpoints. In addition, Escondido has passed a string of restrictive laws targeting undocumented immigrants over the last decade, including a ban on rental housing for undocumented residents, daytime driver's license checkpoints, and a formalized collaboration between local police and ICE.

Police/ICE collaboration in a locality greatly increases the chances that undocumented migrants will be deported, thereby increasing fear among undocumented migrants and their family members in that community. Although local law enforcement officers do not have the ability to place a person in deportation proceedings, if local laws allow for it, they can call a CBP or ICE agent to come arrest a person they suspect is in the country illegally. In some jurisdictions, local law enforcement agents are enthusiastic about cooperating with ICE agents, and use their discretion to funnel more undocumented immigrants into the deportation dragnet. For example, if a driver is caught speeding, a police officer has the discretion to decide whether they will simply issue a citation or instead take the driver downtown to the local jail. For most minor offenses such as speeding or having a broken taillight, police officers are supposed to issue a citation rather than make an arrest. However, the officer may arrest a person if he or she is unable to produce acceptable identification or if the officer believes the suspect will not appear in court. If the officer arrests a person, in some localities, the authorities can then run the arrestee's fingerprints through a database to discover if they are in the country legally or if they are wanted by immigration authorities. Of course, if the police officer chooses to simply issue a citation or a warning, the driver will never be taken downtown and thus his or her immigration status may never be revealed. Undocumented migrants are often aware that avoiding driving is one of the best ways to avoid detection. Nolan Kline's chapter makes clear the significant consequences of otherwise mundane choices like driving versus walking. His chapter also raises important questions about the effects of being undocumented. Miguel, the subject of the essay, was arrested for driving without a license, but was fortunate to avoid deportation. This arrest shook him enough that he decided to walk to work instead of driving. This in turn led to a pedestrian accident that left him injured and unable to work. As you read this essay, think about the extent to which the events in Miguel's life can be attributed to being undocumented.

In Angela García's essay, she explains how local restrictive laws can curtail access to employment, housing, higher education, driver's licenses and identification, and social services and can facilitate local police co-operation in immigration law enforcement. Whereas in some localities, casual encounters with local law enforcement are unlikely to lead to deportation, in other localities, any encounter with local law enforcement could be the first stop in the deportation timeline. The couple introduced in García's essay is well aware of this possibility and structures their lives around the fear of deportation.

State and local laws can make undocumented migrants' lives more challenging. At the same time, some state laws can make their lives easier. California laws providing access to higher education are one example: Since 2001, in California, undocumented youth pay in-state tuition at public colleges and universities. However, other states do not provide this benefit, making it much more difficult to attend college, as we saw in several instances in the previous section. California has since passed two additional laws which have changed the conditions for undocumented youth attending college: The California DREAM Act (2011) provided access to state financial aid at California state institutions of higher education, and California AB-60 (2015) provided access to driver's licenses for all undocumented migrants. These changes in state laws have coincided with DACA, which grants temporary reprieve from deportation as well as a work permit to youth who arrived in the United States prior to the age of fifteen. These laws have created a more favorable context for some undocumented youth. The effects of these changes can be seen in John Park's essay, where he compares three California youth entering college at distinct time periods, who have profoundly different experiences.

Similar to the last section, the chapters in this section also make it clear how deportability affects the lives not only of undocumented immigrants, but also of their family members who often have legal status. Lorena, who appears in Angela García's essay, is a US citizen, yet she worries each day about whether or not her husband will be arrested and subsequently deported. As explained in the last section, when an undocumented migrant marries a US citizen, he or she may apply for legalization on the basis of this family tie. However, for those undocumented migrants who do not have a legal entry stamped on their passport, the last step in the legalization process requires leaving the United States to get a new entry visa at the consulate in one's home country. When the undocumented person leaves the United States, their departure triggers a ten-year bar on admission. Thus, even if the undocumented person is granted an adjustment of status, they have to wait ten years before being able to re-enter the country. These minutiae of immigration law, notably, are constantly in flux. For example, in 2013 a "Lockbox" program was instituted for waivers to be submitted inside the United States, rather than at the consulate abroad. This allows for undocumented migrants to avoid the ten-year bar. Additionally, DACA recipients who leave the country and return under Advance Parole are able to get a legal entry stamped onto their visa and thus may be eligible for adjustment of status. However, both the Lockbox program and the Advance Parole are temporary measures that could again change their rules at any moment.

The essays in this section help us to think through the concept of "illegality" and the extent to which illegality is a legal construction that significantly impacts people's lives. They also permit us to think about how illegality is similar to or different from other ascribed statuses such as gender, race, and sexuality. Additionally, they allow us to consider how undocumented status interacts with these other statuses—how it is different to be an undocumented female college student in California versus an older undocumented male in Georgia. Cecilia Menjívar and Leisy Abrego (2012, 1382) argue that "immigration laws today create a new axis of stratification that, like other forms of stratification, significantly shapes life chances and future prospects." Roberto Gonzales describes being undocumented as a "master status" (2015, 15). The chapters in this section help us to think about some of the ways that illegality shapes immigrants' lives, as well as how illegality interacts with other important statuses such as age, class, gender, regional location, and ethnicity.

References

Gonzales, Roberto G. 2015. *Lives in Limbo: Undocumented and Coming of Age in America*. University of California Press.

Menjívar, Cecilia, and Leisy Abrego. 2012. "Legal Violence: Immigration Law and the Lives of Central American Immigrants." *American Journal of Sociology* 117 (5): 1380–421.

8

The Law Doesn't Care About Love:
Intimate Relationships in Cities with Restrictive Immigration Laws

Angela S. García

The author, Angela S. García, is a sociologist and an assistant professor in the School of Social Service Administration at the University of Chicago. Her work has been published in the International Migration Review, Ethnic and Racial Studies *and the* Journal of Ethnic and Migration Studies. *Her forthcoming book manuscript is tentatively titled* Legal Passing: Navigating Undocumented Life and Local Immigration Law.

Lorena fanned herself in the cramped hot kitchen. Her dark hair was piled on top of her head, and her feet, slipped into yellow flip flops, tapped out a quick rhythm on the worn linoleum floor. Full of anxious energy, Lorena didn't seem to relax until her husband, Pancho, arrived home from work a couple of hours later. It was an August afternoon in Escondido, an inland, working class city just north of San Diego and 40 miles from the United States–Mexico border. With a dwindling but politically dominant white majority, conservative Escondido has passed a string of restrictive laws targeting undocumented immigrants over the last decade, including a ban on rental housing for undocumented residents, daytime driver's license checkpoints, and a formalized collaboration between local police and Immigration and Customs Enforcement (ICE)—the federal agency charged with detecting and deporting undocumented immigrants—dubbed "Operation Joint Effort." I was sitting at Lorena's small kitchen table to ask how Escondido's tough local immigration laws affect the everyday lives of undocumented residents. What I learned from Lorena and Pancho, however, also told me about the ripple effects of these hostile laws on community members across immigration statuses and within intimate relationships.

Escondido's effort to restrict undocumented residents is not new, nor is the city alone in its development of exclusionary immigration laws. State and local immigration laws actually predate federal efforts to control migration. In the more contemporary period, state and local, or subnational, immigration laws re-emerged in force after the federal Immigration Reform and Control Act (IRCA) of 1986, as jurisdictions along the southwest border reacted to IRCA's perceived failure at halting undocumented immigration into their communities.[1] The years between 2005 and 2015 saw an over-tenfold increase in the enactment of immigration-related legislation at the state level (see Figure 8.1 below). There is no comprehensive database of contemporary local level immigration laws. Between July 2006 and July 2007, however, cities, towns, and counties across the country actively considered 118 restrictive immigration enforcement proposals. In the period from 2000 and 2010, an estimated 107 local jurisdictions approved such measures (Chishti and Bergeron 2014). With heavy involvement from states and localities, the contemporary landscape of immigration law in the United States is akin to a "multi-jurisdictional patchwork," wherein the laws governing immigrants' access to rights and benefits vary tremendously across state, city, and county boundaries (Varsanyi et al. 2012).

State and local immigration laws are often (though certainly not always) restrictive, seeking to reduce the rights and benefits available to undocumented immigrants. The goal of these measures is to advance attrition through enforcement—making life difficult in order to push undesired immigrant groups out, either to their communities of origin or, at the very least, to other jurisdictions in the United States. Restrictive laws typically center on curtailing access to employment, housing, higher education, driver's licenses and identification, and social services. They also frequently involve *local* police in the enforcement of *federal* immigration laws, such as unlawful entry and presence (NCSL 2016). Unlike federal, state, and local measures of the past, today's restrictions are facially

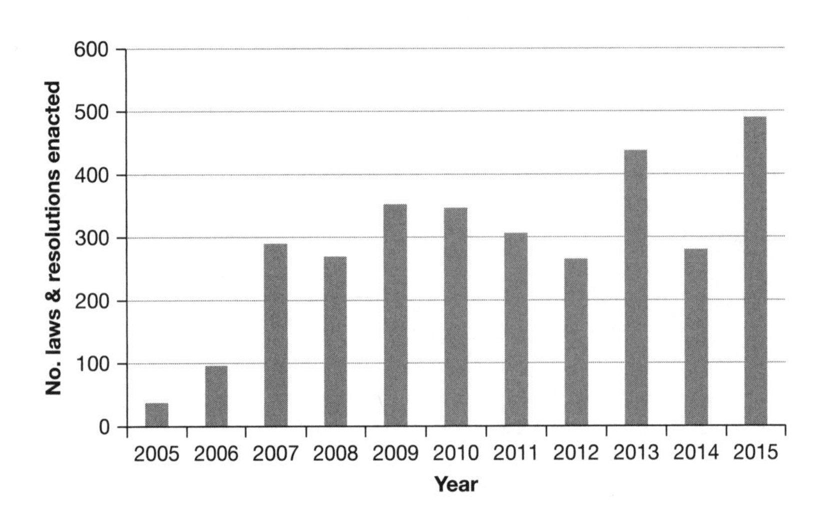

Figure 8.1. Enacted Immigration Legislation in the States, 2005–2015.

Source: National Conference of State Legislatures (NCSL), 2015.

neutral: They do not explicitly target particular racial, ethnic, or national origin groups, but rather unauthorized immigrants in general. By focusing on immigration status, such measures contribute to the criminalization of undocumented immigrants despite the reality that unauthorized presence is a civil—and not criminal—violation according to federal law. Nonetheless, the clear targets of these laws are Latin Americans generally, and—especially in Southern California—Mexican nationals. In Escondido, Operation Joint Effort led to over eight hundred arrests of undocumented immigrants in its first two years of operation. The Escondido Police Department does not keep track of the people it turns over to ICE, and ICE has declined requests to release information about those arrested (Sifuentes 2012), yet given the city's demographics, it is likely that Mexicans make up the bulk of apprehensions.

Categories like "documented" and "undocumented" facilitate the separation of people by immigration laws enacted by the states, cities, and towns that they call home. But in everyday life, relationships form between and across citizenship and immigration statuses. Most immigrants in the crosshairs of restrictive subnational immigration laws are not devoid of social ties within their immediate destinations just because they are undocumented. Indeed, "mixed status" immigrant families, or those that are composed of members with different immigration statues, are quite prevalent across the United States. Passel and Cohen (2009) estimate that 53 percent of unauthorized immigrants live in mixed-status families, which means that a total of 16.6 million people are members of such households (Taylor et al. 2011). Scholars usually focus on the children of mixed-status families—often those who have US citizenship and who live with one or more undocumented parents (Dreby 2015; Fix and Zimmerman 2001). But Lorena and Pancho's story shows the repercussions of these restrictive subnational measures on intimate partnerships that straddle the documented/undocumented divide (see also Lilly López 2015).

Lorena has been a legal permanent resident in the United States for over two decades. She received her green card after legalizing through the 1986 IRCA immigration reform, which regularized the immigration status of over 2.5 million undocumented immigrants, more than 70 percent of whom were Mexican nationals (Chishti, Meissner, and Bergeron 2011). The first chapter of Lorena's life in the United States was spent in Los Angeles, where she lived with her husband, who was a childhood friend from her home village in Chihuahua. Several months after her wedding in 1980, Lorena followed her husband across the border. Lorena had never worked outside her parents' home, but her spouse was convinced that they could not make a livelihood in their small community, where job opportunities outside of small scale agriculture were slim to none. It was better to follow the stream of young men migrating out of the village to the United States, he argued. Lorena was wary of crossing the border illegally and frightened about being so far away from her immediate family, but she headed north. Once in Los Angeles, Lorena learned she was unable to bear children after several miscarriages. Soon afterward, the couple separated.

Determined to start over, Lorena moved to Escondido to be near members of her extended family who had settled in the city. There, she met Pancho, an undocumented immigrant originally from Aguascalientes, at a church event. Pancho had also come out of a long-term relationship with the mother of his daughter, a seven-year-old born in Escondido. Lorena and Pancho's partnership began slowly, but his immigration status was never a sticking point. "Of course, I knew he didn't have papers. That I always knew. It was because of our age, our maturity that we did not move quickly, not because he is undocumented," Lorena recalled. "With our strong foundation as friends, I knew this marriage would truly last." Nonetheless, as Escondido's immigration restrictions ratcheted up, Pancho's undocumented status became one of the most significant factors of their relationship as a married couple.

Just after they got married in 2010, the same year Escondido's police department and ICE began Operation Joint Effort, Pancho got work as a landscaper in town. Combined with the modest salary Lorena earned in her clerical job at a local nonprofit organization, Pancho's wages would help the couple save toward their goal of buying their own home. The small company employing him took care of the upkeep of yards in neighborhoods on the periphery of Escondido, areas that tend to be wealthier and whiter than the central city, where Latinos and immigrants are concentrated. The job was steady and paid well. In Pancho's reckoning, these benefits outweighed the risk of having to drive a company truck around town without a license.[2] Lorena was not convinced. She followed the anti-immigrant politics of Escondido far more closely than Pancho, and worried constantly about him being picked up by police, ICE, or the Border Patrol.

Lorena began to seriously explore the possibility of legalizing Pancho's immigration status. Under current law, both US citizens and legal permanent residents can sponsor spouses for a green card. The problem in Pancho's case, however, hinged upon a section of the Illegal Immigration Reform and Immigrant Responsibility Act (IIRIRA), federal legislation passed in 1996, which requires immigrants in the United States unlawfully to complete the process for obtaining a green card in their home countries. Once they leave the United States, however, an automatic bar of legal re-entry is triggered, ranging from three years to a lifetime for those with a history of illegal entries. Unfortunately for the couple, Pancho was caught crossing the United States–Mexico border illicitly in 2001 by the Border Patrol. He signed a voluntary departure and was quickly returned to Mexico. His second border crossing attempt just a week afterward was successful, but Pancho now had a record of unauthorized entry. After speaking to several immigration lawyers, Lorena understood that the possibility of securing Pancho a green card was a dead end, and that embarking on the process would likely end in a lengthy bar on his presence in the United States. "The law doesn't care about love," she said in a steady but muted voice. "Not the law of the federal government, and not the law here in Escondido that goes after men like Pancho as if they were terrible criminals." Frustrated with her inability to legalize her husband and frightened by Escondido's immigration restrictions, Lorena realized that Pancho's immigration status had taken a front seat in their marriage.

Lorena turned her efforts to keeping Pancho safe while living and working in Escondido's restrictive socio-legal climate. The stakes were high for the couple: Because Pancho had been apprehended by the Border Patrol in the past, another apprehension would result in time in federal prison to be followed by deportation. Immigration offenders are one of the fastest growing groups of federal prisoners, and most are there for criminal re-entry convictions (Light, López, González-Barrera 2014). Like many of the undocumented immigrants I have interviewed in anti-immigrant destinations, Lorena and Pancho began to use strategies to navigate the city to minimize the risk of encounters with police and immigration enforcement.

Often these preventions had to do with driving, which is essential due to San Diego County's limited public transportation infrastructure. Before they traveled together in their car, for instance, Lorena and Pancho performed a series of checks: Do all brake lights, headlights, and turn signals work? Are there any cracks in the windshield? Are both license plates firmly attached and free of debris? Does the car look well-kept and maintained? Addressing the condition of their car, they believed, helped them avoid any pretextual police stops. Lorena was also always behind the wheel. She was fastidiously cautious about obeying the speed limit and other rules of the road, and her valid California driver's license was the couple's first line of defense in case they were pulled over. Both Lorena and Pancho also subscribed to a texting service which alerts users to police checkpoints in the area. Run by a coalition of human rights groups, student groups, and community members in San Diego's North County, the texts served as guideposts for when and where Lorena and Pancho would travel around Escondido.

Another set of strategies used by the couple involved physical appearance, particularly around how Pancho looked on his drive home after a long day's work. "He spends all day outside in the sun blowing leaves and cutting grass. Of course he's dirty and sweaty at the end of the day. But he could get pulled over for just that, for looking like a *mojado* [wetback]," Lorena explained to me in her kitchen. Despite Pancho's repeated promises to drive carefully and obey the speed limit, Lorena remained anxious. Eventually, she hit upon a plan: Every morning she packed him khakis and a dress shirt to wear on his commute home in the evening—the white collar standard for men—rather than his dirty landscaping uniform. Reflecting on this, Lorena said "maybe it means nothing. But I think that he calls less attention to himself with the clean clothes. . . . It makes him look like he's from here."

Legal status is, of course, an invisible trait. In multi-ethnic America, is impossible to know whether someone is a United States–born citizen, a naturalized immigrant, a legal permanent resident, a visa holder, or an undocumented immigrant by simply appraising their appearance. But the noncriminal social characteristics of Mexicans—the language they speak and their physical appearance—associate them with undocumented immigration status in popular consciousness (Chavez 2001 and 2008) and, perhaps more urgently, in the view of law enforcement (Romero 2006). Such profiling can leave undocumented Latinos with the perception of ethnically-biased policing. Thus Lorena's effort to help pass Pancho off as a nonsuspect native by changing his appearance through the afternoon clothing brought the couple a sense of security, regardless of whether it was truly effective. Somewhat surprisingly, I also learned that the exchange of clothes in the morning had become a nuanced ritual for the couple. The moment expressed both the intimate care and affection of their relationship and the broader context of anxiety and worry prompted by Escondido's restrictive immigration laws.

This sense of connection around the change of clothes was best expressed by Pancho himself. Listening to Lorena explain it, I became curious about interviewing her husband. As the undocumented partner in the marriage, I thought Pancho would have a distinct perspective on his relationship with Lorena and the effects of the Escondido's immigration laws. As luck would have it, I was interviewing Lorena in the couple's apartment in the late afternoon, not long before the time Pancho normally came home from work. As we sat talking in the kitchen, Lorena welcomed me to wait there for him. After around an hour, I heard Pancho coming in the front door. He rounded the corner and entered the kitchen: A medium-build man, Pancho was indeed dressed in tan khaki pants and a white, long-sleeve, button-down shirt. He carried a small cooler in one hand and a brown grocery bag in the other; later Pancho explained that it contained his dirty uniform from the landscaping company. Lorena facilitated introductions, offering a quick explanation of who I was and what we'd been discussing. Pancho glanced between me and Lorena and, with a sigh, sat down at the kitchen table. We began to talk about his change of clothes for his afternoon commute back to the apartment.

AG: When Lorena had the idea of you wearing different clothes to drive home, what did you think?

P: That she was worrying too much.

AG: But you do it anyway . . .

P: Yes. Every day, for years now. And she's right in a way. Things are bad in Escondido if you're undocumented like me.

A bit later in the interview, I asked Pancho to explain to me how the exchange of clothes he undertakes with his wife unfolds in the morning. He reached across the table toward Lorena and, finding her hand, held it firmly. "It's early when I wake for work," Pancho said. "But Lorena is up with me. We eat breakfast together, and she packs me lunch and coffee for the road. The last thing she hands me—every day she has it ready—is my change of clothes. Always in a paper bag from the grocery store. For the drive home, you understand? We embrace, and she tells me to be careful and to entrust myself to God. And I always tell her not to worry." As Pancho spoke, it became clear that the ritual exchange of clothes represented a comfortable, even tender daily moment between him and his wife:

> In a way it [receiving the clothes] reminds me. . . . It helps me know every morning that she loves me and wants to keep me safe. So I leave my home knowing this, and this sustains me during difficult moments. . . . In the afternoon when I change I am reminded again of Lorena. This late in life, we are blessed to have found each other. We'll do what it takes to stay together.

Scholars who study restrictive state and local immigration laws demonstrate the many ways that these measures cause fear and social suffering within undocumented communities. Lorena and Pancho's relationship is a case in point, showing the long reach of hostile laws within the city they call home. Reverberations of Escondido's restrictions have a clear impact beyond the undocumented residents they target, affecting legal immigrants like Lorena and, though not covered in this chapter, US citizens like Pancho's daughter. At the same time, these laws also have some unexpected counterintuitive effects. The restrictions in Escondido were developed to isolate and exclude undocumented immigrants, and not to spark a deeper connection between them and their intimate partners. While some mixed-status couples may be driven apart by the difficult sociolegal circumstances of a city like Escondido, for others their social connections deepen and broaden, rooting them more firmly in destinations that would shut them out.

Notes

1. Some contemporary subnational restrictions predate IRCA. Texas, for example, revised education laws in 1975 to withhold state funds from local school districts that educate undocumented children. In 1982, the Supreme Court ruled against the state in *Plyler v. Doe*.
2. California's approach to offering driver's licenses to undocumented immigrants has shifted several times since the 1990s. The most recent change as of writing was Assembly Bill 60, which allowed the state to issue driver's licenses to undocumented immigrants in January 2015.

References

Chishti, Muzaffar and Claire Bergeron.2014. "Hazleton Immigration Ordinance That Began with a Bang Goes Out with a Whimper." Washington DC: Migration Policy Institute, March 28. Online: http://www.migrationpolicy.org/article/hazleton-immigration-ordinance-began-bang-goes-out-whimper

Chishti, Muzaffar, Doris Meissner, and Claire Bergeron.2011. "At its 25th Anniversary, IRCA's Legacy Lives On." Washington DC: Migration Policy Institute, November 16. Online: http://www.migrationpolicy.org/article/its-25th-anniversary-ircas-legacy-lives

Chavez, Leo. 2001. *Covering Immigration: Popular Images and the Politics of the Nation*. Berkeley: University of California Press.

Chavez, Leo. 2008. *The Latino Threat: Constructing Immigrants, Citizens, and the Nation*. Stanford, CA: Stanford University Press.

Dreby, Joanna. 2015. *Everyday Illegal: When Policies Undermine Immigrant Families*. Berkeley: University of California Press.

Fix, Michael, and Wendy Zimmerman. 2001. "All Under One Roof: Mixed-Status Families in an Era of Reform." *International Migration Review* 35 (2): 397–419.

Light, Michael T., Mark Hugo López, and Ana González-Barrera. March 18, 2014. "The Rise of Federal Immigration Crimes: Unlawful Re-entry Drives Growth." Washington DC: Pew Research Center. Online: http://www.pewhispanic.org/2014/03/18/the-rise-of-federal-immigration-crimes/#fn-20132-3

Lilly López, Jane. 2015. "'Impossible Families': Mixed-Citizenship Status Couples and the Law." *Law & Policy* 37 (1–2): 93–118.

National Conference of State Legislatures. February 2016. "Report on 2015 State Immigration Laws." Washington DC. Online: http://www.ncsl.org/research/immigration/report-on-2015-state-immigration-laws.aspx

Passel, Jeffrey and D'Vera Cohen. 2009. *A Portrait of Unauthorized Immigrants in the United States*. Washington, DC: Pew Hispanic Center. Online: http://pewhispanic.org/files/reports/107.pdf

Romero, Mary. 2006. "Racial Profiling and Immigration Law Enforcement: Rounding Up of Usual Suspects in the Latino Community." *Critical Sociology* 32 (2): 447–73.

Sifuentes, Edward. 2012. "Names of Illegal Immigrants Withheld, Citing Privacy Rights." *San Diego Union-Tribune*, July 14. Online: http://www.sandiegouniontribune.com/sdut-exclusive-names-of-illegal-immigrants-withheld-2012jul14-story.html

Taylor, Paul, Mark Hugo Lopez, Jeffrey S. Passel, and Seth Motel. 2011. "Unauthorized Immigrants: Length of Residency, Patters of Parenthood." Washington DC: Pew Research Center. Online: http://www.pewhispanic.org/2011/12/01/unauthorized-immigrants-length-of-residency-patterns-of-parenthood/

Varsanyi, Monica, Paul Lewis, Doris Marie Provine, and Scott Decker. 2012. "A Multilayered Jurisdictional Patchwork: Immigration Federalism in the United States." *Law and Policy* 34 (2): 138–58.

9

"It's a Strange Condition": Being in College Under a Cloud of Uncertainty

John S. W. Park

John S. W. Park is professor of Asian American studies at the University of California, Santa Barbara. In 2013, Temple University Press published his third book, Illegal Migrations and the Huckleberry Finn Problem.

Ever since I became a professor in 2000, I've taught classes on immigration law and policy, including a larger introductory class on the Immigration Act of 1965 and its consequences. I've so enjoyed teaching this larger class: Every fall, as the young freshmen come to campus, I've used this ten-week course to help acclimate my students to life in college, and I've liked explaining why California looks the way it does to an audience of young Californians, as well as to students new to this state. Many different kinds of students take this class—very wealthy students from China, first-generation college students from places like Bakersfield and Salinas, kids from the affluent suburbs, and kids from urban high schools, some small, private, and excellent and others large, public, and not so great. Because it's a general education class, and one that fulfills the ethnicity class requirement, engineering kids, bio majors, econ kids, feminists, tree huggers, hippies, English and comp lit people, and surfers will take it, too, and although they're mostly first-year students, juniors and seniors who've avoided the ethnicity requirement also sit in, sometimes in the back. I notice that many of them move to the front as the term goes on, and I've taken some pleasure in seeing, on my evaluations, that they "didn't expect to like the class." A certain kind of student might seek out ethnic studies classes, but a smaller classroom full of these students is like preaching to the choir, and so a big tent class, with lots of different people, allows me to stretch my skills and to experience a much broader cross-section of campus.

This class is about immigration rules, migration trends, and subsequent rules and laws since 1965, and so it's about how American society has been reshaped over the past five decades. After 1965, hundreds of thousands of skilled migrants have come to the United States, such that major hospitals, universities, and information technology companies are chock full of highly-paid, well-connected immigrants; but over that same time, entire countries have collapsed from civil wars, people in poorer countries have sought to leave for better opportunities, either by reuniting with family members already in the United States, or by coming and staying unlawfully. Students in my classroom are from both worlds: They are the sons and daughters of hyper-privileged immigrants, sitting right next to the sons and daughters of refugees and low-wage migrants. There are significant gaps among them: They may dress alike and even have the same mannerisms, but by the time that my teaching assistants and I grade the first midterms, we can usually tell which ones have had better schooling. The kids from suburban high schools and private schools aren't as overwhelmed with the reading load and the course materials, compared to the ones whose schooling was, well, not as robust. This class is about inequality, and yet as the professor, I can *see* the inequality as well, and I encourage my students to consider their family backgrounds, and to draw from the materials in the class to consider how they came to America and onto my campus.

Many different kinds of students come to office hours, but this essay is about just three of them—Nancy, Philip, and Carlos—because these three students were all "out of status," and, as Nancy said, "it's a strange condition," because you really can't tell, just by looking at these students, that they were prone to such huge disadvantages compared to their peers. Under the prevailing federal law, all of them were deportable. But in 2005, Nancy seemed like every other Chinese American woman in college, with her JanSport backpack and her Hello Kitty cell phone cover. She was from Los Angeles, and her parents worked in the San Gabriel Valley, her mother in a nail salon and her father at a restaurant. Philip was from the Philippines, he went to high school in San Francisco, and he wanted to be a lawyer, and so he was going to be a political science major. Philip had enormous horn-rimmed glasses, rather popular again for young people in 2010, and he even had that annoying pre-law demeanor common among some college-age men. Carlos was from Santa Ana in Orange County, his parents were both farm workers, which meant that Carlos didn't see his parents as they worked up and down the state throughout the year. He was raised by his aunt, in a three-bedroom house with twelve other "relatives." Many kids complain that the dorm rooms are too small compared to the bedrooms that they were leaving, but for Carlos, in 2013, his room on campus was about the largest private space he'd had in his life, even though he was sharing it with another kid. College was a place of breathtaking freedom.

About two hundred students enroll in my lower division class every year, but I remember Nancy, Philip, and Carlos in particular because they were so attentive to the class, and because the class itself, especially in weeks six through eight, was about them and their families.

It's a strange thing in general, that persons who were not legally entitled to remain in the United States were attending colleges and universities at all in 2001. During that year, the state legislatures in Texas and in California approved similar set of rules to allow "residents" of these states to pay in-state tuition, even though some of these "residents" were not lawfully admitted to the United States. In California, the law began as State Assembly Bill 540, sponsored by Marco Firebaugh, and so the students who'd benefited were called "AB 540" students, and by 2003, a significant number of them had matriculated at the undergraduate campuses of the University of California, including my campus in Santa Barbara. This marked a significant change in law and politics: in 1994, California voters had approved Proposition 187 by a 2–3 margin. The law would have banned "illegal aliens'" and "undocumented immigrants" access to important public services, including public education and most forms of publicly financed health care. The federal courts did not allow Proposition 187 to go into effect, as it contradicted a number of important federal laws and Supreme Court precedents, including a major case from Texas that dated to 1975; in *Plyler v. Doe* (1982), Texas had allowed public school districts to charge tuition to any student who could not prove legal residency.

The United States Supreme Court had overturned the rule in Texas, thus allowing undocumented minors to attend the public schools throughout the country, and the lower federal courts blocked Proposition 187 in California in December 1994, based in large part on that ruling. Yet the anger and frustration of many Texans and Californians was a palpable thing in the mid-1990s. Prominent politicians, including Governor Pete Wilson, had railed against the federal government for failing to enforce the nation's borders, allowing for "dangerous" and "expensive" illegal immigrants to consume state services, and then shifting those costs onto taxpayers in states like California and Texas. Nancy remembered the political ads supporting Proposition 187—so many of them, so hostile—if only because her parents switched off the television during that political season, when these things appeared in a constant cycle. We have to wonder whether the sponsors of these ads, including Governor Wilson, considered what they might be doing to kids like Nancy.

Governor Wilson's approach prevailed in 1994, but it was not uniformly popular: Within a relatively short period, the state legislatures in Texas and in California had shifted, as if reversing themselves, they now supported some undocumented students, and even conservative politicians favored allowing the highest-achieving students to continue in the state colleges and universities. Gray Davis, a Democratic governor, had signed AB 540, but in Texas, Rick Perry, a Republican governor, had signed House Bill 1403, a very similar rule as the one in California. In 2001, prominent senators of the United States sponsored the DREAM Act, a federal law that would have allowed undocumented students across the country to adjust to legal status, and to attend college with their peers, under the twin theories that these children were not "at fault" for their immigration status, nor did it make sense to deny them a higher education for which they were otherwise well-qualified. The federal version of the DREAM Act encountered stiff resistance; yet through 2008, state governments in

Washington, Oklahoma, Kansas, New Mexico, and Illinois also passed rules similar to AB 540. States like Virginia, Arizona, South Carolina, and Alabama had rejected these same policies by 2013. A few states behaved like yo-yos: Wisconsin allowed in 2009, then repealed in 2011, and Colorado rejected in 2008, then approved in 2013. This patchwork of state and federal laws was so confusing and unpredictable, even for specialists, that it must have been near impossible to predict from the perspective of college-bound eighteen-year-olds and their parents. More than other immigration issues, the fate of undocumented children perhaps represented best the torn heart of immigration policy and politics in the United States over the past two decades.

Even though she was, in 2005, an AB 540 student in California, and thus lawfully attending UC Santa Barbara, Nancy was not exactly sharing this information with everyone. After all, from 1994 to 2001, California had behaved like a yo-yo, too, and so who could blame Nancy for being cautious? Nancy was beyond cautious. Many students are nervous about attending office hours, but very few ask me to close the door because they don't want others to hear what they have to say. Nancy asked me to close the door. She turned slightly in her chair, and without looking me in the eye, she said that she and her family were "undocumented aliens," although she was quick to point out that she herself was an AB 540 student. Now, I'm a Roman Catholic, albeit a very bad Roman Catholic in recent years, and so there was something about the *way* she told me that reminded me of a confession. In this case, I suppose she was the penitent and I was the priest to whom she was confessing. I will never forget the manner in which she told me this aspect of her identity, and then also the worried look on her face that followed it. Nancy was not the first student I'd had who was out of status, but she was the most memorable for very sad reasons, because she was so nervous and angry and confused about what this meant for her and for her parents and her younger brother. Her worries poured forth upon our first meeting, as she told me sensitive things that were difficult to hear, and hard for her to speak. She said, through her nervous laughter, that she was confident that I wasn't going to call the police or the immigration service to report her (had she worried that I would?), and she talked at length about feeling a pervasive sense of shame, as though she wasn't "normal," and as though she didn't belong in college.

Nancy didn't learn that she was out of status until she had applied for college. She'd assumed that her parents didn't want to get her a car because they couldn't afford it, or that they were just afraid of the police like other immigrants. She didn't think it unusual that they didn't want her to get a driver's license, or when they themselves slowed their car to a crawl when they saw the police. When she was applying to college, though, her mother wept, and she said that this might not be possible for her. Her family had come from China on tourist visas. They overstayed on purpose, because her parents didn't want to raise them in China, and they'd been in Los Angeles ever since, having fallen out of status.

All of a sudden, small and large things made sense: she understood why her parents had switched off Governor Wilson whenever he appeared on the television to complain about "illegal aliens"; and she also got why the family never ventured far from their home. Santa Barbara was about as far as they could imagine. Her parents took the bus to work at their jobs in the San Gabriel Valley because they didn't like taking the freeways. Nancy said that her mother was at once proud and despondent—she was so proud that Nancy had done so well in school, that she was now able to go to college, and she was so sorry that going to a "good college" may not be possible in light of their family's immigration status. This revelation shocked Nancy, and I could tell that she was still processing it here in college.

Many times, I have felt an overwhelming desire to help my students in whatever way I can, perhaps because my own late mother was a working class immigrant, and because I can still remember the expectations and hopes that she'd invested in her two boys. Nancy may have been an AB 540 student, but in 2005, there were no private or state scholarships for such students, and Nancy didn't have a Social Security number, and so she couldn't file the Free Application for Federal Student Aid, even though her family's income likely qualified her for significant amounts of assistance. A sympathetic high school counselor had helped Nancy with her UC applications, and Nancy chose UCSB because of its economics and accounting program, but paying for UCSB was a huge challenge, with tuition alone being about $7,000 that year. Nancy's parents were very supportive of her attending UCSB, but they'd also told her up-front that they'd had enough in savings for one, maybe two years. Plus, there was her brother to consider, and he'd be ready for college, too, in about three years.

In Fall 2005, Nancy came to my office hours quite often, and her visits were always a mix of emotions. Sometimes, she seemed bitter at her parents—why hadn't they come legally? Then she could have applied for financial aid, they wouldn't have to worry about trying to pay for everything themselves, and she wouldn't be so ashamed and she could be "like everyone else." She felt "so guilty" asking her parents for money, and she was never sure if they had any to give. She was grateful to her parents, she said, but they didn't understand what it felt like to be in college with this thing hanging over her, and it was all very frustrating and horrible. Moreover, the more she'd learned about immigration law and policy, the more she felt despondent and hopeless. My class was not helping. When we discussed the Immigration Reform and Control Act of 1986, for example, the last major piece of legislation through which Congress had offered "amnesty" to some undocumented persons, Nancy asked if the federal government might repeat another IRCA. I told her that in fact, President George Bush was trying to persuade his fellow Republicans to pass something like this, just as Ronald Reagan had done in 1986, but that President

Bush was having no luck. President Bush had supported the DREAM Act in 2001, too, and that also went nowhere. Nancy looked crestfallen.

Nancy did very well in my class, we agreed to stay in touch, and I know that she finished out that first year. Then, in Fall 2006, I got this email from her:

> Hey Professor Park,
> I've decided not to return to UCSB. Thank you for all of your help!
> My mom really needs me here.

I wrote back to her twice, and asked her to give me a call, but she never answered, and she never called.

At the UC campuses, about 5 to 10 percent of first-year students will not finish a bachelor's degree in six years, and for reasons that are as diverse as the students themselves. Sometimes, my students seem so affluent and privileged that they do not try very hard, and they appear instead to suffer from an affluenza so severe that their GPAs fall well below a 2.0 by the Spring term. Under these circumstances, they must take "some time off," which is a euphemism for "Please try for good grades at a community college, and then we'll consider you for readmission." About half come back, the other half does not.

Much more often, poorer students struggle one or two or three jobs to help themselves or their parents finance what's becoming a much more expensive education. Tuition now is about double what Nancy was paying. On top of that significant hurdle, these same students often have, through no fault of their own, less than stellar reading and writing skills, coming as they do from poorer districts that are underfunded and don't really prepare them well for college level courses. I tell my students that the first term in college is like taking four Advanced Placement courses—the kids from the suburbs have a much better idea what that means, while the kids from poorer urban and rural districts sometimes have no idea. Quite often, their high schools offered few or no AP courses at all.

Philip was so ambitious and eager, so convinced that he was going to be a lawyer, that he had a hard time accepting that his D was a fair grade for the first midterm. He said that he did not go to a fantastic high school, he admitted that his exam was a string of spelling and grammar problems, but he insisted that he was going to make it by working hard. "I took your class because it had 'Law' in it," he said. He was interested in immigration law because he was from a family of immigrants, and he was also the first in his family to attend college. For a lot of reasons, I tried to like Philip, but he was annoying, even argumentative, and I also had that feeling that he might not make it through his first year. He just couldn't write or think in paragraphs. He came to office hours every single week after the second week, though, and he stayed well past the point where we might have anything else to talk about. After discussing his second midterm (a C−) in great detail, in the seventh week, Philip suggested that we have lunch together, and my first reaction was that I was rather grateful that day for the two-hour committee meeting. Philip felt overwhelming.

Philip didn't tell me that he was out of status until the end of the term, after final exams. He did not pass my class, but he had passed most of his classes in the fall, and he was using the on-campus tutoring center every week. Grades were not at the forefront of his mind, however; in San Francisco, his older brother had been arrested for a serious drug offense over the winter break. His brother was in big trouble: In January 2011, Philip did not come to see me to discuss the class or his final exam or law school, he came to my office to see if I could recommend a good lawyer.

From my class, he remembered that the threshold for "removal"—what we used to call deportation—was much lower now, after Congress had approved a series of rules in 1996. If his brother could be convicted for an offense that *could* trigger a one-year prison term, he would be removable. In addition, anyone facing removal based on a criminal conviction would be ineligible for any kind of relief from deportation, and such a person could be barred permanently from the United States. As an undocumented immigrant, Philip's brother had even fewer procedural rights than a lawful permanent resident. He was indeed in a bad place. Over the winter break, Philip was the closest that his family had had to a lawyer. His mother was despondent: afraid that she or her husband would also be put into removal proceedings, they hadn't visited or even called their eldest son in the county jail.

Philip's parents called the lawyers that I'd recommended, but as in many of these cases, things didn't go well, and his brother did end up serving time in a state penitentiary. But immigration officials didn't come to Philip's house, nor did anyone take his mother and father and put them into removal proceedings. This was only because the lawyers had advised distance between them and their eldest son. Philip had given me regular updates about his brother and his brother's case, as did my lawyer friends, until he didn't do that anymore, and sometime in his third year, he stopped mentioning his brother altogether and I stopped asking. It hadn't gone well, what was there to discuss?

Philip did continue to study political science, his grades improved, and by the beginning of his fourth year, he received state aid under the California DREAM Act, which Governor Jerry Brown had signed into law in 2011. In Fall 2013, Philip received a few smaller private scholarships, but he also got a Cal Grant, a crucial form of state aid now available to undocumented students. He said that these pieces of financial aid greatly alleviated the burdens that he had been putting on his parents, and he was working hard enough to carry a B− average over sixteen units of coursework every term. Philip also joined a few campus organizations as well, including Kapatirang Pilipino, and then IDEAS, the acronym for Improving Dreams, Equality, Access, and Success, a campus organization and support group for students who were out of status. I saw Philip at several campus events for IDEAS, and I was very pleased to see that he was going to finish his degree at UCSB.

In June 2014, Philip filled out his cap and gown nicely, in those big horn-rimmed glasses. I met his parents for two minutes. We shook hands, politely, and I congratulated them on that special day, but there was a sorrow in her demeanor, the way Philip's mother held my hand to thank me, maybe to thank me for trying. I knew their son's lawyers very well, they had taken his case pro bono, and I knew Philip better than I knew most of my students, and I also knew that Philip had told his parents about me in some detail, too. But as sometimes happens when people have known each other from a distance, and then had their expectations dashed, the face-to-face meeting turned into an awkward thing, as it was on that day. Philip had done something amazing, against heavy odds: From a poor, urban school, with working class parents and very little money, he was now the first in his family with a bachelor's degree from the University of California. Yet he wasn't going to law school right away, as he'd once hoped, and the state that had given him generous scholarships during his last year had also turned over his brother to Immigration and Customs Enforcement that same year. Philip's brother had served just one year of a three-year term in a California state prison. He had then been transferred into an immigration detention facility, and he was going to be "returned" to the Philippines.

Philip had been an endlessly, relentlessly optimistic young man in 2010, so gregarious and affable to the point of annoying, and yet at his graduation, he was more like his father, quiet, reserved, even reticent. I invited them to come to my office for refreshments, it's just right there, and I have soda, but they declined. Politely, graciously, they made their leave. For a moment, it occurred to me to express my deepest regrets that they hadn't seen their eldest son, Philip's brother, in about three years, but then it also occurred to me that I might sound very stupid saying that to them, on that occasion. We all knew about the sadness overhanging the joy, about the other son who wasn't there.

When Carlos came to UCSB in 2013, his parents were thrilled, his aunt even more so. He explained how his aunt was more like his "second mother," because his *tia* took care of him for most of the year, over many years. His *tia* had three children of her own, one older and two younger than Carlos, but the cousins joked that their mother loved Carlos most of all. He was the *"inteligente,"* the smarty-pants, the one who walked to the public library in Santa Ana two blocks from their house to read just about everything he could read. His aunt's house was too crowded: during some months, more than a dozen people lived there. "You know how you hear about Mexican houses with cars all parked in the lawn and a ton of people inside? That was my tia's house." If you didn't mind the homeless people, Carlos said, the library was quiet and spacious and full of books. Carlos was indeed a smart young man: He didn't get a single B in high school. His high school offered six AP classes, he took them all, and he pretty much aced everything.

One of the great pleasures of teaching at a great research university is that, on many occasions, we professors get to meet nerdy young people who give us hope for the future, if only because they appear like more studious, more mature versions of ourselves at that age. Carlos was a neat guy: He enjoyed math, bio, chem, soc, lit, everything—he was pretty good at everything, too, and he seemed a taller, better-looking, smarter Mexican American version of me at that age. In Fall 2013, he came to my office hours during the second week, he introduced himself and said how much he liked my class, and I liked him back right away.

He appeared to know a lot about me, but I think this was because UCSB was changing, and its network of staff and faculty was better prepared to acclimate and orient students like Carlos. By 2013, IDEAS had partnered with my colleagues in student affairs, including key staff members in financial aid, orientation programs, and the office of student life. For about two years, with the support of the chancellor and the vice chancellor of student affairs, lead administrators in that division had formed a DREAM Scholars Resource Team, and they had invited professors, staff members, and even the UCSB Police Department to partner with them to raise awareness about, and to assist, the new incoming class of "Dream Scholars." There were now about eighty or ninety students like Carlos at UCSB in the Fall, and they received a special orientation to help them adjust to UCSB. On the other UC campuses, administrators, professors and staff, and students also collaborated to help more undocumented students feel welcome and accepted on campus.

There was some irony in all of this: In 2013, the regents of the University of California had selected Janet Napolitano to serve as the systemwide president. Just before, Ms. Napolitano had served as the secretary of Homeland Security under President Barack Obama, during a time when President Obama had directed the secretary to "remove" more undocumented persons from the United States, including anyone with a criminal record. Although he'd criticized President Bush severely for separating families and for deporting many thousands of people, President Obama and Secretary Napolitano themselves approved and implemented policies that would accelerate deportations at a pace that would far surpass the Bush administration. Janet Napolitano had served as secretary through September 2013, the same month she was named as the new UC president. Student protests erupted on many campuses that fall, including at Santa Barbara, where our chancellor was hosting a welcome event for President Napolitano that turned ugly and visceral even before Ms. Napolitano got there.

In subsequent months, Ms. Napolitano reminded everyone who would listen that she had supported and helped to design DACA, Deferred

Action for Childhood Arrivals, the program that President Obama had approval in June 2012. Under DACA, President Obama directed the Secretary of Homeland Security to exempt from deportation anyone who had arrived in the United States before his or her sixteenth birthday, and before June 2007. These young adults would be eligible for renewable, two-year work permits as well. This program was President Obama's version of the DREAM Act, approved without the support of many members of Congress, including several Republicans who insisted that DACA was illegal. President Obama and Secretary Napolitano agreed that only Congress could provide a comprehensive solution to our nation's immigration problems, but they also said that they were not going to deport minors and people who posed no threat to the United States while waiting (forever?) for Congress. The president and the future president of the UC system had implemented DACA through the summer of 2012, and since that summer and into the fall of 2013, about 200,000 young adults had become "DACA-mented," including my student Carlos.

Carlos was fascinated by all of these developments, and we've been talking about them ever since. He aced my class, of course, but he aced all of his classes, and he's been doing well in his classes through 2014 and 2015, and now that he's a junior, double majoring in chemistry and sociology, I'm still impressed with his intellectual rigor and easy manner. Nancy had been concerned and angry about her immigration status, and Philip hadn't mentioned it at all, and Carlos was quite the opposite in every respect—he loved his family, especially his *tia*, and even though he hadn't seen much of parents, his experience in college deepened his appreciation for the many sacrifices they'd made. He knew that his mother and father did back-breaking work, and that they did this in part to make sure that he had a stable home and access to decent schools. Last fall, Carlos mentioned that his mother and his *tia* both cried when he took a screen shot of his grades and sent them by text message—a string of A's, better than a string of pearls. Carlos said that he did this not so much to brag (well, maybe a little), but to say thank you to his mom, dad, *tia*, and his cousins. He joked that he was taking Spanish, and so maybe that one of the A's shouldn't count as much, but I noticed that he was reading Cervantes now, this *inteligente*.

I do not know what will happen to Carlos, and neither does he. I know that he complained about the horrible renewal process that he had to go through in 2015, when the first DACA ran out and he had to apply for another one. "It was a pain, it was so stupid and so expensive, too." For the DACA renewal, I had sent Carlos over to see our new Undocumented Student Services Coordinator, a paid staff member whose primary mission was to help students like Carlos. Our coordinator had been hired in 2014, with funds coming directly from the UC President's Office. She had a law degree from Berkeley, she was fantastic with our students, and she had also agreed that the renewal process was too long, too expensive, and very time-consuming. Because this process was all-encompassing for a while, Carlos took a few courses at UCSB about government and immigration policy, and he also won an internship at a nonprofit immigration advocacy group in Washington, DC, through the UC DC program. But he found biochemistry just as fascinating, though, perhaps even more so, because "it's not impossibly political."

The last time we spoke, Carlos was considering medical school, perhaps a PhD in biophysics or bioengineering. His father, mother, and *tia* were pulling for medical school: "You'd be the first doctor we'll be able to see on a regular basis," said his *tia*, with a chuckle. Whatever pressure they're putting on him, it's a good pressure: I don't think Carlos has ever felt that his parents were at fault for his immigration issues, nor does he for a moment believe that he is the social problem that some Americans have continued to fear. I think the bonds he feels for his family are as strong as those of any Confucian gentleman. And something had shifted in our politics, between Nancy and Carlos, such that Carlos believed, like many of my own fellow Americans, that our immigration rules don't do justice to people like him or his parents, that the problem isn't him or his family, but with law and policy, with the inability of my own fellow citizens to figure these things out for their benefit and for our own. His parents and his aunt were decent, hard-working people—they made him proud and he made them proud.

In time, I will meet his parents, very likely next year, when Carlos graduates and I will be sad to see him leave. I am so excited to meet his parents and his *tia*, and I'm going to stock my office with refreshments and special treats for them when they visit next June. When I became a professor, I envisioned having students like Carlos, and I'm very eager to tell his parents just that. Between now and then, there will be an election, Carlos will become a slam dunk candidate for Phi Beta Kappa (because I am president of the UCSB chapter), and he will also have to see about renewing his DACA for a second time, if there is a second time. I've already offered to write Carlos a recommendation letter for a graduate program of his choice, but Carlos doesn't really need me, and from the sound of things, a few of his professors would rather like to adopt him. I'm sure that they'll help him into a good medical school, at least in the states where Carlos might be eligible to attend. No matter the obstacles, I would like to believe that in many respects, Carlos is the kind of young person who would do fine anywhere—plop him in any country, surround him with loving relatives, and he would rise to the top.

Under different, perhaps more favorable circumstances, Nancy may have finished college, too, and Philip's family might have recovered as well. Without question, Philip's brother had done a stupid thing, and he had made a serious mistake, and yet in its own way, as a drug offense, that too was a distinctively American kind of mistake. And how many affluent students have I had, some of whom have also made similar mistakes, who aren't then banished for the rest of their lives? Carlos will make a fine physician, a fine professor, maybe one or maybe both—without question, my colleagues on my campus have helped him and many others like him, but how many more renewals must he complete, and really, for what purpose? It's absurd, how even those immigration rules designed to help young people often devolve into structured forms of harassment. I've been an academic for many years now, and it's a strange perspective, being a professor and seeing a full range of college students, so eager, smart, and mostly wonderful, and seeing also such a variety of families, all with their unique struggles and aspirations. As to why this country must treat some of them so, clouding the best of them with such profound uncertainty, and then making difficult things ever more difficult, I still do not know.

10

"How Will I Get My Skull Back?"

The Embodied Consequences of Immigrant Policing

Nolan Kline

Nolan Kline is a medical anthropologist and Assistant Professor in the Department of Anthropology at Rollins College. He earned his PhD in applied anthropology and a master of public health from the University of South Florida. His most recent work examines the health-related consequences of immigrant policing in the United States.

"Come inside," Miguel said when we met in his driveway on a sunny but chilly morning in February. He welcomed me into his suburban Atlanta home and sat next to me on a cold, tan leather couch, keeping on a black, puffy coat and a skullcap with a combined texture and coloring of black, white, and gray that reminded me of static from a television channel that didn't work. Like many other Latino immigrants in Atlanta, Miguel immigrated to Atlanta in the early 2000s. He left Guatemala in 2004 and built a life in Georgia, fathering two children, five and two years old. In many ways, his background is comparable to numerous other immigrants living in the United States South and across the country; he immigrated for a broadly-conceived "better life" that included improved economic and political situations, and he describes himself as hard-working and as a loving father and spouse. Despite Miguel's commonalities with other immigrants in the United States, his story has at least one remarkable difference because of an eventful day near his home that forever changed his life and the life of his family.

Before Miguel's two-year-old was born, Miguel worked in a chicken wing restaurant in the nearby upscale town of Decatur and commuted from another affluent Atlanta suburb. His commute was a reasonable driving distance, and since Atlanta lacks a comprehensive, efficient public transportation system, immigrants and nonimmigrants alike rely on their automobiles as a means for navigating the ninth largest metropolitan area in the United States. Despite the mundaneness of driving, however, for undocumented immigrants like Miguel, driving—to work, to pick up his children, to the grocery store, or to pick up dinner—is a risky endeavor. Because of Georgia's harsh immigration laws, police can stop any person suspected of being undocumented and request proof of their legal status. Moreover, Georgia's driver's license laws prohibit immigrants like Miguel from obtaining a driver's license, so if Miguel is stopped for speeding, not using a turn signal, having a non-working brake light, a broken taillight, or any other reason, he can be arrested for driving without a license. Driving home from work one evening, a patrol car stopped Miguel; he doesn't recall speeding. Numerous immigrant rights organizations describe how men and women who look Hispanic, like Miguel, get stopped for no apparent reason, asserting that law enforcement practices create widespread racial profiling. The evening he was pulled over, Miguel was arrested for driving without a license.

As a result of federal immigration laws, Miguel's arrest for driving without a license could have resulted in him being deported. Through the Secure Communities Program, Miguel's fingerprints were sent to a federal database to examine whether his fingerprints matched any existing fingerprints present in the database. As Guevara, Stuesse, and Coleman (this volume) describe, through this program, Immigration and Customs Enforcement (ICE) places "holds" on arrestees it suspects may be undocumented and interviews them in jailhouses, attempting to determine their immigration status. ICE has three days until the hold expires and, by law, if they are unable to complete their interview in three days, the hold is lifted and the arrestee is released after resolving their initial reason for arrest. Numerous scholars have pointed out that state and federal immigration laws form a new type of immigrant policing that alters immigrants' mobility, shapes their health decisions, and impacts their daily lives and communities by increasing fear of deportation and weakening trust in local law enforcement officials (Rhodes, et al. 2015; Alexander and Fernandez 2014).[1] Miguel was fortunate that ICE never interviewed him because his family was able to bail him out before he had an ICE hold placed on him. Miguel paid his fine and left the local jail where he had been held, unlike some of his friends who ultimately were deported for doing what Miguel had been: driving home from work.

After his arrest, Miguel decided to move to a neighborhood with job opportunities within walking distance. He moved into the house where I met him and took a job in a shopping center near his current neighborhood. "I used to drive a car, but now they put me on probation, so I could no longer do that," he explained. "After [being arrested], I knew that I didn't want to get a car. It's better to walk than drive, so I looked for a job close to home and worked close by." I asked Miguel where he worked since there were numerous possibilities in the shopping center closer than half a mile from the house. It was a large strip mall with several national chain stores, including a grocery store, coffee shop, a tax service, and several small businesses focused on personal services, including a nail salon and beauty supply shop. There were also several restaurants, and Miguel could have feasibly worked in any of these possible sites.

"I used to work; now I don't because of the wound I have. But I used to work just across the street," Miguel said, gesturing to a wall in his living room. Puzzled, I asked—tilting my head as I repeated the word back to him—"the wound?"

"Yes," Miguel answered matter-of-factly, pointing to the fuzzy television channel skullcap. Seeing my perplexed looks, he continued. "So one day, on my day off, I went to get a few things for breakfast." On the morning in question, Miguel walked the five to eight minutes to the nearby shopping center to visit the grocery store. He crossed the busy but navigable four-lane street with cross walks that divided his neighborhood from the row of shops and meandered the parking lot designed for automobiles rather than pedestrians until he made his way to his destination. He quickly passed through the grocery store aisles knowing what he needed; his wife and children waited for him at home, and he wanted it to be a speedy trip. After purchasing what he wanted for his family's breakfast, Miguel began his short trip back home—a walk so mundane he had no reason to expect anything out of the ordinary.

"But when I was coming back," Miguel explained, "crossing the street here [by the house], a car passed by me, hit me, and knocked me onto the ground." My eyes widened as Miguel told his story—I was incredulous. "While you were walking?!" I asked, thinking I had somehow misunderstood his story.

"When I was walking," Miguel reiterated. "They hit me, and I fell to the ground." The motorist who struck Miguel sped away after Miguel fell, hitting his head on the hard, black pavement. "When I fell, I never knew who it was or how they hit me. I don't know if it was a drunk driver or what."

Pedestrian traffic accidents like the one Miguel was in can be fatal. In the United States, over 4,000 pedestrian deaths occur yearly due to cars, and more than 66,000 pedestrians are injured annually due to traffic incidents.[2] Miguel was fortunate to survive being hit that day and, although he was awake when he walked back to his home after being hit by the car, Miguel fell into a coma in the ambulance his brother called for him. He recalled vague memories of receiving injections in the ambulance before slipping into the coma, and heard that he had been rushed to surgery immediately upon arriving to the hospital.

"I woke up in the hospital," Miguel recalled, "but I woke up about seven days after [the accident] and didn't know where I was. When someone falls like that they die because a blow to the head like that—nobody can recover from that kind of blow to the head, nobody can withstand it, so I didn't know anything." When Miguel awoke from his week-long coma, he was confused about his surroundings and who he was. "After it happened, I woke up, but I never understood what was happening and I couldn't talk."

For more than two weeks, loved ones surrounded Miguel, but he couldn't recognize them: He was living a horrific version of a plot device seen on television dramas. "For about fifteen days I couldn't really see who was around; my family was there with me, my wife was there, my two brothers, but I told them that I didn't know who they were because that was my understanding: The wound did that to me." Miguel's wound, in his words, took his memory of his family—the most important people in his life. "I said, 'Who are these people? Who are you?' I didn't know they were my family."

Eventually Miguel began to recognize his brothers, children, and his wife. As he regained some of his memory, he began asking what happened to him, still unable to understand why he was in the hospital and how he had lost his memory. "When I started to recognize them, I said, 'What happened to me yesterday?' and they told me, 'It wasn't yesterday. You've been in the hospital for almost two weeks.'"

Miguel's family was unsure what happened to him and explained to him how he arrived at the hospital. "They told me, 'We don't know what happened to you because you came home, walking, vomiting blood; blood coming out of your mouth, blood in your nose, blood coming out of your ears; dripping blood.'" Miguel showed me from the couch where he had gotten blood all over the floor in house: "There was blood all over there, and all through there," he said, pointing to the foyer, kitchen, and hallway leading to the bathroom. "They told me, 'When you came home we were worried but never knew what happened to you; we never knew. All we knew was that you went to buy something.'"

I looked at Miguel in shock, unable to fully comprehend not only how he survived the accident he described to me and still trying to fathom how his wife, children, and brothers must have felt seeing him walk through the door of their home like that, vomiting blood, without understanding why. As an anthropologist dedicated to immigrant rights, I was accustomed to hearing stories of hardship related to labor exploitation, police abuses, and poverty. Like other immigrants, Miguel's story included a type of bodily harm that continues to haunt him.

As we sat on the cold leather couches, I began to wonder if Miguel's static-television-looking hat served more purposes than just keeping his head warm on a chilly day in Georgia. Could he have suffered severe bruises and deep scratches from his fall that he was embarrassed to show? Perhaps he experienced brain trauma or needed a procedure done while he was comatose that resulted in scars on his head?

Taking off the fuzzy channel skullcap, Miguel revealed the damage to his head. Rather than having a scar, bruise, or deep scratch, Miguel instead was missing a large portion of his skull, possibly as much as a quarter, giving his head a crescent shape. "They've removed all of this," he said, drawing a circle around the large, concave portion of his head. "The operation was up to here," he gestured up toward the center of his head, which seemed to have been recently shaved and hair was starting to grow back. Pointing to the crown of his head he looked at me in surprise. "Up to here, they took this piece out of me! I don't have this piece of my skull."

Miguel and I had spoken over the phone before we met in person, and had suggested we meet the week we did because he said he had an operation scheduled for the following week. "Right now I'm waiting for them to operate on this. . . . I told you it was Monday [when we talked on the phone], but that's not going to happen." I asked Miguel what he meant—what was the operation, and why would it not happen?

"It turns out that Sunday they called me and told me, 'No, we can't operate on you because [that portion of your skull] is in the Suburban Atlanta Health Center.'" (Suburban Atlanta Health Center is a pseudonym for the nearby hospital where Miguel was taken after his accident.) Miguel's surgery was scheduled at Grady Memorial Hospital, the largest public hospital in Atlanta, eighth largest in the United States, and a historically significant institution with deep connections to Atlanta's civil rights movement. I never learned the exact reason for Miguel's surgery being scheduled at Grady, but some hospital administrators and providers unfamiliar with Miguel's case suggested the skull surgery might be used as a teaching case for Emory University medical students, who shadow their Emory provider/professors in the hospital. Alternatively, Miguel might have qualified for reduced-cost services as a resident of one of two Atlanta counties Grady provides care for at a discount. Regardless of how he found Grady, however, Miguel's surgery ended up being canceled. "They said, 'Your bone wasn't sent here; [The other hospital] didn't want to send it. . . . They don't want to send your bone because you have a balance due.'" Because Miguel owed Suburban Atlanta Health Center money for the emergency operation that removed the piece of his skull, the hospital would not release his bone to Grady for the operation that would restore Miguel's head to its original shape. Miguel would happily pay for his skull, but he is currently out of work. "I have no money to pay that hospital because I am not working and they want me to pay them." Since his accident, finding work has been difficult for Miguel. "If I go to whatever job and they say to me, 'Are you okay?' And I say, 'Yes,' they say, 'You don't have a skull!' Bosses don't want to give me a job because I am a person that's already an invalid. . . . I can't work anymore with this injury."

Not only has Miguel's appearance made it difficult to find work, the accident itself left lasting physical damage. He has lost his sense of smell and taste and explained he cannot hear as well as he used to. Still, Miguel is thankful that he can walk and speak. "Through the grace of God I'm like this because I have seen cases where someone had a head injury smaller than this one and couldn't walk, but I can walk, I can talk, I can go to the store and buy something, I can pick up my kids."

The accident that left Miguel missing a portion of his skull happened only five months before he and I met. Miguel's attempts to contact

Suburban Atlanta Health Center often left him frustrated; he claimed to be on hold for two hours or longer waiting to speak to someone who spoke Spanish before giving up or needing to take care of his children. "I take care of the kids because my wife works now, and I can't stay on the phone if they're fighting or something," he explained. Overall, the frustration mounts and takes a toll on Miguel. "Sometimes I feel like a weight is over me. Sometimes I cry; if I cry sometimes I start to cry hard because sometimes I see no way out. How am I going to get my bone? And then I start to pray and ask God to take this sadness from me and move on, and I'm okay."

When we spoke, Suburban Atlanta Health Center still had the large portion of his skull, and Miguel worried he may never be able to have his surgery if he must pay his entire medical bill before getting back what was removed from his head. He has already borrowed large sums of money from friends and family members to cover medical procedures related to his accident, including $3,500 for removing staples put in his head that the surgeon had forgotten to take out. "I paid the neurosurgeon and I told him I'm in pain [where the staples were] and I had thought he put them there to support the wound, and he told me no, just that he forgot [to take them out]. He forgot them! I had been putting up with this pain for almost two months, suffering with this, and when I paid the $3,500 all they did was take out the staples and that was all. Then they told me 'for your other surgery you need to bring $3,800 more.'"

Paying $3,800 more for a surgery to put the portion of bone back in Miguel's head was a challenge because Miguel had already tapped into family and friends for financial support. "Where will I get that money? My brother already gave me $1,700, the friends we live with gave us $200 and $150, and so after they said 'Bring the other $3,800,' where will I get it? I don't have it."

Miguel's story raises alarming questions related to biological rights, ownership over portions of the body, and a number of moral, ethical, and legal considerations surrounding this situation of holding a bone hostage. A hospital keeping a portion of Miguel's skull also speaks to concerns regarding the health system in the United States. A growing number of hospitals in the United States are requiring up-front payments prior to treatment, even for patients with health insurance. This is partly due to health insurance plans increasingly featuring high deductibles, prompting hospital administrators to provide treatment costs and payment option with patients before they receive their bills. Undocumented immigrants typically lack health insurance, however, and they are prohibited from purchasing insurance created through the Patient Protection and Affordable Care Act. Moreover, undocumented immigrants are banned from receiving Medicaid benefits, effectively leaving them to cover all health care treatment costs on their own. Furthermore, there are extremely limited legal responsibilities for hospitals like Suburban Atlanta Health Center to provide care related to payment. A federal law, the Emergency Medical Treatment and Labor Act (EMTALA), prohibits hospitals from denying patients treatment based on their ability to pay when they seek care from an emergency room, but the law's requirements do not apply to nonemergent care. As Miguel's condition is stable, Suburban Atlanta Health Center has no legal responsibility under EMTALA to put the remainder of his skull in his head. Hospital policies and restrictions to health insurance and entitlement programs are not the only elements in advancing Miguel's suffering, however; Miguel's situation is also linked to immigration laws.

Miguel's predicament directly implicates immigrant policing in not only impacting overall health and well-being of undocumented immigrants, but directly playing a role in shaping some immigrants' bodily integrity. If it were not for the harsh immigrant policing regime that restricts immigrants' mobility by denying them driver's licenses and operates through local law enforcement who can arrest undocumented immigrants through routine traffic stops, Miguel would not have limited his own mobility to walking. Immigrant policing regimes and Miguel's need to walk to work shaped large and small decisions in Miguel's life based on his need to avoid police on roadways, such as moving to where he did, and walking to the store the day he was struck by a car. In other words, if it were not for the harsh immigrant policing regime in Atlanta, Miguel might not have a quarter of his skull being held ransom by a local hospital. While a car accident could have resulted in the same outcome, immigrant policing regimes nevertheless augmented Miguel's risk of a *pedestrian* injury. Miguel has thus embodied the issue of immigrant policing—his body wears the signs of harsh immigration regimes that have shaped his life and ultimately impacted it in potentially irreparable ways. This is not to suggest immigrant policing regimes are entirely responsible for Miguel's condition, but rather to bring into view how immigrant policing can shape individual actions that have indirect health impacts.

Overall, Miguel's situation is rooted in intersecting health and immigration policies that require scholarly and activist attention. Undocumented immigrants' prohibition from certain types of health insurance prevent Miguel an affordable way to defray the cost of his treatment, and hospitals like Suburban Atlanta Health Center have no legal obligation to further operate on Miguel. These policy vulnerabilities that undocumented immigrants, and to some extent all poor, uninsured people face, are exacerbated by harsh immigration regimes. The layered immigrant policing efforts in Atlanta ultimately shaped Miguel's decisions to stop driving, and as a result of that decision, he was involved in a pedestrian accident that funneled him into the United States health care system that is designed just to keep uninsured patients alive and do barely more than that. Specific legislative interventions are needed to respond to this policy constellation of that can impact undocumented immigrants' health.

To respond to the intersecting impacts of immigration and health policy that can result in embodied consequences, legislation reducing undocumented immigrants sweeping social vulnerabilities is needed. Such legislation should include possible forms of health care financing for immigrants like Miguel, permitting driver's licenses to undocumented immigrants, and ending the harsh immigrant policing regimes that govern immigrants through fear. Such steps may allow for immigrants like Miguel to feel safe living their lives and avoid having to take drastic measures such as moving to a place where they can walk to work, which for Miguel, ultimately resulted in long-term, biological effects.

Notes

1. In the United States, undocumented immigrants, who comprise the largest uninsured patient population, are ineligible for public entitlement programs to subsidize the cost of care. They often must rely on charitable organizations or hospital emergency rooms for health services, and immigrant policing efforts have made accessing care more precarious in certain areas.
2. These estimates come from the 2013 National Highway Traffic Safety Administration report and more information can be found here: http://www-nrd.nhtsa.dot.gov/Pubs/812124.pdf.

References

Alexander, William L., and Magdalena Fernandez. 2014. "Immigration Policing and Medical Care for Farmworkers: Uncertainties and Anxieties in the East Coast Migrant Stream." *North American Dialogue* 17 (1): 13–30.

Guevara, Juan Carlos, Angela Stuesse, and Mathew Coleman. 2017. "I Used to Believe in Justice." This Volume.

Rhodes, Scott D., Lilli Mann, Florence M. Simán, Eunyoung Song, Jorge Alonzo, Mario Downs, Emma Lawlor, et al. 2015. "The Impact of Local Immigration Enforcement Policies on the Health of Immigrant Hispanics/Latinos in the United States." *American Journal of Public Health* 105 (2): 329–37.

PART 4

SEEKING REFUGE:
What Does It Take to Get Asylum in the United States?

In the spring of 2015, news headlines informed us that Central American women and often-unaccompanied children were surging across the border between the United States and Mexico. Many people asked: Why would mothers send their children on such a perilous journey? During the Syrian refugee crisis in Europe a few months later, people asked the same thing. What compels people to leave their countries? What responsibilities do countries have when people arrive on their shores seeking refuge?

In 1980, the United States passed the Refugee Act, which aligned our definition of refugees with the United Nations Convention and Protocol on the Status of Refugees. According to the UN Convention, a refugee is a person who has "a well-founded fear of being persecuted for reasons of race, religion, nationality, membership of a particular social group or political opinion" and is in need of a safe haven.[1] As of 2017, there were 21.3 million refugees in the world, the vast majority of whom were awaiting permanent settlement.[2] An additional 1.66 million people submitted applications for asylum worldwide.[3] In the United States, the Refugee Act allows 50,000 refugees to be admitted each year, although the president has the authority to take in more refugees. President Barack Obama increased the United States' allocation for 2016 to 85,000—or 0.44 percent of the world population of refugees. Nevertheless, the United States resettles more refugees than any other country, as most refugees remain in refugee camps in the developing world.[4] In part due to the significant obstacles refugees face, first in being formally classified as a refugee and secondly in being chosen to be among the 85,000 permitted to settle in the United

States, many people who fear persecution come directly to the United States and apply for asylum.

Asylum seekers are people who flee persecution in their home country and seek protection elsewhere. The right to seek and enjoy asylum is enshrined in Article 14 of the Universal Declaration of Human Rights (UDHR). In the United States, asylum-seekers must prove they have a well-founded fear that, if returned to their home country, they will be persecuted based on their race, religion, nationality, membership in a particular social group, or political opinion. People who fear persecution may apply for asylum at the port of entry, after arriving in the United States, or when they are facing deportation. Whereas refugee status is granted abroad, asylum seekers must arrive at the gates of the United States in order to apply. They often have to take circuitous and dangerous land and sea routes; airlines will not sell tickets to anyone lacking proper documentation to enter the United States.

When a person attempts to enter the United States as an asylum-seeker, they must convince the receiving border inspector that they have a credible fear of persecution. Otherwise, they face expedited deportation. If refugees pass the credible fear of persecution test conducted by the border inspector, they are usually placed in detention while their applications are being processed. Some are detained for a few days, yet others are detained for years while awaiting trial. The UDHR states that "the right to seek and enjoy asylum is a basic human right; individuals must never be punished for seeking asylum." The DHS, however, maintains that detention is not punishment; it is a security measure to ensure that people report to their immigration hearing. At this hearing, if the claim is successful, the asylum-seeker will be granted legal status and work authorization in the United States. If their claim is denied, they face deportation.

The stories we have read thus far in this book have been about people who came to the United States seeking a better life. Many of them fled economic deprivation and political turmoil in their countries of origin. However, to be classified as a refugee or to be granted asylum requires more than showing that your life would be better if you moved to the United States. In fact, it requires more than showing that you could be killed if you return home. To be granted asylum in the United States, you have to prove that you have a well-founded fear of persecution on account of race, religion, nationality, membership in a particular social group, or political opinion. You can't just say that you would be persecuted. This persecution has to be personalized toward you. Because of the specificity of asylum laws, these cases are much more likely to be successful if you have a lawyer to help present your case in a way that aligns with US immigration law. However, in the United States, asylum-seekers are not guaranteed legal representation. They can only get representation if they are able to afford it or if a lawyer offers their services *pro bono.*

Sarah Lakhani's chapter in this section explains the myriad obstacles asylum-seekers face as they navigate the complex immigration system in the United States. These stories make it clear why asylum seekers with lawyers are almost five times as likely to win in immigration court as those without representation. Unlike criminal defendants, asylum-seekers do not have the constitutional right to government-appointed legal counsel. The chapter by Tanya Golash-Boza revisits this theme as Rafael's asylum case would have had a better chance of being successful if he had had adequate legal representation. The case of Rafael and his family also points to another critical issue: What are the responsibilities of the United States toward Central Americans when the US government funded the very forces who repressed people in this region? As Maya Barak explains, between 1980 and 1990, 500,000 refugees fled civil war in El Salvador—a war funded in part by the United States. Barak's story of three generations of Salvadorans makes it clear just how deeply El Salvador was affected by that war—as well as the repercussions Salvadorans continue to feel today. This story of three generations of family separation may sound exceptional. Unfortunately, it has become the norm for many Central American families, due to ongoing violence in the region as well as the impasse on immigration reform in the United States.

The people discussed in these chapters all feared for their lives in their country of birth. However, the criteria for asylum is not simply that you might be killed if you are forced to return home, but that your fear of persecution must be based on "race, religion, nationality, membership in a particular social group, or political opinion." As you read these essays, think about the ramifications of granting asylum only on this basis.

Notes

1. *United Nations Convention and Protocol Related to the Status of Refugees*, http://www.unhcr.org/3b66c2aa10.html
2. http://www.unhcr.org/en-us/figures-at-a-glance.html
3. Ibid.
4. *UNHCR Global Resettlement Statistical Report*, http://www.unhcr.org/52693bd09.html

11

"Is This America?": Asylum-Seeking in an Era of Humanitarian Decline

Sarah M. Lakhani

The author, Sarah M. Lakhani, is a JD candidate at the University of California, Berkeley School of Law and an Affiliated Scholar at the American Bar Foundation. She completed her PhD in sociology at the University of California–Los Angeles.

Azzeza, a schoolteacher from Eritrea, was tortured and imprisoned for months for explaining menstruation to curious adolescent girls in defiance of government authorities. After her release from captivity, Azzeza left her two young children with a friend and fled the country,[1] afraid for her life. She trekked across Africa, took a boat to Latin America, and traveled by train and on foot north through Mexico, where she attempted to cross the border into Texas. At that point, Azzeza was apprehended by Immigration and Customs Enforcement and detained. After passing a credible fear screening,[2] a sister in Los Angeles paid Azzeza's bond and she was released. She went to Southern California before reporting to immigration court for her removal hearing several weeks later.

Having miraculously made it safely to Los Angeles, Azzeza was optimistic about her prospects for starting over in the United States, a place she associated with freedom, opportunity, and acceptance of immigrants. She planned to attend school to learn English, get her high school equivalency degree, and pursue a nursing career. Meanwhile, she would find a job to save money for her children's transport to the country. Although her immigration hearing loomed over her, Azzeza recalled that, for the most part, she was not thinking about her legal permission to remain in the country. She assumed she could explain her situation to the judge, who would tell her how to resolve any issues so that she could stay. However, Azzeza's early experiences in American society opened her eyes to the importance of legal status for immigrants.

> When I came here, I came directly to my sister's house, and I lived with my sister, and I wanted to start a class, get a job, and start my work. But [when I tried to enroll at] West L.A. College, they sa[id] to me, "If you haven't any residency, you can't take the

> class." Wow, it's hard in America. I tr[ied] to take the GED[3] test, and the teacher told me, "Oh, if you don't have [a] California I.D., you can't take [it]." Wow, American is very hard. I want[ed] to [look for] some jobs. The [employers] t[old] me, "If you don't have your work permit, you can't start a job." I don't have a work permit. Wow. Is this America? Everything is closed for me at first, because I must ask [for] asylum.

It was not until several months after her arrival that Azzeza became fully aware of the US government's political asylum program, through which she could apply for her own legalization and the legal passage of her children. When she was apprehended at the border, she told immigration officers that she was scared to return to Eritrea because she had been tortured there. As a result, Azzeza was referred to an asylum officer for a credible fear interview. Notwithstanding that she completed and passed the evaluation, she described that her first few days in the United States were "confusing." The officer told her a few details about political asylum, but Azzeza's physical and emotional exhaustion from her long journey and her limited English skills prevented total comprehension of the events of this stressful period. It was not until she met with a lawyer that she began to understand the asylum program.

The US Congress passed the Refugee Act in 1980. Under this law, the State Department annually selects tens of thousands of refugees, many of them living abroad in camps run by the United Nations, and resettles them in the United States. The Act also provides a system through which people who flee to our shores can apply for asylum. Any foreign national who comes to the United States, with or without a visa, may seek protection. To win asylum, the individual must prove that the reason for fleeing his or her country is a well-founded fear of persecution on account of race, religion, nationality, membership in a particular social group, or political opinion.[4] Asylum holders may remain in the country and are authorized to work. They are also entitled to benefits that include employment assistance, a Social Security card, social services, and the ability to apply for the immigration of certain family members.

Although *political asylum* is similar to *refugee status* and is often confused with it, the two programs are different in several ways. Importantly, while eligibility for each program hinges on the same set of past circumstances, refugees and asylees are welcomed to the United States differently. Refugees receive more resources than asylees before and after their arrival, and they retain access to aid for a more sustained period of time.[5] For instance, refugees receive cultural orientation to the United States and help with their overseas travel. They are also entitled to medical and cash assistance in the United States.[6]

No such orientation is offered to potential asylees upon their arrival in the United States, regardless of immigration status or country of origin. In part, this is because some of them enter the United States without immigration status of any kind, having escaped detection at the border. The US government is unaware of their presence until they apply for asylum, making any organized, targeted orientation logistically difficult, if not impossible, to administer. Other asylum-seekers enter the United States with some form of immigration status, such as a tourist or student visa, but the government has no way of knowing they intend to seek asylum and so cannot provide any cultural or sociolegal settlement assistance. Others, like Azzeza, arrive without immigration status and are immediately apprehended; knowing little or nothing about the political asylum program, they may nevertheless voice a fear of returning to their home countries and undergo credible fear interviews without fully comprehending what is happening.

"Political asylum" is one of several types of immigration legal status granted on a humanitarian basis that are supposed to protect and support individuals who endure violence, persecution, or other extreme events in their countries of origin and escape to other nations. However, the current sociolegal reception that the United States gives to potential asylees falls drastically short of those aspirations. In reality, asylees face convoluted routes to accurate information about legal status and social services opportunities and to competent, nonexploitative, and affordable assistance. The experiences of Azzeza and others during their initial months and years in the country point to the need for improved information dissemination to immigrants about the political asylum program and legal and other aid for applicants.

Like Azzeza, some immigrant newcomers are unaware of the socioeconomic problems a lack of legal standing can pose to their incorporation and mobility in the United States. They expect that the United States, a politically stable country with humanitarian policies and a robust social welfare infrastructure, will accommodate their presence and pursuit of better lives. Other newly arrived immigrants without legal status understand the importance of getting their legal "papers" in order as soon as possible. They know that legal standing is a gateway to desirable social opportunities and protections in the United States, and appreciate that having stable legal status will enhance their psychological well-being.

> *Habtom, 25–44, Eritrea, legal permanent resident (former asylum holder):*[7]
> In this place . . . you have to have a paper. You have to have legal [status] to do anything. I believe if you don't have this paper, or if you are not a resident . . . you cannot do anything.

> *Roberto, 45–64, Colombia, legal permanent resident (former asylum holder):*
> Of all of the things that I was scared of most [when I arrived in the United States], it was going around without papers here.

Lucia, 45–64, Peru, US citizen (former asylum holder):
Among the things that one wants upon arriving here, first it's to have your documents. . . . Once you have your documents, the language [comes], you [gain] your work capacity. . . . One can start to unwind in the city, in everything . . . and after one can think of other things, [like] housing.

Even if immigrants perceive the value of acquiring US legal status and want to regularize their standing, many do not know how to do so, including what opportunities they could qualify for or how to apply. Financial issues can prevent immigrants from pursuing legal assistance, since many are unaware that free or low-cost legal aid may be available. For potential asylees, the trauma associated with the circumstances from which they escaped can also impair help-seeking behavior.

Valeria, 25–44, Colombia, asylum holder:
I arrived here two years ago. . . . I didn't have information about who to turn to and I had just as many social problems as those stemming from why I came here, and also economic ones because starting the process was expensive. . . . It's difficult to find the information, and [also] to be able to take the step that one needs to take [once one has the information], both because of money reasons and because of personal reasons.

Lucia, 45–64, Peru, US citizen (former asylum holder):
I arrived here in 1994, and really because of fear I didn't look for help because I came hiding myself from the Shining Path [group] from my country. A few years went by, my oldest daughter arrived, but she didn't get the visa and she came through Tijuana. Then she was arrested by Immigration. Seeing the situation that I found myself in, out of desperation I went to a particular immigration lawyer, paying the money for the consultation and everything.

Immigrants who know of the political asylum program and believe they may be eligible for it remain in a precarious position vis-à-vis the law. The uncoordinated reception that the US government provides to immigrants about legalization and social opportunities often leads migrants to rely on family members, friends, or others in their co-ethnic communities for information. This process can certainly bring about positive outcomes, but information about immigration drawn from informal social networks of lay people can be inaccurate or misconstrued. It is common for family and friends to refer newly arrived immigrants to lawyers they know personally, or to individuals whom they believe are lawyers but are not. This can create problems for people with potential asylum claims.

Rodrigo, a civil engineer from Colombia, fled his country in 2008 after receiving repeated death threats from members of an antigovernment guerrilla because of work he had done with the government. When he arrived in Los Angeles, a cousin introduced Rodrigo to someone who presented himself as an immigration lawyer, but who was actually a *notario*[8] and unauthorized to practice law in the United States. While non-lawyers may assist individuals in their own completion of asylum and other immigration forms, the complexities of immigration law often cause non-experts—including those pretending to be lawyers and lawyers who do not specialize in immigration law—to err in their advice. Petition mistakes can prevent asylum approvals. As Rodrigo articulated,

> When he [the notario] saw one of the documents that was sent to me by the guerrilla, he told me, "With the document you have and the others, in this country they can give you the opportunity of political asylum." [But] all he really did was lie to me and cause me problems. I had just arrived here, [and] I didn't know there were people who would do something like this. One of the mistakes made was that I didn't include my wife on the political asylum application. . . . I was going to get help from this great country like school and all these things, but due to [the notario's] lack of knowledge, time went by and I lost these benefits. I also lost a lot of money.

After surviving traumatic ordeals in their countries of origin, many asylum seekers reach the United States with little money, limited or no English language skills, and scant knowledge about where or whom to turn to for help. While some immigrants wind up in the hands of unscrupulous *notarios*, others locate bona fide lawyers who have the technical wherewithal to assist immigrants in the complex asylum application process. Unfortunately, some of them exploit immigrants' naivety and legal, social, and psychological vulnerability. Frances, a journalist from Sierra Leone whose advocacy against genital mutilation led to government-supported torture and death threats, described her initial experiences with lawyers in the United States.

> I started [my asylum case at] a legal organization [in Northern California]. [At first] they were not charging me for anything. But when it [came time to pick up] my status [from them], [they told me that] I had to pay [them] a thousand and some hundred dollars to get [it at their office]. My second experience was with another

> foundation. I was with them, I applied for food stamps [and] cash aid, [and] they were buying me clothes. They [even] sent me to see a new school, all that. But later on, there were problems because they wanted to use my story . . . to make money. [T]hey introduced me to several organizations . . . and I spoke briefly about my story. Then all these media people started running after me. [B]ecause my story was pathetic, [people] started to give [the organizations] money. . . . [A]t first they raised my hope that they would give me some of the money to help me bring my sister [from Sierra Leone], because now she too is [dealing with] the same thing [as I did]. But they didn't.

Not all asylees experience the same challenges as Rodrigo or Frances when trying to apply for asylum. Azzeza, for example, found a good lawyer who successfully navigated her case to approval on the first try. As she explained,

> [After] I paid [my] bond [to be released from ICE detention], I came here [Los Angeles]. After that, my sister asked some people what to do, because I didn't know what to do. Some people gave her the phone [number] of [the] public defender, and she called them. At first they did an interview, then they saw my papers, and they accepted me. I did everything what they told me, and then I got my paper.

As the above accounts suggest, grants or denials of relief under the political asylum status quo can depend heavily on random chance, independent of migrants' qualifying experiences in their countries of origin. This kind of jeopardous justice does not reflect the humanitarian ethos of the asylum program.

The twists and turns of asylees' paths to legal and social services convey the importance of quality, affordable, and holistic sociolegal advice in immigrants' lives. Unfortunately, many asylum seekers do not have access to this sort of effective, comprehensive representation. The United States does not guarantee asylum seekers the help of a lawyer.[9] Given the complexities of the US asylum system, this constitutes a significant barrier to access to justice. A recent national study found that fewer than 40 percent of immigrants in deportation court proceedings were represented by an attorney in cases decided on the merits.[10] The same study found that approximately 86 percent of immigrants in detention facilities were without representation. Lack of attorney representation has dire consequences for immigrants, as illustrated by another study finding that asylum seekers without lawyers were almost five times less likely to win in immigration court than those with representation.[11]

The representation gap in asylum and other immigration legal cases has received national attention of late. Considering the extremely high stakes involved, this is a sign of progress. The consequences of deportation can be just as, if not more, devastating for immigrants and their families as criminal conviction.[12] Asylum seekers can face detention, torture, or even death if forced to return to their countries of origin. However, unlike indigent criminal defendants, poor asylum seekers do not have a constitutionally recognized right to government-appointed legal counsel.

As the narratives presented here convey, access to lawyers or other legal aid may be insufficient to deliver justice to asylum seekers because of unethical or unskilled immigration law practitioners. The reluctance of some asylum seekers to pursue aid in the first place due to past trauma and a lack of orientation to American society and its legal system may also prevent them from regularizing their status. For those asylum seekers who feel able to talk about their experiences and seek remediation, the paucity of free and low-cost legal aid[13] represents another challenge to achieving the ideals of US asylum policy.

> *David, 25–44, Uganda, asylum holder:*
> My experiences are horrible. I'd been arrested numerous times, tortured, beaten, until I finally managed to escape. So many challenges along the way. So when you come over here, you say, "Oh my, at least I'm going to get some relief." Then you get over here, [and there are] new challenges altogether. You know, you can't even work, can't even feed yourself. You can't give too much information to people about home and all that, and you can't go back. It's really, really difficult. . . . [Many] people just give up. They're on the streets. They have no help. . . . [T]hey couldn't get anywhere ahead, you know, they are stranded. . . . So, I did my best and when I got in touch with the assistance that they[14] gave me, it's really impacting my life very positive[ly]. [Now] I can work legally. . . . I have several jobs, part-time here and there, and I'm not scared of being arrested. I'm legal in the United States and I have documentation.

> *Joseph, 45-64, Ethiopia, legal permanent resident (former asylum holder):*
> In Ethiopia, my sister and I were trying to overthrow the bourgeois democratic government and avoid communism. And repeatedly three times I ended up as a suspect, and I was going to be killed. They kept breaking into my place and searching [for me] always. . . . When I got here [United States], I was in San Pedro Detention Center. I didn't want to get help from the attorneys that were coming. They were trying to help me to have rights, telling me, "You are not supposed to be in [this] detention center. [We

> want to help] take you out from here. Let us help you. We are getting nothing from you, [so] let us help you." But [for me] it [felt] dangerous to open [myself]. I [felt like I would be] a suspect for life. From the church also, they came once a week to help us, but I could not trust anyone. I could not trust the American government. They may kill me. They may deport me. [The attorneys told me,] "But you have rights; we are trying to help you legally." I avoided them like four or five times, but finally I signed. That's how I met Equal Justice. And they introduced me to Dr. Lopez [a psychologist from a mental health organization] and I got X-rays [to demonstrate my injuries from torture in Ethiopia], and they accompanied me to court.

Asylees' narratives show that access to justice for this population often requires more than legal assistance. Asylum seekers are frequently battling the psychological ramifications of severe trauma, and they may need counseling and support from mental health professionals in order to adequately explain their experiences to lawyers and government officers. Language barriers and cross-cultural differences can also affect asylum seekers' ability to recount their experiences with the kind of detail that immigration lawyers need and immigration officers expect, as can a limited understanding of the law.

Meeting the needs of the asylum-seeking population in the United States is difficult but not impossible. Arguably, the humanitarian mission of the asylum project demands that a certain level of assistance and care be devoted to orienting potential asylum seekers to the availability of legal and social resources in the country and to connecting them to competent, ethical, and affordable aid providers.

Beyond the realm of asylum, similar dynamics play out in the legalization trajectories of other immigrant groups. Immigration law is notoriously tricky for laypeople and lawyers alike. Not surprisingly, immigrants' independent understanding of legalization opportunities is often inaccurate. Yet locating reputable, economical legal advice can be difficult. In turn, many immigrants other than asylees have undergone traumatic experiences in their countries of origin and the United States and may struggle to share their situations with attorneys and immigration officials. Therefore, the challenges of Azzeza, Rodrigo, Frances, and the other asylees discussed here are realities for myriad immigrants in the country.

Notes

1. This was no simple task for Azzeza, as Eritrea is one of a handful of countries in the world that requires an exit visa to leave.

2. An arriving immigrant without authorization to enter the United States who expresses a fear of returning to his or her country of origin because of persecution or torture and an interest in applying for asylum is supposed to be interviewed by an asylum officer before being deported. If the officer determines that the individual's fear is "credible," he or she may seek asylum before an immigration judge during a subsequent removal hearing. See https://www.uscis.gov/humanitarian/refugees-asylum/asylum/questions-answers-credible-fear-screening (accessed May 12, 2016).
3. The "GED," or General Educational Development test, is the high school equivalency exam in the United States.
4. See http://www.uscis.gov/humanitarian/refugees-asylum (accessed December 30, 2015).
5. This is not to say that the refugee experience is at all easy. In fact, the refugee selection process is very rigorous and lengthy. See https://www.state.gov/j/prm/ra/admissions/index.htm (accessed February 4, 2017).
6. See http://www.uscis.gov/humanitarian/refugees-asylum/refugees (accessed December 30, 2015).
7. Most of the research I draw on in this chapter comes from focus groups I conducted in 2011 with asylum seekers and holders, some of whom had become legal permanent residents and US citizens. I collected data on participants' age (in ranges), country of origin, and current legal status, and include it here for context.
8. A *notario*, shorthand for *notario público*, is a Spanish language term for "notary public." In the United States, *notarios* are nonlawyers who engage in the unauthorized practice of law. While a notary public in the United States is authorized to serve the public as an impartial witness in executing various fraud-deterrent acts related to the signing of important documents, a notary public in many Latin American countries refers to an individual who has received the equivalent of a law license and who is authorized to represent others before the government. As a result, Latin American immigrants can be deceived into believing that *notarios* in the United States have the authority and skills to provide legal advice. See, e.g., http://www.americanbar.org/groups/public_services/immigration/projects_initiatives/fightnotariofraud.html and https://www.nationalnotary.org/knowledge-center/about-notaries (accessed May 17, 2016).
9. Because immigration proceedings in the United States are considered civil, not criminal, in nature, asylum seekers facing removal from the country do not have the same constitutional protections as defendants in criminal proceedings. This includes the right to appointed counsel. See, e.g., Golash-Boza 2012.
10. Eagly and Shafer 2015.
11. TRAC 2010.
12. See, e.g., Ardalan 2015; Golash-Boza 2015; Kanstroom and Lykes 2015; Markowitz 2011; Mills, Echemendia, and Yale-Loehr 2009.
13. See, e.g., Heeren 2011.
14. David is referring to the assistance he received at Equal Justice of Los Angeles ("Equal Justice"), a nonprofit legal organization in Los Angeles, California where I conducted most of my research with asylum seekers and holders.

References

Ardalan, Sabrineh. 2015. "Access to Justice for Asylum Seekers: Developing an Effective Model of Holistic Asylum Representation." *University of Michigan Journal of Law Reform* 48 (4): 1001–38.

Eagly, Ingrid V. and Steven Shafer. 2015. "A National Study of Access to Counsel in Immigration Court." *University of Pennsylvania Law Review* 164 (1): 1–91.

Golash-Boza, Tanya. 2015. *Deported: Immigrant Policing, Disposable Labor, and Global Capitalism.* New York: New York University Press.

Golash-Boza, Tanya. 2012. *Due Process Denied: Detentions and Deportations in the United States.* New York: Routledge.

Heeren, Geoffrey. 2011. "Illegal Aid: Legal Assistance to Immigrants in the United States." *Cardozo Law Review* 33 (2): 619–74.

Kanstroom, Daniel and M. Brinton Lykes. 2015. *The New Deportations Delirium.* New York: New York University Press.

Markowitz, Peter L. 2011. "Deportation is Different." *University of Pennsylvania Journal of Constitutional Law* 13: 1299–361.

Mills, John R., Kristen M. Echemendia, and Stephen Yale-Loehr. 2009. "Death is Different and a Refugee's Right to Counsel." *Cornell International Law Journal* 42 (3): 361–85.

Transactional Records Access Clearinghouse (TRAC). 2010. "Asylum Denial Rate Reaches All-Time Low: FY 2010 Results, A Twenty-Five Year Perspective." Transactional Records Access Clearinghouse. Retrieved March 21, 2016 at http://trac.syr.edu/immigration/reports/240/.

12

When American Dreams Are Shattered

Tanya Golash-Boza

The author, Tanya Golash-Boza, is a professor of sociology at the University of California–Merced. She is the author of several books, including Deported: Immigrant Policing, Disposable Labor, and Global Capitalism *(New York University Press, 2015).*

"My last Christmas in the United States, I couldn't even think of anything to ask for; I had everything," Katy told me. I met Katy in a popular chicken restaurant in Guatemala City, Pollo Campero, in 2009, where she reminisced on her life in the United States. The interview was difficult for both of us as she shed tears throughout our conversation. Katy grew up with her parents and older sister in a spacious home in a suburb of New Orleans, Louisiana. Her parents moved to the United States when she was two years old, and had achieved the American Dream: they had a house, several cars, and two daughters headed for success. Katy's father owned a lucrative business, her mother was a housewife, and Katy was a typical American teenager who loved going to the mall and the movies with her friends. Katy was fourteen years old when immigration agents told her family they had a week to leave the country. She was in her final year of middle school, and her sister was enrolled in college. Deportation was their worst nightmare.

The story of Katy's family makes it clear that even immigrants who do everything right can be deported. Katy's father, Rafael, fled persecution in Guatemala. He entered the United States legally, as he had a multiple-entry visa. He applied for asylum and, even though he had a solid case, his petition was not granted. Instead of working illegally in the United States, Rafael and Mariluna started several successful businesses, which is permitted under US law. Although they led law-abiding lives in the United States, they were arrested in their home and deported to Guatemala. Katy's family is unusual among Guatemalan immigrants for several reasons: Rafael is of Jewish descent, Rafael and Mariluna come from elite families and have college degrees, and they achieved financial success in the United States. Their reasons for coming to and leaving the United States, however, make them more typical. Hundreds of thousands of

Guatemalans fled the country during the civil war in the 1980s and 1990s. And, in the twenty-first century, hundreds of thousands of Guatemalans have been deported from the United States.

Guatemala had been in turmoil for much of Rafael's life—between 1960 and 1996 there were over 30,000 documented killings and disappearances in Guatemala, carried out as part of a "deliberate government policy of extrajudicial killings."[1] The armed conflict began with the overthrow of socialist President Jacobo Árbenz in 1954, organized by the US Central Intelligence Agency (CIA) and carried out by military officials trained in the United States.[2] Over the course of the war, the United States supplied arms and military support to the Guatemalan military, even as reports of massive terror spread.

The vast majority of people killed were peasants, but there were targeted killings of students and professionals in urban areas as well. Between 1956 and 1996, there were 492 confirmed murders of university professors and students in Guatemala. Right-wing militants saw universities as hotbeds of activism and insurgency. Rafael had attended the University of San Carlos, which was the most heavily targeted university. Four hundred twenty-three of those assassinated were affiliated with San Carlos—ninety of them in the law school alone.[3]

In 1986, Rafael witnessed one of these extrajudicial killings. He went to the house of one of his professors and accompanied the professor and his sons to the school bus stop. As they were walking back to the house, armed gunmen leapt out from a parked vehicle and began to shoot at the professor. Rafael managed to escape the crime scene, but not without seeing the men who shot and killed the professor. The killers found out who Rafael was, which meant his life was in danger.

During the 1980s, clandestine death squads routinely carried out targeted assassinations in Guatemala City. Most of the victims in the capital were people working in defense of human rights in Guatemala and who were organizing against widespread repression.[4] Rafael was not a political activist, but became a target because his friendship with a left-wing professor led to him witnessing an assassination.

Terrified he would be the next victim of a targeted assassination, Rafael fled the country. He had a visa to enter the United States and took the next plane out of Guatemala. His wife, Mariluna, stayed behind to settle their affairs but, concerned she would also be targeted, soon packed her bags and took their children to the United States to join their father. Katy was two and her sister was seven years old.

When this family left Guatemala for the United States in 1986, they joined thousands of Guatemalans who had also left the country. During the twentieth century Guatemalans had many reasons to leave their country: economic turmoil, violence, and political disorder. Guatemalans began to migrate to the United States in large numbers during their long and bloody civil war, in which the United States was heavily involved. During the forty-two-year civil war, a series of military officers ruled the country. Guerilla armies frequently challenged their rule, and this conflict caused intense violence. Rural inhabitants suspected of involvement in guerilla activity were killed *en masse*. In cities, anyone suspected of leftist activity could be a target for assassination. The brutal practices of the Guatemalan military created an exodus of refugees, particularly in the 1980s.[5]

Rafael had spent time in the United States before his forced exile: He completed two years of university in Florida and had previously operated a Mercedes Benz import company located in the United States. When the Mercedes business was doing well, Mariluna and Rafael contemplated staying in the United States. However, they missed their families and their homeland and ultimately decided they would make their lives in Guatemala. Once Rafael's life was threatened, however, they felt they had no choice but to flee to the United States.

Rafael went to Louisiana, where he had lived previously. He applied for political asylum, and his lawyer advised him not to work while his application was pending. Mariluna and Rafael were able to live off of their savings for several months. When their money ran out, they began to get desperate. Rafael contemplated returning to Guatemala. He called his mother to ask her for help. However, Rafael had converted to Christianity from Judaism when he married Mariluna. His embittered mother told him he should ask Jesus Christ to help him, as she was not willing to.

Eventually, the family ended up in a homeless shelter. This was quite a fall from grace. Both Rafael and Mariluna are from elite families in Guatemala City. Mariluna was born into a wealthy family that had lived in the center of Guatemala City back when rich people still lived in the city center. She reminisced about her childhood:

> It was very clean. Before, people were very elegant. When I was small, I went out in the afternoons with a hat and gloves to visit friends and take tea with them. I am related to the vice president of Guatemala. . . . My mother is from an upper-class family and I was raised well. In those days, rich people lived in the historic center. That is why the houses are very large. . . . Doctors and other honorable families used to live here in the center. But, things have changed.

Mariluna went to a private French school, another signal of her class status. Her mother was a pediatrician and her father a psychiatrist. Mariluna and Rafael met at the University of San Carlos, when they were both students. Once Mariluna became pregnant, she left university, although she was able to teach primary school once her daughter was born.

Rafael and Mariluna, who were from elite families in Guatemala, never imagined they would end up in a homeless shelter in the United States. Nevertheless, the homeless shelter turned out to be their saving grace, because that is where Rafael met his future business partner. Rafael befriended the director of the homeless shelter and, once the director realized Rafael had experience in the import/export business, they came up with the idea of starting a new business. Although Rafael did not have a work permit, he could legally operate a business in the United States. They began to import shoes from Mexico and sell them on the local market. Within a few months, they had enough money to move out of the homeless shelter and into an apartment.

Rafael's next business venture was a bilingual school that did asbestos safety training in Spanish and English for laborers. After Rafael received training in environmental quality management and asbestos safety, he realized that few Spanish-speaking people were qualified to work with asbestos due to a lack of training programs in Spanish. He and Mariluna opened and ran a school where they granted asbestos certificates with options for classes in Spanish and English. The school was very successful, as trained asbestos workers were in demand.

Rafael's school was profitable, but he and Mariluna worked constantly to keep it running. He decided to close the school and went to work for his brother, who had done very well for himself in the United States. Rafael's brother, Rodrigo, had a successful car-detailing business and wanted an employee he could trust. Rafael hoped that, as an employee, he would be able to make ends meet without having the time pressures and stress of operating his own business. Things went well at first, but Rodrigo did not pay Rafael as much as he thought he deserved. Eventually, Rafael decided to open his own detailing business.

One major reason the family needed more money was so that their older daughter could attend university. She had been offered a scholarship to a private university. However, the scholarship required a Social Security number, which she did not have. Thus, they had to pay her tuition in full.

Rafael's business did tremendously well. He was able to buy a spacious home, purchase five cars, and pay his oldest daughter's college tuition. However, Rafael and his family, like many other Central Americans, found themselves in legal limbo for many years, awaiting the outcome of their asylum case.

People who face persecution in their country of origin can apply for asylum in the United States. During the 1980s and 1990s, the United States routinely granted asylum to Cubans and Nicaraguans who were fleeing Communist regimes. Due to the politics of the Cold War and the US support for right-wing regimes in Guatemala and El Salvador, however, refugees from these countries were rarely granted asylum. Thus, although Rafael applied for asylum on the basis of his fear of being killed by death squads in Guatemala, his application was denied—a decade after his arrival in the United States, after he had built a life for himself and his family.

Rafael may have qualified for an extension or another appeal, based on changes to US immigration laws in the 1990s, but, he was deported before that occurred. Rafael's deportation occurred in a highly unusual manner. Many people think that you can simply call immigration and report people, but in reality immigration agents rarely follow up on these reports. In Rafael's case, a call to immigration agents worked because the caller—his brother—had important political connections.

Rafael's brother, Rodrigo, resented the fact that Rafael had opened a business in the same industry as him, and vowed revenge. Moreover, Rodrigo was friends with the then-governor of Louisiana and was able to pull some strings to ensure that immigration agents found out about Rafael's denied application for asylum and his failure to depart. Immigration agents came to their house and ordered the family deported.

When immigration agents came to tell them they had to leave the country, Rafael and Mariluna were preparing to move into a new house. Mariluna was having a fabulous time choosing the new furnishings, dishware, and decorations. Tears fell from her eyes as she recalled decorating her new house, making her dream home exactly as she wanted it. Mariluna went to bed tired one evening after hanging the curtains in their new home. They hoped to move in the following week.

At six in the morning the next day, when Mariluna was still sleeping and Katy was getting ready for school, they heard a loud knock on the door of their home and someone shouting, "Does Rafael Gutierrez live here?" She told me, "They came in, as if we were criminals, as if we were murderers."

The immigration agents told the family they had thirty days to leave the country. The family panicked. They decided to move into their new home with the hope that immigration agents would not go so far as to try and figure out where they had moved to.

When Mariluna recounted the story of what happened the second time immigration agents came to her house, her voice broke and tears streamed down her face. The immigration agents were upset that they tried to flee and told them that this time, they would have to take two of them into custody to ensure the family would depart. Rafael surrendered, but they had to choose whether to send Mariluna to immigration detention, leaving their children to fend for themselves, or to send their daughter Alejandra. Alejandra volunteered, and was taken to a county jail.

The immigration agents took Rafael to an immigration detention center. However, there was not a similar center for women close by, so Alejandra had to spend four days in county jail. She was twenty years old. Nine years later, she still has nightmares about the experience. Another inmate tried to rape her while she was detained, but she waited years before telling her parents about the sexual assault as she did not want them to feel guilty.

With Alejandra and Rafael in custody and her life in shambles, Mariluna was in shock. Her friends helped her pack her things, but she could barely think straight. With just four days to pack, Mariluna was not able to get all of their belongings shipped to Guatemala. She was able to get a few things into a container and to fill eight suitcases, only six of which she was able to take with her. They left the house and five cars in Louisiana.

When I spoke with Katy, and later with Rafael and Mariluna, they had been back in Guatemala for nine years, but the wounds were very deep. When they were deported to Guatemala, Katy could not believe how drastically her life had changed. They were fortunate they had a place to go—Katy's grandmother had passed away and left them a house. However, it was a simple dwelling, with adobe walls and a tin roof. The bathroom was outside on the patio. Katy went from living in a spacious, luxurious home in Louisiana to a one-bedroom shack with an outdoor toilet in Guatemala City. It is always difficult to be an adolescent and Katy did not deal well with this fall from riches to rags. She fell into a deep depression, and barely left the house for over a year.

In Louisiana, Katy excelled in school, was popular with her classmates, and never got into trouble. She had dreams of becoming a veterinarian and her sister was already studying to be a doctor. When they were deported to Guatemala, her dreams were shattered.

When they first were deported, both girls became deeply depressed and spent their days sleeping. Mariluna tried to enroll Katy in school. However, with no record of ever having studied in Guatemala, the public schools refused to enroll her. Private schools were beyond their means. Unable to read or write Spanish, she never went back to school. In the United States, Katy had only finished the ninth grade. Katy had big plans for herself in the United States. In Guatemala, once she finally was able to pull herself out of her depression, she secured a job in a call center, where her fluency in English was an asset. Her job paid Q3500 ($400) a month—enough to survive, but not to provide her with the lifestyle she enjoyed in the United States.

Katy resigned from her job after she married her husband, who is a videographer for a local news channel. Although they have been married for several years and have three children together, she still has not told him that her family was deported. The shame is too much to bear.

Katy plans to go back to work, as she hopes to be able to provide her children with a private education. It is not within her means to send her children to the schools her parents attended, but she does not want to send them to public school either. For now, they make ends meet with her husband's salary and her parents' earnings from the small hardware shop they have opened in downtown Guatemala City.

Among deportees, Katy is relatively well-off, as her parents' families have left them inheritances. Her father inherited a large building in the downtown area, where they now live, and where he is able to rent rooms and open a shop of his own. At the same time, Katy is among the most distressed of the deportees I met, as she was deported at a very fragile age and compares herself both to her friends in the United States and her relatively well-off cousins in Guatemala.

Rafael has not been able to secure employment in Guatemala City. He was nearly fifty years old when they were deported, and is too old or over-qualified for every position he sought. Mariluna learned that, since she had worked as a teacher before leaving Guatemala, she could collect a pension. She spent a year getting the papers together before she finally was able to collect the payments. In the meantime, they depended on the charity of their family members, who lent them furniture and gave them bags of rice and beans to eat.

Rafael explained to me that he has the opportunity to move to other countries. His mother was born in Germany, so he could move there. With his Jewish lineage, he could move to Israel. He also could go to Spain. However, he would rather stay in Guatemala than move to a country where he knows no one. In contrast, he would move back to the United States in a heartbeat. He loves America. In the United States, he was able to build a successful business. He received help from many kind and generous people. He would love to return.

Mariluna feels the same way. She told me, "I love the United States as I have never loved Guatemala. . . . My home is there and I still ask God for me to be able to live there, for my grandchildren to be able to grow up over there, because it is better over there. It is a truly blessed country." She went on to tell me a story:

> Once I read a beautiful book about a bird that lived in a swamp. The bird lived with its wings covered with mud, completely dirty. One day, the bird saw a beautiful forest filled with flowers and luscious fruits. Once he saw it, he told himself he wanted to fly there. He struggled to fly because his wings were covered with mud. Eventually, he was able to get himself out of the swamp and into the paradise. In the paradise, he took a bath in the clean water. When he emerged from the water, he saw that he also was beautiful. His wings were colorful and long. He said to himself: "How could I have stayed in that swamp for so long?" That is how I feel. Like the bird, I left the swamp and arrived in the beautiful United States. The problem is that they threw me back in the swamp. Nevertheless, I have to lift my wings and return to paradise. This is what I ask God for each day.

Katy feels just as strongly about returning to the United States. I asked her what she would say to the president if given the opportunity to speak to him. With tears streaming down her face, she told me:

> Please let me go back. It was unfair. It was unjustified. We actually, well my dad, he actually provided money to the United States and we never stole or anything. So please just give me one more chance. I can prove to you that I am going to be a good fit. That I will show my kids what a wonderful country this is. Just please let us go back. I will leave everything here in one second, for me and my family to go back. You know what? It is so hard [voice breaks], because my mom always prays. She is like, "You know what? God told me we are going to back someday." And I see my mom. She is getting older and older, and that's her dream, to go back [voice breaks]. And I wished I could provide her that before she leaves and I have no idea how to.

When I met this family, it had been nearly a decade since they were deported. Rafael and Mariluna told me that they hoped that, since ten years had passed, they could ask for a pardon and be able to return. They all dream of returning to the United States and rebuilding their lives there.

Notes

1. Patrick Ball, Paul Kobrak, and Herbert F. Spirer, *State Violence in Guatemala, 1960–1996: A Quantitative Reflection* (Washington, DC: American Association for the Advancement of Science (AAAS) Science and Human Rights Program; International Center for Human Rights Research, 1999). Online at: https://www.hrdag.org/wp-content/uploads/2013/01/state-violence-guate-1999.pdf
2. Ibid.
3. Paul Kobrak, *En pie de lucha: Organización y represión en la Universidad de San Carlos, Guatemala 1944–1996* (Guatemala: CIIDH y GAM, 1999).
4. Ball and Spirer 1999.
5. María Cristina García, *Seeking Refuge: Central American Migration to Mexico, the United States, and Canada* (Berkeley: University of California Press, 2006).

References

Ball, Patrick, Paul Kobrak, and Herbert F. Spirer, 1999. *State Violence in Guatemala, 1960–1996: A Quantitative Reflection* Washington, DC: American Association for the Advancement of Science (AAAS) Science and Human Rights Program; International Center for Human Rights Research. Online at: https://www.hrdag.org/wp-content/uploads/2013/01/state-violence-guate-1999.pdf

Kobrak, Paul. 1999. *En pie de lucha: Organización y represión en la Universidad de San Carlos, Guatemala 1944–1996* Guatemala: CIIDH y GAM.

García, María Cristina. 2006. *Seeking Refuge: Central American Migration to Mexico, the United States, and Canada* Berkeley: University of California Press.

13

The Power of Law:
How Immigration Policy Shapes Salvadorans' Experience of Family and Motherhood

Maya Pagni Barak

Maya Pagni Barak is an assistant professor of criminology and criminal justice at the University of Michigan–Dearborn. Her most recent work focuses on the relationship between legal consciousness and procedural justice assessments in the context of Central American removal proceedings.

While many are familiar with the plight of immigrant families in the United States devastated by the deportation of a parent, the separation of children from their US-bound parents often receives less attention in US immigration debates. Migration *to* the United States, however, can be just as disruptive to families as can be deportation *from* the United States.[1] Constrained by immigration law, family members are separated, reorganized and, at times, reunited, in dynamic transnational family formations (discussed in detail in Chapters 8 and 9).[2] Such re-formations can have detrimental impacts on the emotional and psychological well-being of family members, especially children and parents.[3] Yet immigration law not only impacts individual family members, it (re)shapes understandings of family altogether.[4] As immigration law produces transnational families,[5] it also produces new *experiences* of family. As immigration law (re)defines individuals' positionality toward the state and shapes immigrants' daily lives (as examined in Chapter 6),[6] it also (re)defines individuals' positionality toward the family. Thus immigration law has the potential to drastically alter family roles, as well as one's ability to fulfill the duties and obligations of such roles; the role of "mother" is no exception.

Between 1980 and 1990, over 300,000 refugees fled civil war in El Salvador. Many were forced to leave behind young children to be raised by relatives. This is the story of three generations of Salvadorans seeking safety and prosperity in the United States. It is also a story about motherhood and migration and, more specifically, how understandings of "motherhood" are challenged and reaffirmed in the context of transnational families constrained by immigration law. More than this, it is a demonstration of the power immigration law has in shaping experiences of family in the United States and abroad.

Jessica's smile is contagious. Sitting across from her on a large green sofa in the dimly lit apartment, I cannot help but be enamored with her bubbly personality. Somehow she manages to make light of her and her son's immigration situations in the United States. She inserts little jokes here and there into our conversation, recalling the occasional positive tangent now and again. Although we have just met, I do not get the sense that she does this out of embarrassment or nerves—she genuinely has a positive attitude despite the long odds she and her family face.

Although I have come to Jessica's apartment to discuss her teenage son's pending removal hearing, I am told that this is not where the story begins. Instead, we must start with Jessica's mother Maribel's decision to come to the United States. Jessica was born in El Salvador during the civil war, which began in 1980. It came on the heels of five decades of military rule, seven military coup d'états, and nearly twenty years of social unrest. The war, fought between the Farabundo Martí National Liberation Front (FMLN) and the Salvadoran government, lasted twelve years and resulted in mass internal displacement and external migration, as well as the deaths of more than 75,000 Salvadorans.

It is estimated that upward of 300,000 Salvadorans fled to the United States during the war.[7] The United States supported the Salvadoran government during the war, making it politically difficult to extend Salvadoran migrants fleeing the war refugee status.[8] Hence most of the 300,000 Salvadorans who came to the United States during the war did so illegally. Some Salvadorans came on their own or with the assistance of *coyotes*, paid smugglers familiar with border-crossing routes. Others came to the United States as part of the Sanctuary Movement, a multi-denominational network of religious organizations that assisted undocumented immigrants with their resettlement in the United States, often providing legal advice, material goods like clothing and food, and temporary shelter.

Among this group of unrecognized refugees was Jessica's mother, Maribel. Given the limited migration options at the time, Maribel left Jessica in El Salvador with her grandparents. She hoped to start a better life for the two in America and eventually bring Jessica to live with her. Like many of the Salvadorans fleeing the war, Maribel entered the United States without permission by crossing the United States–Mexico border; she was not apprehended. Once in the United States, Maribel eventually found work and a husband, with whom she would have three more children, all US citizens.

The passage of the Immigration Reform and Control Act of 1986 (IRCA) provided Maribel and her husband, also an undocumented immigrant, with a path to legalization. IRCA served three primary functions: to increase Border Patrol funding, to create employer sanctions for the hiring of undocumented immigrants, and to grant amnesty to several million undocumented immigrants residing in the United States. Through IRCA, Maribel and her husband acquired green cards and were eligible for citizenship. With her immigration status "fixed," Maribel now had the opportunity to bring Jessica to the United States legally. However, achieving this goal would be neither cheap nor easy.

In the summer of 2003, Jessica, along with a small group of other undocumented immigrants, attempted to cross the United States–Mexico border into Texas to no avail. As Jessica explains, it was like a scene out of a movie. All of a sudden, two large helicopters appeared in the sky, shining bright spotlights down upon them. Before the group fully realized what was going on, they were surrounded by Border Patrol agents.

Yet unlike most of those she was traveling with, Jessica had had another option. She was already in line for a family-sponsored visa—a visa her mother had promised her years earlier, but for which she had waited years to apply—that would have allowed her to enter the United States legally and would have put her on a path toward citizenship. The problem was that her visa was not materializing quickly enough. Because the number of visa applications far surpasses the number of available visas each year, Jessica could expect to wait nearly a decade for her family-based visa.[9] Making matters more complicated, Jessica, a self-described housewife, was in what she refers to as an abusive relationship. Her family situation in El Salvador was quickly deteriorating and she had a toddler to think about. After discussing her options, Jessica and Maribel decided their best option was for Maribel pay a *coyote* to bring Jessica to the United States illegally. Like her mother before her, Jessica would leave her son with his paternal grandparents and make the arduous trek through Guatemala and Mexico to the United States. Like her mother before her, Jessica intended to create a better life for her and her son, whom she hoped would join her once she was established in the United States. However, the trip ended with Jessica detained and in the custody of the US Border Patrol.

Jessica did not mind being detained. Although it was difficult to adjust—the detention facility was always freezing cold, the food was no good, and the employees were certainly not the friendliest—Jessica managed to build several strong friendships with other detained women. She even celebrated a birthday with these women. Jessica watched as, over time, many of the same women accepted Voluntary Departure (VD), which permits eligible noncitizens to leave the country on their own without some of the negative consequences associated with removal (deportation). Yet, many opted for this alternative to removal under extreme pressure from *la migra* ("immigration"). Immigration officers repeatedly told detainees—including Jessica—that they had no chance at remaining in the United States legally and would have to spend months, even years, in detention if they chose to take their cases to court, where they were told that they would eventually lose. Jessica remembers various immigration officers yelling at her, "No matter where you go or where you try to hide, we have your fingerprints and we will find you." The strain of detention coupled with the constant intimidation of *la migra* was simply too much for many to handle. Jessica, on the other hand, was determined to remain in the United States. After several months in detention, she was finally given a hearing date and released to her mother.

In retrospect, Jessica realizes she made a grave mistake once reunited with her mother: she failed to appear for her hearing with the immigration court. The court was over two hours away from her mother's home and she did not have a driver's license or speak any English. When she asked her parents about getting to her hearing, her stepfather told her it was a waste of time and refused to drive her. "Forget about going to court and try to find a job," she recalls him saying. Jessica was already nervous about going to court—she had never been in court before and was afraid that if she went, she would be deported. Between her fear and, as she explained, not knowing any better, she did not argue with the advice.

Only after having spent some time in the United States and making friends who were a bit more familiar with the immigration system did Jessica learn of the consequences of her actions, but it was too late. It is standard practice for immigration court judges to order individuals removed if they fail to appear for a hearing. Without being sure, Jessica assumed this was what had happened in her case—as she explains, she had ignored multiple letters from the court after all. She was still hopeful that her visa, sponsored by her mother, would eventually come through. In the meantime, she decided to get a job and dedicate herself to bringing her son to the United States as quickly as possible—she did not want to repeat her mother's mistakes.

Today, Jessica remains undocumented. Despite her positive attitude, it is clear that, to a certain extent, she resents her mother. Not only did Maribel leave Jessica in El Salvador to be raised by grandparents, but she waited years to file her immigration paperwork properly. Jessica has never been able to comprehend her mother's capacity to leave her in "limbo" in El Salvador for so many years. Nor can Jessica understand her mother's seemingly nonchalant mismanagement of Jessica's visa application. She has often found herself wondering what kind of *mother* could do this to her child? Although Jessica's mother did eventually pay for a *coyote* to bring Jessica to the United States, Jessica felt—and still feels—a deep divide between herself and her mother, as well as her US-citizen half-siblings. She cannot not help but think that her mother abandoned her in favor of a new life and family in the United States. After struggling to build a relationship with her mother, stepfather, and siblings in Texas—all of whom, Jessica is quick to point out, enjoy the privileges of being "legal," privileges she would have been entitled to as well were it not for her mother's mishandling of her immigration case—an uncle suggested Jessica try her luck in Virginia.

Jessica took her uncle up on the offer. She left Texas for Virginia and eventually found a new partner—an undocumented Guatemalan man—with whom she has a four-year old son, a US citizen. One day, when he is an adult, she points out, he will be able to be sponsor visas for her and his father to in live in the United States legally. Jessica has managed to find restaurant work on and off over the years. She notes that her precarious employment situation is the direct result of her immigration status. She laments missing the opportunity at legalization that she would have been afforded had she shown up for her removal hearing. As Jessica sees things, if she had papers, she could have found stable employment, as well as been able to bring her older son, Eddie, to the United States legally.

Reuniting with Eddie in the United States was always part of Jessica's plan, just as it had always been her mother's plan to bring Jessica to America. Unfortunately, the realities of daily life, coupled with the workings of immigration policy, made this more difficult than Jessica expected. She began asking around and wound up in several consultations with immigration attorneys regarding her case and the possibility of bringing Eddie to live with her. It was during one such consultation that Jessica learned that, due to her illegal entry into the United States, the visa process her mother had begun for her was essentially ruined. At some point, her application would reach the top of the pile and immigration (USCIS) would request copies of her fingerprints. A fingerprint search would quickly reveal her past encounter with the Border Patrol and her missed immigration hearing, as well as the fact that she had given the Border Patrol a fake name when she was caught. Numerous lawyers told Jessica that all she could do was hope for comprehensive immigration reform. In the meantime, both she and her son, Eddie, would simply have to wait.

By the fall of 2014, Eddie, who had just turned fourteen, could wait no longer. Harassment by MS-13, a notorious Salvadoran street gang, had become commonplace in El Salvador. MS-13, along with rival Barrio 18, both trace their origins to 1980s Los Angeles, where groups of young Salvadoran civil war refugees began forming cliques to protect themselves from L.A.'s existing black and Hispanic gangs. Over time, these Salvadoran cliques adopted the practices of US gangs. Many members of MS-13 and Barrio 18 were deported back to El Salvador after being arrested on gang-related charges. Once in El Salvador, the two street gangs quickly proliferated, uniting with former FMLN and government combatants—many of whom had been child soldiers—who not only had military training, but also weapons left over from the war.[10] Today, entire neighborhoods, as well as many prisons and jails, across El Salvador are gang-controlled.[11] Citizens are often forced to pay "rent" or join the gangs. Failing to cooperate can lead to death. Moreover, many police and military either tolerate or collaborate with the gangs.

Hence when Eddie—and his half-brother—began facing MS-13 harassment, it was seen as a fact of life. Eddie continued going to school but stopped spending unnecessary time outside his grandmother's home. Then, after refusing to join the gang, Eddie's half-brother was killed. Jessica panicked. She realized that her son's life was in imminent danger. She felt she had no choice but to send money for him to be smuggled to the United States. Eddie made the dangerous journey from El Salvador to the United States in the fall of 2014, joining tens of thousands of unaccompanied minors who have sought refuge in the United States from gang violence in Central America over the last three years.[12] This recent surge in Central American migration is one of the largest since the 1980s, when Eddie's grandmother, Maribel, fled the violence of civil war.

Like the Salvadoran civil war refugees of the 1980s, the refugees of El Salvador's current gang violence have yet to be recognized as a group eligible for asylum by the US government. The United States has also failed to recognize its role in facilitating El Salvador's current gang problem through the deportation of American gang culture to El Salvador, just as it neglected to acknowledge the part it played in El Salvador's bloody civil war by intervening in Salvadoran politics. While many who have come to the United States as part of this recent wave of migrants hope to be granted asylum—including Eddie—uncontrollable gang violence, the driving force behind their migration, often fails to meet the basic requirements of asylum.[13]

Applying for and receiving asylum, as discussed by Lakhani (this volume), is often a complicated and difficult process. Specifically, in order to qualify for asylum, individuals must establish that they experienced persecution in the past, or that they have a well-founded fear of future persecution. Importantly, this persecution must occur on account of one's race, religion, nationality, political opinion, or membership in a particular social group. This "nexus" requirement is often the greatest hurdle for gang-based asylum claims, leaving many Central American immigrants with little recourse for relief.

Jessica stresses that she does not want to be guilty of the same mistakes her mother made. When her son was released into her custody after being briefly detained by immigration, Jessica made sure to carefully collect and store any documents they gave him, as well as any that arrived by mail. Today, instead of being afraid of immigration court, Jessica sees it as a valuable entity with the power to help immigrants, not just harm them. She also sees her role as Eddie's mother as being crucial to his success in immigration court and the United States. She put Eddie's first hearing date in her calendar, coordinated rides to and from the court as she still does not have a driver's license, and made sure that he attended—she was by his side.

Following Eddie's first hearing, Jessica heeded the judge's advice and began searching for an attorney to take his case. A woman of little means, she knew that most immigration attorneys would be cost-prohibitive. Recalling the hundreds of dollars she spent on mere consultations in the past, Jessica asked around and was finally referred to a local nonprofit legal organization specializing in youth cases. She was successful in obtaining a lawyer for Eddie, free of cost. The lawyer believes that Eddie has a viable case and a real shot at relief.

Jessica and Eddie are currently awaiting his next court date, which has been postponed three times in the past year. Eddie's experience with the court is not unique—as of this writing, there are a total of 463,627 pending immigration court cases across the country, and the court that is assigned Eddie's case is currently scheduling cases as far out as 2020.[14] It is unclear when Eddie will finally have his merit hearing, let alone when he might be able to legalize his status in the United States. In the meantime, his hearing—and the family's future—is pending.

As exemplified by Jessica's story, immigration policy has the ability to tear families apart and bring them back together again, producing transnational families along the way. The resulting transnational families, comprised of individuals like Jessica and her mother Maribel, are forced to navigate complex legal systems—replete with ever-changing immigration requirements and ever-expanding immigration backlogs—as well as complicated cultural, sociolegal, and political boundaries. Yet such policies not only impact individuals' ability to keep their families united, they redefine the meaning of family itself and drastically alter relationships between individuals.

In some cases, these policies result in near-insurmountable wedges between family members, including mothers—like Maribel—and their children—like Jessica. It is well-established that immigration law, through assigning various rights, responsibilities, and limitations to various categories of immigrants, shapes immigrants' daily lives, at times constraining their ability to participate in society.[15] Similarly, through the production of transnational families, immigration law (re)defines family roles and, at times, constrains individuals' ability to fulfill such roles. It is apparent that, although managed quite differently, immigration law presented significant challenges to both Maribel's and Jessica's abilities to perform the role of "mother." Jessica's experience of motherhood—both from the perspective of a child separated from her migrant mother and the perspective of a migrant mother separated from her child—has thus been unavoidably shaped by US immigration policy in the greater sociopolitical context of civil war, gang violence, and United States–El Salvador relations. Through Jessica's life story, one appreciates how immigration law produces "legal" and "illegal" immigrants and redefines the meaning—and experience—of denizenship. Of equal importance, one also understands how immigration law produces "good" and "bad" mothers and, ultimately, has the power to redefine the meaning and experience of motherhood altogether.

Notes

1. Leisy J. Abrego, *Sacrificing Families: Navigating Laws, Labor, and Love Across Borders* (Stanford, CA: Stanford University Press, 2014); Joanna Dreby, *Dividing Borders: Mexican Migrants and Their Children* (Berkeley: University of California Press, 2010).
2. Judith K. Bernhard, Patricia Landolt, and Luin Goldring, "Transnationalizing Families: Canadian Immigration Policy and the Spatial Fragmentation of Care-giving Among Latin American Newcomers," *International Migration* 47, no. 2 (2009): 3–31.
3. Ibid.; Carola Suárez-Orozco, Irina L.G. Todorova, and Josephine Louie, "Making Up for Lost Time: The Experience of Separation and Reunification among Immigrant Families," *Family Process* 41, no. 4 (2002): 625–43; Valentina Mazzucato, "Transnational Families and the Well-Being of Children and Caregivers who Stay in Origin Countries." *Social Science & Medicine* 132 (2015): 208–14.
4. Michelle J. Moran-Taylor, "When Mothers and Fathers Migrate North: Caretakers, Children, and Child-Rearing in Guatemala," *Latin American Perspectives* 35, no. 4 (2008): 79–95.
5. Valentina Mazzucato and Djamila Schans. "Transnational Families and the Well-Being of Children: Conceptual and Methodological Challenges," *Journal of Marriage and Family* 73, no. 4 (2011): 704–12.
6. Leisy Abrego, "Legal Consciousness of Undocumented Latinos: Fear and Stigma as Barriers to Claims-Making for First- and 1.5-Generation Immigrants," *Law & Society Review* 45, no. 2 (2011): 337–70; Susan B. Coutin, *Nations of Emigrants: Shifting Boundaries of Citizenship in El Salvador and the United States* (Ithaca, NY: Cornell University Press, 2007); Roberto G. Gonzales, "Learning to Be Illegal: Undocumented Youth and Shifting Legal Contexts in the Transition to Adulthood," *American Sociological Review* 74, no. 4 (2011): 602–19; Cecilia Menjívar, "Liminal Legality: Salvadoran and Guatemalan Immigrants' Lives in the United States," *American Journal of Sociology* 111, no. 4 (2006): 999–1037; Cecilia Menjívar, "The Power of the Law: Central Americans' Legality and Everyday Life in Phoenix, Arizona," *Latino Studies* 9, no. 4 (2011): 377–95.
7. Steve Hobden, "El Salvador: Civil War, Civil Society and the State," *Civil Wars* 3, no. 2 (2000): 106–20.
8. Susan B. Coutin, *Legalizing Moves: Salvadoran Immigrants' Struggle for U.S. Residency* (Ann Arbor: University of Michigan Press, 2000).
9. Christina A. Pryor, "'Aging Out' of Immigration: Analyzing Family Preference Visa Petitions Under the Child Status Protection Act," *Fordham Law Review* 80, no. 5 (2012): 2199–239.
10. Jocelyn Courtney, "The Civil War That Was Fought by Children: Understanding the Role of Child Combatants in El Salvador's Civil War, 1980–1992," *Journal of Military History* 74, no. 2 (2010): 523–56.
11. Dennis Stinchcomb, and Eric Hershberg, "Unaccompanied Migrant Children from Central America: Context, Causes, and Responses" (Center for Latin American and Latino Studies, American University, 2014).
12. Ibid.
13. Kevin R. Johnson, Raquel E. Aldana, Bill Ong Hing, Leticia Saucedo, and Enid Trucios-Haynes, *Understanding Immigration Law* (LexisNexis, 2009).
14. http://trac.syr.edu/phptools/immigration/court_backlog/
15. Abrego, "Legal Consciousness of Undocumented Latinos"; Coutin, *Nations of Emigrants*; Menjívar, "Liminal Legality"; Menjívar, "The Power of the Law."

PART 5

GENDERED EXCLUSIONS:
How Are Deportation Experiences Gendered?

In a 2013 article, Tanya Golash-Boza and Pierrette Hondagneu-Sotelo described deportation as a "gendered racial removal program," due to the fact that 90 percent of deportees are men, 97 percent are Latin American, and the discourses surrounding these deportations are often raced and gendered through the demonization of Latino "criminal aliens" and Muslim terrorists, both of which are imagined as male. Any study of deportation from the United States must pay attention to the fact that nearly all deportees are Latin American. Additionally, it is critical to explore how deportation is gendered, both because it primarily targets men who leave women and children behind—and because when deportation happens to women the consequences can be particularly pernicious, for reasons that will become clear in the chapters in this section.

Yolanda Martin's essay presents the stories of three Dominican women whose lives have been torn asunder by deportation. Two of the women—Carmen and Nicole—were legal permanent residents deported after pleading guilty to weapons charges. Carmen pled guilty to protect her son and Nicole pled guilty with the hope that she would be released from prison. Neither woman knew this guilty plea would lead to deportation nor how drastically their lives would change as a consequence. Carmen is a graduate of Harvard University and was working as an accountant when her home was raided by police officers who believed her son was involved in the drug trade. When the officers found an unregistered weapon in the home, she claimed ownership of it to protect her son from prison. Her desire to protect her son, however, led to her spending time in prison and subsequently being deported. Even though she had lived legally in the United States for forty years, a weapons charge such as this is grounds for deportation. Back in her country of birth, her Harvard degree did not translate into stable employment due to her relative lack of Spanish skills, her complete lack of connections, her age, and her gender. This sudden change in her life circumstances after deportation—from a middle-class Bostonian to a homeless person in Santo Domingo—led her into a downward spiral. The other women profiled in Martin's essay encountered and sometimes overcame other obstacles, but gender-based violence is a constant in their lives.

Heidy Sarabia's essay continues with the theme of domestic violence and abuse that often haunts the lives of female deportees, in addition to the extreme pain of family separation for mothers who are their children's primary caretakers. The differences between the stories in Sarabia's and Martin's essay also reflect distinct regional realities. In New York, where Carmen lived, it is more common for legal permanent residents to be funneled into the deportation system through the criminal justice system. In San Diego, where Paloma lives, it is more common for migrants to be deported after an encounter with Customs and Border Patrol (CBP) (Golash-Boza 2015). Migrants' lives are policed in both places, but in distinct ways. In New York, suspicions of criminal activity can lead to deportation, whereas in San Diego, the omnipresence of the Border Patrol facilitates deportations. As you read these essays, think about the ways that gender played a role in how these women were funneled into the deportation pipeline.

Christine Wheatley's contribution brings in gender from a distinct perspective—that of a *travesti*[1] who was deported from Detroit to Mexico after getting into a car accident. His deportation experience was shaped by gender from the moment he was arrested, through his experiences in gender-segregated prisons and immigration detention centers and back to how he was treated once he was in Mexico again.

Reading these essays, it becomes clear that it is critical to pay attention to gender as we think about deportation and immigration law enforcement. Women and men face distinct societal pressures to nurture and to provide. Male and female deportees face different obstacles post-deportation. And, both women and gender-nonconforming people have to navigate gendered discrimination and violence both behind bars and once released.

Yolanda Martin's essay also highlight the nexus between criminal law enforcement and immigration law enforcement through a discussion of the effects of IIRAIRA on legal permanent residents, commonly referred to as "green card holders." Under IIRAIRA, legal permanent residents face mandatory deportation if they are convicted of "aggravated felonies." These include crimes where the person is sentenced to at least one year in prison, regardless of whether the sentence is served or suspended. These crimes can also be relatively minor, such as petty theft, or two counts of minor drug possession. These cases do not require judicial review, meaning people do not have the right to ask a judge to consider the specifics of the case or the ties that person has to the United States. As we will see in the cases discussed by Martin, even fairly minor charges can lead to deportation of people who have lived their entire lives in the United States legally.

In Heidy Sarabia's essay, we can see how the complex web of laws that creates illegality for an immigrant named Paloma interacts with another complex web of gender oppression that kept her in an abusive relationship and rendered her feeling powerless in confronting the state. Patriarchy is a "system of social structures and practices in which men dominate, oppress, and exploit women" (Walby 1989, 214). Paloma's husband's abuse toward her is not solely a result of his individual pathologies, but also is part of a broader patriarchal system of oppression in which men have more power than women and use violence to exert this power. Like many women, Paloma's life choices have been severely constrained by the ever-present threat of male violence. It is somewhat straightforward to conceptualize how patriarchy has affected Paloma's life, yet it is also important to consider the role of patriarchy in Nico's life—the deported *travesti* discussed in Christine Wheatley's contribution. Patriarchy prescribes certain norms of femininity and masculinity that men and women are compelled to conform to. Wheatley's essay allows us to consider how patriarchy also can affect men, particularly when they are gender-nonconforming. As you read these contributions, think about how patriarchy has played a role in these migrants' lives.

Notes

1. *Travesti* refers to "people who are designated male at birth but live according to the female gender. They perform a series of bodily changes but generally reject sex-reassignment surgery" (Silva and Ornat 2016, 225). In this case, Quetzal identifies as a man yet wears women's clothes and makeup. Unlike men who participate in drag shows in the United States, being a *travesti* is a way of life, not a show or an occasional practice. There is no direct translation of *travesti* into English so we have kept the original Spanish word, which is used in several Latin American countries.

References

Golash-Boza, Tanya. 2015. *Deported: Immigrant Policing, Disposable Labor, and Global Capitalism*. New York: New York University Press.

Silva, Joseli Maria, and Marcio Jose Ornat. 2016. "Transfeminism and Decolonial Thought: The Contribution of Brazilian Travestis." *TSQ: Transgender Studies Quarterly* 3 (1–2): 220–27.

Walby, Sylvia. "Theorising Patriarchy." *Sociology* 23, no. 2 (1989): 213–34.

14

Gendered Exclusion:

Three Generations of Women Deported to the Dominican Republic

Yolanda C. Martin

The author, Yolanda C. Martin, holds a PhD in Sociology and is an assistant professor of criminology at Borough of Manhattan Community College, of the City University of New York. Her research interests are critical criminology, forced migration and deportations, ethnographic methodology, and linkages between structural inequality and criminalization of Latino communities.

Because immigrant removal rates are highly disproportionate in terms of gender, with nine out of ten deportees being male, existing scholarly work is heavily focused on repatriated men (e.g., Golash-Boza and Hondagneu-Sotelo, 2013; Brotherton and Barrios, 2011, among others). But women too are deported and endure deportation stigma. In this essay I introduce three generations of women from the same family: Carmen (62), Nicole (47), and Milagros[1] (18)—all turned into forced migrants and sufferers of deportation trauma. Their narratives, drawn from an extensive study I conducted in Santo Domingo, Dominican Republic, from 2008 to 2016, illustrate how gender contributes to negative life outcomes. They reveal the social marginalization and a range of negative life events Dominican female deportees face upon repatriation to their homeland, including sexual abuse, legal separation from their children, chronic depression, substance abuse, and HIV infection, outcomes to some extent forced on them by gender expectations in Dominican society.

According to aggregate statistics released annually by US Immigration and Customs Enforcement, between 1997 and 2015, a total of 5,066,413 immigrants were expelled from the United States (ICE 2015). Notably, out of the almost 369,000 deportees expelled in 2013, more than half (56 percent) did not have a criminal record at all but were expelled mostly due to visa status offenses. Interestingly, despite his support for the DREAM Act, President Barack Obama's administration has forcibly removed more noncitizens than any previous president. The Dominican Republic, the Caribbean country with the highest repatriation numbers, received an average of 2,450 deportees annually between 2012 and 2015 (ICE 2015).

The Illegal Immigration Reform and Immigrant Responsibility Act of 1996 (IIRIRA) eliminated judicial review of many deportation orders, turned visa violations into crimes, and enforced mandatory detention and deportation for immigrants who committed various nonviolent drug felonies. IIRIRA was enhanced during the War on Terror after September 2001, as immigration law became intertwined with law enforcement, leading to what Stumpf (2006) has coined *crimmigration*. The concept of crimmigration refers to the intersection of immigration law and criminal law, resulting in the lives of noncitizens rigidly regulated through a two-fold phenomenon: the increase in the number of law-breaking activities that result in immigration-related infractions, as well as in the number of immigration-related violations that may lead to criminal charges. President George W. Bush institutionalized this new approach in 2003 when he merged the Immigration and Naturalization Service into the Department of Homeland Security (DHS), a single agency responsible for overseeing both immigration control and counterterrorism efforts. The message in this restructuring was obvious: Immigration constitutes a potential threat to the United States, even though all available data indicate that immigrants are less likely than US citizens to commit crimes (Rumbaut and Ewing, 2007). In the twenty years since the passage of IIRIRA, deportation levels have become so massive and alarming that it is easy to focus on the numbers alone, detaching ourselves from the individual victims of mass deportation.

Carmen is a Harvard University graduate who worked as a certified public accountant for the Boston Housing Authority for more than a decade. She is also a deportee, forcibly returned to the Dominican Republic in 2001 after she claimed ownership of an unregistered weapon found in her home. Though a noncitizen, Carmen had held a green card and lived in the United States since she was seven years old. When the police raided her house in search of her son's stash of drugs, Carmen had no idea that she was at risk for deportation—she simply sought to protect her only son from arrest by any means necessary.

Carmen described the trauma of her deportation to the Dominican Republic. From the moment of her arrival, she felt she was branded as a criminal by the media, Dominican law enforcement, and her own family. She struggled to adjust to her new life, completely disoriented and unable to pay for basic necessities:

> I was depressed and I felt vulnerable. When I came here, nobody oriented me. Nobody said, "Listen, it's gonna be hard to get a job, because you don't have any referrals." And as soon as you come, even though you didn't do anything in this country, you have to pass by the drug enforcement agency, and they take your fingerprints . . . you're gonna be here as a criminal, even if you've never done anything here. You are deported once, and you've paid your

> dues. But as soon as you get off the plane, you are under arrest again. A bus was waiting here, with the newspapers, with cuffs . . . that was a shock. I wanted to die. My family was there, and nobody uses drugs or anything, and they had to see me like that. They were there, and the press was there. . . . It was total culture shock. When people come to visit, they stay in good places. When you come here to stay, without any money and without speaking any Spanish, with the heat and the sweat, the blackouts, lack of water so many hours every day, you can't go to the bathroom without any water. It doesn't feel safe at night without light. And it's all of it, all of it at the same time. To get a job, I had to speak correct Spanish, and I couldn't. I felt lost. I felt completely lost, out of my territory. Like this was a foreign country to me. I would go to bed hungry because everyone around me was so poor. I had no way out.

Carmen tried to find a job in the formal economy, which one might expect would be fairly easy given her prestigious education. In Santo Domingo, however, one needs social capital —networks of relationships built around trust and reciprocity, which increase the chances for social and professional advancement—and Carmen was considered "too old" for most service industry positions. Rejection after rejection sent her into a downward spiral of hopelessness and helplessness:

> I could not get a job because of my age: "job available to thirty-eight years or under" . . . I was forty-seven by then. No call center jobs, no connections, no job, regardless of how hard I tried. I didn't have anywhere to go. I slept at a park. I was all alone there. It hurt a lot. After a long time, I was able to get a temporary job at a call center, but it only led me to all the drugs that you could imagine. I did crack. I discovered crack while working at the call center. You can find them all there. I lost my family. I lost everything.

Emotionally shattered and lacking any social support networks, Carmen began self-medicating with crack and shortly thereafter moved on to intravenous heroin. She began spending time with some homeless crack and heroin users, with whom she at least shared a sense of alienation: "I ended up hanging out with some heroin users on the streets. I was ashamed of my turn of luck. I didn't want anybody to know who I was or what I was doing. I didn't want anybody to judge me. I had sold everything that I owned. I felt very lonely." Loneliness and a sense of helplessness threw Carmen into a loop of substance abuse and social withdrawal.

The stigma and shame resulting from her loss of status prevented her from reaching out to friends or family who might have helped her. She entered a series of sexually abusive relationships with men and, eventually, turned to sex work to survive: "My life went downhill. I sold my body, since I could not sell my mind. I lost my family. I didn't want them to know anything about me. I ended up getting AIDS. That's not me, Yolanda, that's not me. But that is what I was doing." Eventually she ended up homeless and HIV-positive. Last time I was in Santo Domingo, I could not locate her. She was missing on the streets—an extreme example of the human devastation caused by our draconian system of mandatory deportation of immigrants convicted on felony charges.

Carmen frequently discussed how gender discrimination and societal double standards make it especially hard for female returnees to reinsert into Dominican society:

> Women are treated like garbage. We are seen as dirty, as nasty. . . . the assumption is that since we don't have anything when we get back, we will sell our bodies. And many women do, because here they discriminate against women, especially if you're a bit older. You will not get hired anywhere. At times to go out with men is the only recourse. If you use drugs, that's even worse, because they think you'll sell your body to get your fix.
>
> For men, they'll say things like, "He's a vicious drug addict," or "He's a delinquent." But they don't say anything about him as a failed father. For women, they'll talk like she deserved the worst for not being a good mother. They call us *cuero*, prostitute. They stigmatize us. Society is much harder on the woman.

Nicole, Carmen's niece, was in her early forties when we first met in 2008. She seemed to represent the opposite end of the wide range of deportation case studies one can find in the Dominican Republic. She grew up in the 1970s and 1980s in the New York neighborhood of Corona (Queens). While her single mother worked two jobs, at a factory during the day and cleaning offices at night, Nicole hung out with the "bad boys." She was arrested for the first time at age thirteen, when two boys with whom she regularly spent time stole a car and went joyriding around the neighborhood. The case never went to court and, not wanting to upset her mother, she kept the arrest a secret. A legal permanent resident at the time, her record made Nicole afraid to apply for naturalization as a US citizen, avoiding the risk of having her family learn about her past record.

A gun charge in 1999 led to a second arrest and eventually to deportation when she was twenty-seven and married, with two children and a third on the way. The police raided a friend's home while she was present, along with some other acquaintances. A Colombian man dropped on the floor a gun he had hidden inside a paper bag. The police found a couple of grams of heroin in Nicole's jacket. The prosecutor threatened to give her a two-year sentence on the drug felony unless she pleaded guilty to the gun charge, a class C felony that carried mandatory deportation. Nicole explained that a public defender pressured her into pleading guilty to gun possession, even though she was innocent, without ever explaining that she would be deported:

> They got my little bag, which was nothing, and they said, "Well . . . you had that gun." "No, that gun is not mine." They said, "Well, you're still going to jail, and you have this dope charge . . . and we're gonna make a deal with you. You cop to the gun, and we're gonna give you a year. I had already been in jail for seven months and a half. They said, "You'd have fifteen more days and you're going home." I said, "But that's not my gun." They kept saying, "You cop to the gun; we give you a year, which is really eight months. You have only fifteen more days. Fifteen days and you're going home." I insisted, "But that is not my gun," and they got upset: "If you don't take that, we're gonna give you two years for the drug charge. Take it. You're going home in fifteen days." But they didn't tell me, "as soon as you get that, you get an immigration hold." It's a class C felony, which is a violent felony. I was just thinking "fifteen more days and I'm going home." And I never saw home again. It's your own lawyers that do this. It's a public defender. They don't want anybody to go to court, to reduce cost, so they just want everyone to cop out, cop out, cop out.

Nicole had a troubled upbringing. She suffered traumatic sexual abuse as a small child, which diminished her sense of self-worth and led to a chain of abusive relationships with men beginning in adolescence. These scars prompted her to take a series of wrong turns growing up, including refusing to become a US citizen, for fear of her mother finding out about her criminal record:

> My adolescence was a normal adolescence, but the one thing that happened was that when I was eight I was raped. He was a very good friend of the family. Everybody loved him. I never told anybody that he was raping me for over five years. It lasted until the day he died, when I was thirteen.

Dominican families have strong gender expectations about what constitutes female respectability. As a consequence of being repeatedly raped by a member of her immediate family circle, Nicole believed she did not deserve a positive relationship with a man. She became increasingly alienated and turned to compulsive drug use:

> I felt I was dying inside. I thought that I was damaged. And I was scared. You know, in our culture . . . my grandma—we used to live with my grandma—she would tell me, "If you're not a virgin, your husband will send you back home, and it will be a disgrace." I never thought that I could go out with anybody that was decent, honorable. I always had like, you know, the bad-boy type. Because that was what I thought I deserved. . . . I felt dirty . . . and I started drinking at fourteen . . . marijuana at fourteen, fifteen, LSD and acid at sixteen . . . and it kept escalating—the last I did was heroin at twenty-two.

Immigrant families that lose a father to deportation are often reduced to financial and emotional distress. But the deportation of a mother is often even more damaging to a family, with immigration laws playing a powerful role in shaping families (as documented by Barak and Gomberg-Muñoz in this same volume). Women, especially in traditional Latino communities, are expected to prioritize caring for their children above all other responsibilities. The stigma of being a mother who was arrested on a felony charge, then separated from her children, threw Nicole into a state of despair that stayed with her for years. In addition to a teenage son, Matias, who was already in juvenile detention, and a small daughter, Cristina, at home, Nicole was four months pregnant with her youngest daughter, Milagros, when she was arrested after missing a court date on the gun charge:

> I didn't know that they changed my court date through the mail—because nobody checks mail anymore. So I went on my normal date, and they were waiting to arrest me, without even giving me the benefit of the doubt. "Oh, you missed court; that's it for you." After that, I never saw the streets anymore. When immigration came [to prison] my baby was five months old. They put the baby in foster care, just like my ten-year-old. My husband used to go to court all the time [to request custody], but they would give him the boot [because he was a drug user].

Nicole seemed destined for a similar path as Carmen when she arrived in the Dominican Republic. Her two older children were living in New York with their maternal grandmother and on and off with their father, while the younger child, Milagros, continued to live with a foster care family for seven years. Nicole began working in a call center six months after her arrival to Santo Domingo, where she soon got hooked on drugs again. After a few years of heavy heroin use, however, she entered a drug rehabilitation center. Though she struggled with unemployment after finishing the program, she stayed clean, eventually landing a stable and (by Dominican standards) decent-paying job. Her husband, too, was eventually deported and moved to Santiago, the second largest city in the country, while Nicole stayed in Santo Domingo. She is separated from him because he continues to use drugs today.

Nicole's older daughter, Cristina, experienced a series of economic and emotional hardships in foster care, culminating with a teenage pregnancy:

> After staying with her father for a while, my fifteen-year-old daughter, who had just had a baby, was placed with a foster family too. And she called me and said, "Mommy, this place only takes the money for the kids, and she [foster parent] doesn't do nothing. She has me here like a maid. I'm the one that she orders "Come here, go there; clean this, clean that. . . . I don't have any help. She doesn't give me any money, and I look and my baby's milk is not there." Over the phone, I was able to get her a lawyer to request emancipation. . . . That's when she moved in with her boyfriend, at fifteen.

Cristina still relies on Nicole, regularly calling to ask for money. Nicole cried as she described the pain she feels when Cristina requests her help, given her own limited resources living on a humble Dominican salary:

> I'm always helping her out. She calls me, "Mom, I'm feeling down, because of my life." Sometimes she asks for money, "Mom, I need $200 to get this or that." . . . I save whatever I have, $20 or $30, and send it to her, because she doesn't have any money. But my daughter doesn't understand that I don't have anything either. I make 8,000 pesos every two weeks [US$200]. One time [after I sent her money] I couldn't pay rent for two weeks.

Meanwhile, Nicole struggled to reunite with her youngest daughter, Milagros. Eventually, Nicole's mother located a family attorney in New York who agreed to help them. Milagros was seven years old by the time Nicole regained custody. Because Nicole could not return to the United States, Milagros was de-facto deported, even though she had a US passport by birthright. She arrived in the Dominican Republic having only had telephone contact with her mother since their separation when she was a few months old:

> My daughter was sent with a little badge with her name, and when she came she didn't speak any Spanish. She didn't really know me at all. She didn't hug me or kiss me, nothing like that. She was not affectionate. She couldn't be. When she was little on the phone she would tell me, "You're a liar. You're not my mommy." She would only tell me things like "I'm hungry" or "I want to watch TV." But we didn't have a real relationship. We didn't talk about

> what she had gone through, her life over there. Now she can't even remember. I was in a permanent state of depression, even though I was happy to have her with me.

Seeking to help her mother financially at age 16, Milagros tried to find employment in a call center. Even though she is fluent in English, she never got called for an interview. Carmen claims that Dominican employers never hire US citizens, in order to avoid the enhanced labor and legal protections extended to those holding a US passport. Only Dominican (or Haitian) applicants were perceived as exploitable workforce: "My daughter, when she went looking for jobs at the call centers, she wouldn't even get hired. They said you have to be Dominican, and you got to speak English. That's because they only want to hire deportees to exploit them without getting in trouble."

Now eighteen years old, Milagros is still searching for a sense of belonging. After graduating from high school, she moved to Florida, intending to enroll at Florida State University. She reunited with her older sister, Cristina, who is twenty-seven and resides in Northern Florida. Having had no experience navigating the US university system, Milagros failed to realize that she would have to document one year of residency in the state before she could qualify for financial aid. Lacking the kind of cultural capital that would have helped her tap into any scholarships available, she had to postpone her college dreams. Still hoping eventually to enroll in college, she stayed with Cristina, her husband, and their three young children, with all three adults working at minimum-wage jobs:

> My daughter [Milagros] found a job in a hotel, but it's working at night. And in Florida you need a car, so she's depending on my daughter's husband to pick her up, and to take her, but he's like, you know, bipolar. So today he's feeling OK, but there have been a few times when he wasn't feeling OK and he wouldn't take her. . . . She is so good and hardworking. I can only speak for her [Milagros]—the other one, I didn't raise her.

Nicole would rarely speak about her eldest son, Matias. On one occasion while we were taking a walk, however, Nicole opened up about how she had suffered over not being able to see him again. Though he refused to talk to her for many years, she tried to assist him from a distance, whenever he would let her:

> Did you know that it's been nineteen years that I haven't seen my son? Sometimes I see him on Facebook or whatever, and I'm like, "I just wish I could hug you and kiss you." And I wasn't a very good role model or good example for him. His life wasn't so great. He went

> to jail when he was like fifteen, and when he came out, his mother was deported, and his father was not around. Matias didn't have no place to go. He had that weight on his heart: "How come I don't have a dad or a mom? I don't have a house. Where am I going? . . . What am I doing?" There were many years when he never called. He knew my number, but he never called. When I found out that he got out of jail, I said, "I'll send you some money." I only had a little bit, but I took it all out and sent it to him. I sent him all I got, like $100. Then, two days later, he asked if I could send him some more, that he wanted to go stay with a friend. I sent it to him. I didn't hear from him for a lot of years. Now he's working, he lives in Virginia and is married. He's thirty-seven years old. We talk on Facebook. Better late than never. I still hope that one day, he'll be man enough to know what he's got to do, to get a passport and come see me before I die. Last time I saw him he was in jail, in a juvenile facility.

Deportation is the ultimate form of forced mobility in international migration. The immigrant *push* is administered by agents of the state who use detention, shackles, and physical punishment to facilitate the physical removal of immigrants. When a noncitizen parent is deported, children often have no choice but to leave their country of birth in order to follow them. Despite their legal status, they too are pushed out. Children like Milagros are collateral damage in the phenomenon of mass deportation, and scholars of deportation ought to include those children as an extension of the deportee category.

Far from providing definite answers, these case studies stand as seemingly paradoxical life histories that raise further sociological questions. On one side, Carmen held a respectable position in society, as a tax-paying and law-abiding member of her community. Yet her sudden, unexpected loss of that master status, and the subsequently internalized criminal label, drove her into law-breaking activities. On the other side, Nicole struggled with substance abuse in the United States but, eventually, she was able to adapt and secure a stable job in the Dominican Republic. Although outcomes seem to contradict social expectations in the case of both women, I would argue that Nicole was able to develop a higher level of resilience through previous episodes of marginalization and emotional trauma she experienced while living in the United States. In addition, age discrimination imposed against Dominican women reduced the already scarce opportunities available to Carmen upon arrival. Finally, we should ponder the cycle of underclass conditions into which Milagros seems to have fallen after being uprooted twice, seeing her family bonds and social networks dismantled, all in the name of a "national security." Milagros was and is entitled to full-fledged citizenship rights in the United States. However, unequal power relations between the state and those affected by the deportation experience void those citizenship rights of any substantial protection.

For Carmen, Nicole, and Milagros, family relationships and societal expectations about the roles of women in their community were central to their life outcomes. Sexual and emotional abuse, drug addiction, and a subsequent loss of self-esteem are at the core of the female deportee experience. Women suffer higher rates of extreme marginalization and stigma, risk-taking behavior, and drug use; they even contract chronic and severely undertreated health conditions upon their return to the Dominican Republic. Deportation, therefore, serves as a structurally violent mechanism for social control, an enhanced tool for the state to punish or discipline noncitizen women that are perceived to violate social and legal norms—most of them women of color from Latin American or Caribbean countries.

Note

1. All names have been changed to protect confidentiality.

15

Caging Paloma:
Illegality and Violence along the United States–Mexico Border

Heidy Sarabia

The author, Heidy Sarabia, is an assistant professor at California State University–Sacramento. She is the author of several articles dealing with the issues of transnational activism, cross-border practices, the long-term consequences of illegality, and citizenship practices along the border.

Paloma[1] was at a *panaderia* (bakery) in Mexicali, Baja California, Mexico—along the United States–Mexico border—and as she was getting ready to pay for her bread, a man entered the store and placed issues of *White Sheet* on the counter—a local publication with ads and coupons from the businesses around the Imperial Valley in Southern California. When Paloma saw the newsletter, she started crying inconsolably. The cashier asked what was wrong but Paloma could not stop to explain her grief. After she finally gained a little composure, she explained to the cashier that seeing *White Sheet* had reminded her of the life she had in Brawley, California: She used to read the *White Sheet* daily, cook breakfast for her children, take them and pick them up from school, do homework and eat dinner with them. But that life was long gone now. She had been deported two years prior and was now living in Mexicali, alone, across the border from Brawley, where her children live. Yet the border had shaped Paloma's life long before the incident at the *panaderia*, and her tears were the result not of one event but of a lifelong struggle to survive the whimsical rules of a border that insisted on caging her on either side of it.

Paloma had been born in Mexicali and her father had attained legal residency in the United States with the 1986 Immigration Reform and Control Act (IRCA). The legislation permitted approximately 3 million unauthorized migrants to adjust their legal status. When her father adjusted his status, Paloma and her mother were living in Mexico. When Paloma was fourteen years old her mother decided to join her father, move to the United States, and take her with them. At that time, Paloma did not want to migrate. Migrating to the United States meant leaving her friends, extended family, financial security, and her lifelong home. But, as a minor, staying in Mexico by herself was not an option. So, she went to the United States with her parents, Paloma and her mother entered the country with a border-crossing card—a temporary visa for border residents, which allows them to cross to visit the United States for short periods of time—and simply did not return to Mexico. She overstayed her visa and became unauthorized. But her status did not prevent her from enrolling in a high school due to the legal ruling of *Plyler v. Doe* that grants free public education to all children regardless of legal status, and she quickly learned English. Due to her unauthorized status in the United States, however, she was unable to cross back and forth over the border: She was fenced in. She had to choose a side: either the United States or Mexico. When she turned eighteen, after three years in the United States, she decided to return by herself to Mexico, her home.

Back in Mexico again, she studied nursing. She was able to enroll at a technical school without much trouble because she had only been in the United States for a couple of years. Eventually she fell in love, and got married. In 1993, at the age of twenty, Paloma migrated to the United States again with her husband, this time because of economic hardships in Mexico. In the United States her husband was able to get work; she had three US-born children, and became a stay-at-home mom. But her life was not easy. Paloma's husband was physically and emotionally abusive. In one instance, he corralled her in the laundry room, choking her, while telling her, *"Muerete cabrona"* ("Die, bitch"). Paloma saw hate in his eyes and thought he was not going to let go, so she hit him in the groin and escaped. In part due to the abuse, Paloma became a private person; she did not know her neighbors, and focused all her efforts on her children, as she hoped for a better life for them. Paloma thought that if her husband had done better in school, their lives would be easier. She was convinced her children could have a better future through education, so she tried to make sure they succeeded in school. Even though one of her children was diagnosed with ADHD, she made sure that he did all his homework and behaved well in school. Her children did do well: they consistently received awards for their excellent performance and behavior. Though Paloma felt proud for their success and development, the situation at home continued to be difficult. Sometimes her husband was violent and at least twice she called the police to intervene.

Paloma could have applied for a U visa to stay in the United States. In 2000, Congress created the U visa with the passage of the Victims of Trafficking and Violence Protection Act (VTVPA), intended to help victims of domestic violence, sexual assault, and trafficking get legal status in the United States. In theory, victims of domestic abuse, like Paloma, could call the police and press charges against their abusers without fear of deportation. Yet, the US Citizenship and Immigration Services (USCIS) issued the regulations and procedures for migrants to apply for U visas in September of 2007; therefore, no U visas were issued until 2008. By 2009, when Paloma was deported, the U visa was so recent that USCIS received only 6,835 visa petitions (USCIS 2015)—not meeting the 10,000 annual cap stipulated by Congress. Neither Paloma nor the lawyer she consulted knew about the U visa, even though Paloma could have qualified for such visa. Given the complex legal terrain, lawyers play a key role in determining eligibility to certain immigration visas, not only by encouraging their clients to apply for these legal remedies, but also in the way they craft their clients' stories in order to persuade immigration officers that their clients qualify and deserve legal status in the United States (Lakhani 2013). Nevertheless, even when these options are available to victims of violence, U visas are a tenuous legal status that often maintains immigrants vulnerable to "blocked mobility, persistent fear of deportation, and instability, confusion, and self-blame" (Abrego and Lakhani 2015, 287).

Adjusting one's legal status is tricky, however, because migrants who enter unauthorized into the United States are not able to apply for "adjustment of status" from within the United States, the migrant has to leave the United States and apply overseas through a US consulate in his or her home country. Another legal option for Paloma was to adjust her status through her father, who had become a US citizen, and had submitted an application for her and her husband. But this path was unsuccessful since family-reunification visas have a very long wait period. For someone like Paloma, the Mexican child of a US citizen, older than twenty-one years of age, the wait could be as long as fifteen years to adjust her legal status. So Paloma and her husband lived unauthorized, waiting for the permits that would change their legal status. But her husband was not patient, he hated living unauthorized, and would often blame his inability to get better jobs on his legal status. He sought an easier and faster way to legalize his status: finding and marrying a US citizen.

Ignoring the legal complications inherent in his strategy, Paloma's husband moved forward with his plan to marry a US citizen. He left her and their three children, moved in with a neighbor (who was a US citizen), and went to see a lawyer. But the lawyer had bad news for him: The record of domestic violence would mean problems for his case, unless he could prove they were lies. As a result, he decided to call social services on Paloma, accused her of being abusive to their children and being addicted to drugs, and requested full custody of the children. He wanted to build a case against Paloma, representing her as an unfit and abusive mother, to discredit her claims of abuse and improve his chances of gaining legal status in the United States. On September 25, 2007, social services took charge of the children and placed them in foster care. Paloma was devastated but she also felt confident. She knew the devotion she had showed to her children throughout the years would demonstrate to the government agency the positive relationship she had with her children. She felt she had been a good mother and was confident the social worker would see how dedicated she had been to her children. Until the day that social services took her children away, she had never spent a single night away from them.

Indeed, after months of inquiries, it was determined that Paloma was a fit guardian and she was granted full custody of her children. The social worker informed her husband of the outcome and asked Paloma to meet her at the court on November 4, 2007. The social worker planned to surprise Paloma with the news that she had prevailed in her case, and she would get her children back later that day. Paloma went to the courthouse on November 4, and saw two officers waiting near the court's entrance. As she approached the building, one of the officers asked, "Are you Paloma Perez?" She quickly replied, "Yes, I am Paloma Perez." To her shock, they turned out to be immigration officers who took her into custody. Paloma was deported that very night. While Paloma later learned that her husband had called immigration authorities to report her, cases around the country have emerged where social service agencies have called immigration authorities to have parents deported (Miller 2009), sometimes to facilitate the adoption of children by white families (AP 2010).

Paloma was dropped off in Mexicali at 3 am and immediately called her mom. "What am I going to do?" Paloma cried on the phone with her mom, "I don't want to stay here, I don't want to stay here, I want to go back, I want my children." Paloma's distress was not just caused by the shock of apprehension and deportation, but also by the further consequences of deportation on her role as a mother (see Barak, this volume). Her mom explained that when she arrived at the detention center to see Paloma, Border Patrol told her that unless they could show Paloma's legal status in the United States, she had to be deported. Paloma was just one of the over 26 million migrants that have been deported since 1993—while most immigrants deported are men, women are affected by deportations in distinct and unique ways (see Martin, this volume).

Once again, she was forced to cross the international boundary—this time to return to Mexico against her will, and legally banned from returning to the United States for ten years. She was told explicitly, "If you come back, we are going to throw you in jail because we are already warning you not to come back illegally." Taking that stern warning to heart, she settled in Mexicali, moving in with her sister, and soon after began considering her options. She wanted to bring her children with her—her 12-year-old son, 8-year-old daughter, and 6-year-old son—and get them out of foster care, but who would take care of them once she got a job? Where would they go to school? What would their future be like if they joined Paloma in Mexico? The State of California had concerns, too. Given Paloma's precarious situation in Mexico—with no work, no income, and no home—they would not allow the children to move in with her. So they stayed in the United States in foster care, and she settled in Mexicali. In 2011, it was estimated that approximately 5,100 children were living in foster care because their parents had either been detain or deported by immigration authorities (Wessler 2011, 6).

Legally, immigration law and family law are often completely divorced, and even in direct contradiction (Thronson 2006). On one hand, from the perspective of immigration law, judges cannot consider family unity and the rights of US-born children when deciding whether or not to deport the immigrant parent, even though detention and deportation cause tremendous psycho-social harm to children and their families (Abbott et al. 2013), and historically, family separation has been a common consequence of the way US immigration law is applied and enforced (see Goodman, this volume and Garcia, this volume). For example, lawsuits that have tried to claim that the deportation of a parent infringes on the right of the child to be raised by the parent and to grow up in the United States have failed. Thus, the courts have found that "a citizen child does not have a legal interest in preventing the deportation of his parent" (Maun 2011, 464). On the other hand, from the perspective of family law, the realities of immigration law enforcement are often ignored. For example, immigration status can have a detrimental influence in family law determinations—such as determining what's best for the child in custody cases (Thronson 2005, 48; Wolozin 2016). In many cases, after being detained and deported, immigrant parents have been found to be "unfit" parents due to their failure to see their children, be present in their children's lives, and failing to reunite with their children (Hall 2010).

The foster parents allowed Paloma's three children to visit her in Mexicali every weekend. One weekend, Paloma took her children back to the border crossing after a visit in Mexicali. On that day, the Border Patrol officer saw Paloma's children and told Paloma she could cross as well. He happened to be the boyfriend of a former foster mom, knew the children well, and was not going to check Paloma's permits to cross. It was a random opportunity that she was not anticipating and she took it. She crossed the border without being inspected. Repeated migrations are common because deported immigrants tend to have many cultural, social, and economic ties to the United States (Sarabia 2016, see also Hiemstra, this volume). Paloma's return was not planned, but she ended up in the United States again. She talked to the social worker, found an apartment, and began arranging for her to get her children back. Since the court had already decided in Paloma's favor, the social worker returned the children to Paloma immediately. Paloma thought things would get back to normal. But three months later immigration officers showed up to her door again.

Paloma could not hide from her husband because legally he had the right to know where their children were living. But Paloma knew he was never going to leave her alone. He had already threatened her, "If I am not going to have the children, neither will you. If I can't fix my papers, neither will you." These were not empty threats; he had already showed once that he was willing to call Border Patrol to get Paloma deported. Three months after, immigration officers showed up at the door to deport her once again. They told her, "Your husband does not want you to have the children. If you can't show your legal status, you will have to leave to Mexico." This time, immigration officers suggested to Paloma that she award the custody of her children to her mom if she did not want them in foster care. Paloma signed the custody papers, and was deported once again. But this second time, it was different.

"Once again, I was in Mexicali," Paloma remembered, "But this time it was worse. Worse because I was deported for twenty years. They did not deport me for life by the pure mercy of God. But the judge told me that he had to punish me for what I had done, for coming back unauthorized." Paloma explained to the judge what had happened, how the immigration officer had allowed her to enter, that she had not planned to come back unauthorized, but that she could not resist the opportunity to be with her children. The judge was not sympathetic. He told her, "If you had been more decent, more legal, more *recta* [straight], you would have told the officer that you did not have papers." The judge implied that Paloma had taken advantage of the situation by not revealing her lack of legal permits to cross into the United States. But Paloma responded, "With all the respect that you deserve, if you had been in my situation, if you had seen the opportunity to return to your children, you would not have cared. You would have done the same thing I did. I am responsible for the consequences but I did what I did for my children—it was an opportunity." The judge's response was empathetic but still severe. "Only for that reason, only because you are a mother I will deport you for twenty years [and not for life]." During the first deportation, and now during this second deportation, Paloma had not been represented by an attorney—she just could not afford one. Yet, having a lawyer is increasingly determining the outcomes of deportations. Those with legal representation are less likely to face deportations. Paloma's lack of legal representation shaped the terrible outcomes.

In Mexico, Paloma is more *resignada* this time. She does not want to end up in jail and living in *perpetual illegality* in the United States was not an option (Sarabia 2011, see also Chapter 21, Garcia, in this volume). The judge told her clearly, *"Me advirtio* [she warned me], that if I cross unauthorized again, they will throw me in jail for three months, without any rights, and they will deport me for life." That legal threat keeps Paloma in Mexico—a threat that now seems much more real, concrete, and severe. Paloma became aware of the legal consequences of her uninspected crossing, and experienced the full force of legal violence (Menjívar and Abrego 2012). *"No le voy a buscar tres pies al gato* [I am not going to tempt my luck], as long as my ex- husband is alive, he is not going to leave me alone." Now Paloma lives and works in Mexicali, resigned to stay here on the long run. But life in Mexico has not been easy. Some days Paloma returns from work to a lonely home where she cries, remembering the things she should be doing with her children. Sometimes she has felt like she could go crazy. But the love of her children keeps her afloat. *"Mis niños me adoran* [my children adore me]," Paloma remembers on the difficult days.

Paloma's children also suffer, and often remind her that they would like to live with her. Paloma knows that they have more opportunities in the United States. She could not even provide for adequate child care while she works at a call center in Mexicali, where she earns $50 to $80 USD per week. Yet, as she reflects upon her children's lives in the United States, Paloma feels that even if the jail is golden it is still a prison: Even if her children have more opportunities in the United States, they remain in a prison because they miss their mother. The border cages her, preventing her from crossing to live with her children, but it also cages her children, preventing them from living with their mother. Her youngest daughter writes her letters asking when she is going to move in with them. Paloma's children are part of the collateral damage of deportation. It has been estimated that between 2010 and 2012, more than 205,000 migrants with US-born children have been deported from the United States (Wessler 2011, 2012).

Paloma's children are growing and often get worried about their mother living alone in Mexico. Her oldest son, a fourteen-year-old now taller than Paloma, saw a television show where they talked about *femicides* in Mexico—that is, the violent and deliberate killings of women in Mexico—and he immediately called her, crying and telling her, "Do not accept rides from strangers, you do not know who they are." Mexico is ranked sixteenth in the incidence of homicides against women globally (CDD and CMDPDH 2012), and *femicides* along the border have become notorious since the 1990s (Fregoso and Bejarano 2010). Her son's fears are not completely unfounded. Paloma thinks her ex-husband has also been deported to Mexico because she has seen him following her to work in a car. One day, he went around the block three times, until finally Paloma turned around and confronted him. She was afraid because she remembered the episodes of physical violence at the hands of her ex-husband, but her nervousness forced her to confront him, "What the fuck do you want? What do you want?" He did not respond and took off, leaving Paloma with memories of the violence she experienced while together. She felt like she had seen *el diablo* [the devil].

Paloma is strong and refuses to be victimized by her circumstances, deportation is not the end of everything, and immigrants learn to adopt to their new reality (see Guevara, Stuesse, and Coleman this volume; Silver, this volume; and Wheatley, this volume). She found a job at a call center in Mexicali (see Anderson, this volume) and goes to work every day with a wide smile on her face thinking, "I can't do much, so I am not going to be *martirizandome, acuchillandome la mente* [I am not going to be a martyr, by abusing my mind]." People at work think she has an easy, problem-free life because she is always happy. But she lives by a poem she read once: "Don't give your enemies the satisfaction of your tears, give them the punishment of your smile." Only she knows what she went through, and she keeps it close to her heart. She keeps her children in her mind, and tries to forget the distance and the barriers that keep them separated. After all, they only live 20 miles apart.

Paloma's story shows how, for many unauthorized migrants, crossing international boundaries is often a forced choice. After coming to the United States with her husband, she stayed because she could not travel back and forth to Mexico freely. Then after she was deported she could not travel back to the United States to be with her children. She was trapped on one side of the border and then the other because she could not get the legal documents to cross freely. She has been both forced out and fenced in. In addition, Paloma's story highlights how immigration law and border policies can become a mechanism of abuse, when her husband used immigration law to have her deported and keep her from her family. At a high emotional cost to her children, her parents, and herself, she is caged in Mexico by the legal threat imposed on her: If she comes back to the United States she will be jailed and banned for life from returning legally to the United States. Paloma endures her pain with the hope that someday, when her children turn twenty-one, they might once again be able to be together. Paloma hopes and waits for the day when the border will no longer dictate the distance between the life she wishes to have and the reality.

Note

1. Paloma, a pseudonym to protect the identity of the subject, is a migrant I interviewed in the border city of Mexicali in 2009 as part of a larger project on life along the United States–Mexico border.

References

Abbott, Charles, Francisco Quintana, Erin Cipolla, Robert Pauw, Jessica E. Chico, Daniel Kanstroom, Jayashri Srikantiah, and Lida Weissman-Ward. 2013. "Request for Public Thematic Hearing Concerning U.S. Deportation Policy and the Rights of Migrants." http://law.stanford.edu/wp-content/uploads/sites/default/files/project/443312/doc/slspublic/13-10-17 US Imm Hearing Summary FINAL.pdf

Abrego, Leisy J. and Sarah M. Lakhani. 2015. "Incomplete Inclusion: Legal Violence and Immigrants in Liminal Legal Statuses." *Law & Policy* 37 (4): 265–93. http://doi.wiley.com/10.1111/lapo.12039

AP. 2010. "Illegal Immigrant Sues over Lost Custody of Child in Mississippi." *NY Daily News*, August 13. http://www.nydailynews.com/news/national/illegal-immigrant-sues-lost-custody-child-mississippi-article-1.206256

CDD and CMDPDH. 2012. *Femicide and Impunity in Mexico: A Context of Structural and Generalized Violence.* http://www2.ohchr.org/english/bodies/cedaw/docs/ngos/CDDandCMDPDH_forthesession_Mexico_CEDAW52.pdf

Fregoso, Rosa Linda and Cynthia Bejarano. 2010. "Introduction: A Cartography of Feminicides in the Americas." in *Terrorizing Women: Feminicide in the Americas*, ed. R.-L. Fregoso and C. Bejarano (Durham, NC: Duke University Press).

Hall, C. E. 2010. "Where Are My Children—And My Rights? Parental Rights Termination as a Consequence of Deportation." *Duke Law Journal* 60: 1459–504. http://heinonlinebackup.com/hol-cgi-bin/get_pdf.cgi?handle=hein.journals/duklr60§ion=41

Lakhani, Sarah Morando. 2013. "Producing Immigrant Victims' 'Right' to Legal Status and the Management of Legal Uncertainty." *Law and Social Inquiry* 38 (2): 442–73.

Maun, Kristin. 2011. "Sanctuary from De Facto Deportation: The New Sanctuary Movement and De Facto Deportation Claims for Children Challenging Illegal Immigrant Parents' Removal Orders." *Richmond Public Interest Law Review* 15 (2): 449–74. Retrieved from http://scholarship.richmond.edu/cgi/viewcontent.cgi?article=1263&context=pilr

Menjívar, Cecilia and Leisy J. Abrego. 2012. "Legal Violence: Immigration Law and the Lives of Central American Immigrants." *American Journal of Sociology* 117 (5): 1380–421.

Miller, Carol Marbin. 2009. "Foster Care Agency Faulted for Calling Immigration Agents." *Miami Herald*, March 25. http://www.freerepublic.com/focus/f-news/2215939/posts

Sarabia, Heidy. 2011. "Perpetual Illegality: Results of Border Enforcement and Policies for Mexican Undocumented Migrants in the United States." *Analyses of Social Issues and Public Policy* (Special collection on Social Psychology and Contemporary Immigration Policy): 1–19.

Sarabia, Heidy. 2016. "Borderland Attachments: Citizenship and Belonging Along the U.S.-Mexico Border." *Citizenship Studies* 20 (3–4): 342–58. http://www.tandfonline.com/doi/full/10.1080/13621025.2016.1158352

Thronson, David B. 2005. "Of Borders and Best Interests: Examining the Experiences of Undocumented Immigrants in U.S. Family Courts." *Texas Hispanic Journal of Law & Policy* 11: 47–77.

Thronson, David B. 2006. "Choiceless Choices: Deportation and the Parent-Child Relationship." *Nevada Law Review* 6 (3): 1165.

USCIS. 2015. *Number of I-918 Petitions for U Nonimmigrant Status (Victims of Certain Criminal Activities and Family Members) by Fiscal Year, Quarter, and Case Status 2009–2015*. http://www.uscis.gov/sites/default/files/USCIS/Resources/Reports and Studies/Immigration Forms Data/Victims/I918u_visastatistics_fy2015_qtr3.pdf

Wessler, Seth Freed. 2011. *Shattered Families: The Perilous Intersection of Immigration Enforcement and the Child Welfare System*. New York: Race Forward: The Center For Racial Justice Innovation. Online at https://www.raceforward.org/research/reports/shattered-families

Wessler, Seth Freed. 2012. "Nearly 205K Deportations of Parents of U.S. Citizens in Just Over Two Years." *Colorlines*, December 17. Online at http://www.colorlines.com/articles/nearly-205k-deportations-parents-us-citizens-just-over-two-years

Wolozin, Becky. 2016. "Doing What's Best: Determining Best Interests for Children Impacted by Immigration Proceedings." *Drake Law Review* 64: 141.

16

The Ripple Effects of US Immigration Enforcement:

A Young Mexican Deportee's Story of Isolation, Precarity, and Resilience

Christine Wheatley

The author, Christine Wheatley, is a lecturer in the department of sociology at Southern Methodist University. Her current work is a bi-national ethnography that investigates the impacts of US deportation laws on the processes of removal taking place in detention centers and immigration courts in Texas and on deportees and other returning migrants in Mexico.

I first met Quetzal in his beauty salon in San Pedro, a small town in the highlands of Jalisco, Mexico, in July 2010. At that time, the salon had been open for business for about a year and a half. He was attending to a woman client who had asked for long, acrylic nails. As we spoke, he painted intricate patterns in bold colors, adding plastic stones that sparkled like jewels. "Right now, the most popular [designs] are flowers, hand-painted flowers," he told me. "And lots and lots of stones!" he laughed. He himself was also wearing long, painted acrylic nails in this style. Quetzal refers to himself as *travesti*, because he identifies as a man who wears clothes and accessories typically associated with women.

He worked intently, hunched over the woman's nails with his small, thin brushes, looking up at me from time to time as he recounted how he came to be here, running his own beauty salon in his hometown. Between 2002 and 2008, Quetzal made two separate unauthorized trips to the United States. During his first trip, he was deported. The second time he came back to Mexico by choice. Each time, he went with the hope of saving money to open his own salon. Realizing this dream came with great costs, not just financial, but also emotional, psychological, and physical. Quetzal's story illustrates the ripple effects of US immigration enforcement, the many facets of life that it touches. His story also illustrates the ways in which his gender identity and expression as a *travesti* and his legal status in the United States as an unauthorized immigrant and deportee together have shaped his life in both the United States and Mexico.

In 2002, Quetzal arranged for a *coyote* to him help him cross the border near Tecate, a border town about 30 miles east of Tijuana, in the Mexican state of Baja California. His mom had been living without authorization in Detroit, Michigan, for two years and offered to loan him $2,800 for the crossing and the flight to Detroit from Los Angeles. Once he arrived in Detroit, he lived with his mother, his cousin, and his cousin's mother.

He got his first job in Detroit "by chance," he said. The day he arrived in Detroit happened to be the fifth of May and there were *Cinco de Mayo* celebrations happening all over town. He decided to go to one such celebration and there he ran into an old friend from San Pedro, someone he'd known since middle school. "I told him that I just got here and was looking for work and he told me, 'I'm a supervisor [at a factory] and I could get you a job. All you need is to get your false identification, and a false Social Security card.'" So the next day, Quetzal contacted someone from Mexico living in Detroit who he knew made false documents and arranged to have a set made for him. He then went to the factory to fill out the application, showed his documents, and was hired. Quetzal's reliance on his social network from his hometown to obtain work in Detroit echoes Chavez's findings from her study which shows that lesbian, gay, transgender, and queer (LGBTQ) migrants tend to depend on friends and family when they have needs[1]. Such reliance diverges, however, from the experiences of transgender individuals who develop supportive social networks defined by their gender and sexual identities and engage in social capital building within such networks.[2]

His new job was at a meat processing factory. After two months, he was promoted to supervisor. He held the supervisor position for a little over a year until he had an accident: His fingers got smashed in one of the machines. "This was a problem for them because they didn't want to give me [workman's compensation] . . . I didn't have insurance, they didn't want to pay for the doctor . . . so the easiest thing was to just let me go."

This type of abuse of undocumented workers happens with alarming frequency.[3] When an accident happens, employers are afraid to report it because doing so could reveal that they are using undocumented labor, which is illegal. The workers themselves have little ability to demand medical care or challenge their firing because of their undocumented status; doing so would put them at risk of deportation.[4]

After he was dismissed from the meat processing factory, Quetzal began working in a beauty salon. He got the job through another connection from his hometown: The owner was also from San Pedro. "I just helped sweep, things like that."

Then came the incident that led to his deportation, when he had been living in the United States for just short of two years. He had bought a car and was out driving when he collided with another driver in an intersection. The other driver was clearly at fault, Quetzal explained, "but because I was an immigrant, I was illegal, against an American, well, I couldn't compete. So he called the police and the one who ended up losing was me." The other driver told the police that the accident was Quetzal's fault. Quetzal felt like he couldn't argue with him. Two police officers had arrived at the scene. One of them was a Mexican man, Quetzal said, and "he wanted to let me go. He told me: 'I'll give you the opportunity to pay a bond or you can pay damages to the other person and you can go.'" But the other officer, a woman, felt differently.

> She thought I was a woman and she treated me really badly. She made me feel uncomfortable because I've always had long hair, always had nails, I've always gone out like this. She thought I was a woman and I told her, 'No, I'm not a woman, *soy travesti*, I just dress like a woman.' She said, 'No, you're a woman,' admonishing me. . . . She treated me so badly. The other police officer said, 'look, just let him pay the driver and there won't be a problem.' But her, no, she wanted to see me go to jail. She handcuffed me, making the handcuffs super tight. But she was the only one who treated me like that. When I went to the immigration [detention], everyone there conducted themselves properly [*se portó muy bien*], it was just that police officer.

After the car accident, Quetzal was placed in deportation proceedings and sent to an immigration detention facility to await his deportation. Quetzal's story demonstrates the vulnerabilities to deportation that undocumented migrants face in the current era of immigration enforcement. Any encounter with law enforcement can result in deportation. After being held for a short period in an immigration detention facility, Quetzal was sent to a prison. "I don't know if it was a state or federal prison but it was much bigger." In Quetzal's case, his only deportable offense was that he was in the United States without authorization. According to US immigration laws, unlawful presence is a civil, not criminal offense, which means that people convicted of unlawful presence can deported, but cannot be imprisoned as a form of punishment for the offense. They can, however, be detained while they await deportation.

With the recent explosion in the number of people placed in detention as part of their deportation proceedings, Immigration and Customs Enforcement (ICE) faces a capacity problem. This had led ICE to rent out bed space in county jails and state and federal prisons to be used for detaining immigrants in deportation proceedings in what it calls "non-dedicated" or "shared-use" detention facilities.[5]

Quetzal was detained for three months before he was deported. Given that Quetzal is a *travesti*, I asked him if they put him with men or with women. He responded, "It was a dilemma—they didn't know where to put me." In the end, they decided that, for his own safety, it was best to put him in solitary confinement.

Gender-nonconforming individuals are victims of assault, including sexual assault, and other forms of harassment at much higher rates in immigration detention[6] and prisons[7,8] as compared to other detainees and inmates. Placing gender-nonconforming individuals in solitary confinement is common practice intended to protect them from these forms of violence. However, studies have shown that solitary confinement can cause severe psychological damage[9,10]. In 2011, the United Nations released a report, calling on countries to ban solitary confinement in most cases. It states that more than fifteen days of solitary confinement could amount to torture.[11]

"So, I was always isolated." Quetzal acknowledged that it would have been dangerous to be put with other inmates. "Actually, right before I came back to Mexico was when they put me with a group of Mexican men and . . . they made me very scared." There was one immigration officer who looked out for him while in detention.

> A woman named Marta Hernandez [pseudonym]. I remember her name perfectly. She would say to me in English, "You are so cute!" and I would say to her, "Thank you!" and she'd say, "You are so nice. I'm going to protect you." And she always protected me, always tried to put me in places where I'd be protected, she never left me with everyone else.

For Quetzal, the worst part about being deported was detention, "months trapped within four walls." It took a psychological toll on him. "Your mind begins to go to very ugly places when you're in prison. You think you're a criminal, that you did something bad, that you did the worst thing ever, and you even begin to believe that you've killed someone."

He felt frustrated, being surrounded by people who had committed serious crimes, violent crimes, thinking to himself, "what am I doing here when I didn't do anything? I just came here to work, that was the only bad thing I did." He also felt frustrated with how long he had to wait in detention before being sent back to Mexico. It'd be one thing if immigration caught you and just put you back across the border, he said, but,

> no, they lock you up, you're there a month, two months, three months, they vaccinate you, inject you, they put you here, put you there, you can't leave, you get sick and you can't [be deported when you're sick] . . . so there's fifty undocumented [immigrants] in the prison. Of those fifty, thirty are sick with something so they can't leave and the plane can't go with only twenty people because the plane isn't full with just twenty people, it has to be full, so they have to wait and so sometimes you can wait a month, two months, there's people who were waiting in prison for more than six months.

He said there was nothing for him to do. He got so bored. He read the Bible every day. He was allowed recreation periods each day, when he'd play cards, poker, and dominos with other detainees to pass the time. Since he was in isolation most of the time, he didn't have anyone to talk to, which made his boredom almost unbearable. Exercise helped him a lot.

While he awaited his deportation from his prison cell, worried thoughts went through his mind. He asked himself,

> What am I going to do when I get to the border? Where will I have to go? Where will I have to walk? What about my clothes? Will my clothes be dirty? Am I going to go in a bus? A plane? Or what? If I don't have money, what am I going to do? I *don't* have money; how am I even going to buy a phone card to talk to my family to let them know where I am?

Not having answers to these questions made him feel very stressed. "It was so much stress, so, so, so much stress." Then, he got an idea: He could ask his father to put money in his commissary, which he did. He felt much better knowing that arriving on the border, he'd have some money to help him get back to San Pedro. "But I didn't count on getting robbed as soon as I crossed the border into Mexico."

When it was finally time for Quetzal to be deported, he was handcuffed, and put on a plane to Laredo, Texas. From the plane, he was transported by bus to the Juárez-Lincoln International Bridge, which connects Laredo to Nuevo Laredo, Tamaulipas, Mexico. He remembers it vividly. "As I was walking across the bridge to Mexico, I saw people who were crossing to get [to the United States], there, in the river down below, you could see people coming across." As soon as he reached the other side, *coyotes*, one after another, approached him, offering him very low fees to cross him back to the United States.

Quetzal wasn't tempted by their offers. He'd already been through enough and didn't want anything else bad to happen. Better to just go back to San Pedro. But before he could do anything, he was assaulted by a group of Mexican men right on the border. "They robbed me, took my clothing, everything. *Me quedé así*. It was horrible." Miraculously, though, he still had his Mexican ID card and a bank account in Mexico. He managed to make a few phone calls to friends and family in San Pedro to ask them to deposit money for him, even a little bit. He said of all of the Mexicans deported with him, he was the only one who had a Mexican ID with him, which meant he was the only one among them who could withdraw money from the bank. The details of Quetzal's deportation share some striking similarities to Juan Carlos's (Guevara, Stuesse, and Coleman, this volume). Both were involved in car accidents which were not their fault, which led to their arrests, detention, and deportation. Both found themselves repatriated to the border, panicked, with no plan and few resources. But both were able to rely on their friends and family to wire them money. These similarities demonstrate just how precarious life can be as an unauthorized immigrant, how forces beyond their control, like a car accident, can rip them from their lives in the United States in an instant and leave them vulnerable in the dangerous border region. Yet they also show the importance of friends and family to help mitigate such vulnerability.

Quetzal managed to pull together enough money to pay for a bus ticket. He first took a bus from Nuevo Laredo to Guadalajara, the capital of Jalisco, a twelve-hour journey. From there, he took a second bus to San Pedro, another two hours. "And I came walking up to my house, greeting everyone, saying 'What's up?! I'm baaaack!'" he recalled, laughing.

Living in San Pedro again under these circumstances was difficult for Quetzal. First of all, he had no money, largely because he was deported before he had the opportunity to build up savings. "The thing is, it was very little time. I just barely paid off the $2,800 debt I had with my mom from the *coyote* so I didn't have anything else [saved]."

His dream of opening his own salon would have to wait. Instead, a friend of his offered him a job in his salon. He stayed in San Pedro for another year and a half, working for his friend. It proved very beneficial to his career as a stylist. It was there that, "I learned to do everything that I now know how to do. I learned how to cut hair, do makeup, style hair—I learned it all."

Although he was content at work, he was not content in other realms of his life. Given that his deportation meant a sudden and unplanned departure from the United States, he didn't have the opportunity to bring any of his possessions. "I didn't have any of my clothing, I couldn't go out on the street because I didn't have anything, everything was there [in Detroit]."

He did not feel well-received by people in town. "People would look at me weird, some would laugh." There was gossip about why he was back. "They'd laugh and others would comment that I was in prison for drugs and things like that . . . it was so uncomfortable because everyone would look at me, stare at me but, little by little, I adjusted."

When the word spread that he was actually deported after being in a car accident, "People would say 'Oh, you were deported because you hit somebody?' and I would say, 'No, it was the other person's fault, they hit me!'" He explained, you'd think something as mundane as a minor car accident would not be fodder for gossip, but not in San Pedro: "They take something so insignificant and make it as big as the world, that's how it is here, *un pueblo chico, infierno grande* [small town, big hell]."

Quetzal missed his life in Detroit. He had made a lot of friends during his two years there and earned good money. Furthermore, in the time that he was away from San Pedro, virtually all of his friends had left town. They had either migrated to the United States themselves or moved to

Guadalajara for work or school. "The only one who was still here was my friend from the salon." Most of his family had left, too; the only ones who remained were his grandmother and cousins, "but I don't spend much time with them."

He fell into a depression, realizing how much he had gotten used to life in Detroit. So, one day, "I said to myself, 'I want to go to the United States again,' and so I decided. I talked to my mom again, told her I wanted to go there. And so, I went again."

Quetzal's second journey to Detroit, in 2005, was less difficult than the first. "I spoke a little more English, I was less afraid, everything was easier." He used a *coyote* again to get across the border. Some relatives of his were also planning to go to the United States and they knew this *coyote*. He arranged to go with them. This time, he paid $3,000—another loan from his mother—which included the flight to Detroit. They crossed via Piedras Negras, a town in the Mexican state of Coahuila, across the border from Eagle Pass, New Mexico.

Once he arrived in Detroit, he lived with his mother again. It wasn't difficult to find work. All he had to do was look through the "Help Wanted" sections of the Spanish-language newspapers in Detroit. He wanted to work in a beauty salon. He was hired at one, where he worked from 4 pm to 9 pm. He also returned to his job at the meat processing factory, working the morning shift. He picked up a third job, working overnight on Fridays, Saturdays, and Sundays at a clothing store at the mall, folding clothes. For three months, he maintained this schedule in order to pay off his debt for the crossing as quickly as possible. "I was sleeping just two hours a night." Once he paid off his debt, he quit the job at the mall.

He held onto the salon job for a little over a year and the factory job a little under a year. The reason he left the factory job: "I'm embarrassed to say but . . . it was because a [male] supervisor and [female] supervisor sexually harassed me." As a gender-nonconforming individual, Quetzal's experience of workplace harassment is, unfortunately, not unique. Sangganjanavanich and Cavazos have found that transgender individuals "face various degrees of aggression, hostility, and discrimination in the workplace."[12]

Now, he was left with just the part-time job at the salon. It was too few hours and he wasn't earning enough to pay his bills or save up. So, he decided to work as a mobile stylist, offering hair and make-up services in clients' homes. He created business cards and left them at businesses all over the city. The mobile beauty salon was a success. He was happy to be, "on my own, not working for anyone, just for myself."

What make his mobile salon possible was the fact that his cousin, also living in Detroit, had sold him a car, allowing him to make payments on it. His cousin also taught him how to drive and to prepare for his driver's exam. Eventually, he got his driver's license. Much like Lorena, (A. García, this volume), it was a great relief to him to have a driver's license. "I was no longer afraid of being pulled over by the police." He recognized that deportation was still a risk for him—if he were fingerprinted at any point, immigration officials would discover that he had violated his deportation bar and he'd be sent to prison for criminal re-entry. Criminal re-entry is felony criminal offense punishable up to two years in federal prison.

Despite the success of his mobile salon, Quetzal had begun abusing drugs and alcohol. His friends had become bad influences on him. "I began to have a lot of friends but these friends were always like 'Let's go get high, c'mon, let's go drink.'" Over time, he abused a variety of drugs—marijuana, cocaine, ecstasy, crystal meth.

> I began to see myself with a terrible addiction [*un vicio muy feo*] that . . . like, I began to deviate from what I actually wanted. Sometimes, if I earned one hundred dollars, sixty dollars would go to buying beer, cigarettes, drugs, all of these kinds of things, and I was no longer saving money. I began to feel frustrated. I said, "I'm no longer doing what I wanted to do."

His mother noticed the change in him. She confronted him, told him that he had to decide what he wanted. Did he want her to see him on the street, high, having vomited and soiled himself, robbing in order to get more drugs? Or would he rather she see him back in Mexico? He wouldn't be earning much but at least he wouldn't be living like this. "And that's when I made the decision to say, 'I'm returning to Mexico, because I don't I want to turn into a drug addict, nor an alcoholic.'"

Before he left, he tried to move to California, so he could get away from his friends in Detroit but still stay in the United States. But it was much more difficult for him to find work in California. Plus, the cost of living was exorbitant. "I thought, okay, I can just go somewhere else but [actually], I don't have any other place to go besides Detroit."

He came back to Mexico in 2008 with a few friends. They drove down in his friend's pickup truck. Arriving in San Pedro felt much different this time. "There was no stress, no fear. . . . I arrived comfortably [*a gusto*], I realized that I was comfortable being back." He still had a lot of questions going through his mind, like "What am I going to do for work? How will I begin? I have just a little bit of money but how can I best invest it?"

His mom, once again, was an immense help to him. He told her that he wanted to open a beauty salon in San Pedro and she offered to put some of her savings with his. Together, it would be enough to get started. "With that ten thousand pesos, I started buying the most important things, started little by little. I've been able to get going, little by little. I have something now but I have still a long ways to go."

He got help for his drug and alcohol abuse. A friend of his told him that her sister works for an organization that offers services like drug and HIV counseling as well as psychological counseling. He started seeing a psychologist, which helped him a lot. He learned how to protect himself from falling back into abuse.

When he first got back, he bought a car with some of his savings and got a job teaching at a beauty academy in a nearby town, about a twenty-minute drive. He started learning how to do acrylic nails. When he worked in the salon in the United States, he never had a chance to practice but saw how they were done. Six months after he returned, Quetzal finally opened his salon in San Pedro. He started out with just a few clients and got more practice. Over time, his clientele grew.

In general, it wasn't as difficult adapting to life in San Pedro the second time. "This time, I have more friends here in Mexico. Many of them have returned after graduating [from college]. I've made new friends, I got to know a lot of people [working in the beauty academy]." Plus, his parents had returned. Given all this, it was hard for him to say whether he'd return to the United States again, if given the option, or stay in Mexico.

Part of him would like to go back to the United States to work and save up another sum of money. Doing so could provide opportunities to create a good future for himself in Mexico. "I'd like to put together money for my small business to make it a little bigger, a little nicer." Also, he could bring back high-quality beauty products from the United States for his salon—products that are either unavailable in Mexico or prohibitively expensive. Doing so would reduce overhead costs and increase his profit margin dramatically.

He also recognized certain benefits of making a life for himself in the United States. "I'd like to go back . . . more than anything, for the economic stability there." He'd also like to go to school for interior design. Becoming an interior designer has been a dream of his for a long time, but one that would be virtually impossible in Mexico, given the high cost of tuition there. And, beyond economic and educational considerations, he feels more comfortable as a *travesti* in the United States.

> People are much more open. People aren't like, 'Look, a man who's dressed like a woman!' and critical. It's more, like, more open minded, just more open. Here it's very difficult because I've tried to get people to respect me but it's not as easy as it is there. There, they look at you like a normal person. . . . We *are* normal people. Actually, it's that people don't pay much attention to you but here, they do. I miss that so much because there, I could do whatever my heart desires and nobody would say anything to me. . . . It's more comfortable there.

His legal status contributes to his conflicted feelings about returning to the United States. When we spoke, his bar was active for two more years. He was hopeful about applying for a visa once it expired. In terms of going back without authorization, he said, "I'm afraid to go back. I don't want to go back illegally anymore." The only circumstance under which he'd consider it is if he mother wanted to go back. She'd been back in San Pedro for eight months but, after living in Detroit for seven years, she'd been having a hard time adjusting. And she hadn't found work yet. "If she decides to go back. . . . I'd want to accompany her. I wouldn't want to let her go on her own."

Quetzal's story demonstrates the ripple effects of US immigration enforcement. His undocumented status in the United States made him vulnerable to the chain of events that occurred on that fateful day when he was involved in a minor car accident. For a legal resident, a minor car accident would indeed be minor—perhaps a police report, followed by an insurance claim, and repairs made to the vehicle. But for Quetzal, it resulted in a series of violent events: time spent in jail, solitary confinement in detention, and deportation to Nuevo Laredo, a notorious dangerous border city, where he was robbed and physically assaulted, only to face scrutiny, judgment, and gossip about his deportation when he finally made it back to San Pedro.

Because Quetzal is a *travesti*, his gender identity and expression may have shaped *how* his legal status in the United States as an unauthorized migrant and deportee impacted his life. Quetzal didn't discuss his gender identity and expression much; it only came up in our conversation a few times: when describing the scene of the car accident where the police officer treated him poorly and insisted on apprehending him, which led to his deportation; being held in solitary confinement; and in reflecting on his desire to live in the United States again, where he felt more comfortable and accepted living as a *travesti*, compared to Mexico. The fact that he mentioned his identity as a *travesti* at these particular points in his story is actually quite telling: It shows the concrete ways in which gender identity and expression can matter for an undocumented migrant. It may have contributed to his deportation, it meant being subjected to incredible psychological distress in solitary confinement, and it served as a source of longing to return to the United States so that he could feel more at ease being himself, a longing that was complicated by the knowledge that an unauthorized return could result in imprisonment and another deportation. The way Quetzal told his story also shows us that he is not defined only by his gender identity and expression, his legal status in the United States, or the hardships he has endured. He is also a talented artist and entrepreneur who is finding his place.

Overall, he said he's content with his life in San Pedro. His business is stable. And the high demand for acrylic nails keeps a steady stream of clients coming through his door. "I wanted to clear a path for myself here in my own *pueblo*," he told me. "So, here I go, little by little, breaking up the stones to see how far I can get."

Notes

1. Karma R. Chávez, "Identifying the Needs of LGBTQ Immigrants and Refugees in Southern Arizona." *Journal of Homosexuality* 58, no. 2 (2011): 189–218.
2. Rogério M. Pinto, Rita M. Melendez, and Anya Y. Spector, "Male-to-Female Transgender Individuals Building Social Support and Capital From Within a Gender-Focused Network," *Journal of Gay & Lesbian Social Services* 20, no. 3 (2008): 203–20.
3. Annette Bernhardt, Ruth Milkman, Nik Theodore, Douglas D. Heckathorn, Mirabai Auer, James Defilippis, et al., "Broken Laws, Unprotected Workers: Violations of Employment and Labor Laws in America's Cities," Institute for Research on Labor and Employment, University of California–Los Angeles, 2009. http://escholarship.org/uc/item/1vn389nh#page-1 Accessed: 3/21/16.
4. Janet E. Benson, "Undocumented Immigrants and the Meatpacking Industry in the Midwest," in *Illegal Immigration in America: A Reference Handbook*, ed. David W. Haines and Karen Elaine Rosenblum, 172–92 (Westport, CT: Greenwood Publishing Group, 1999).
5. Immigration and Customs Enforcement, "Immigration Detention Overview and Recommendations," Department of Homeland Security, 2009. https://www.ice.gov/doclib/about/offices/odpp/pdf/ice-detention-rpt.pdf Accessed March 21, 2016.
6. United States Government Accountability Office. "Immigration Detention: Additional Actions Could Strengthen DHS Efforts to Address Sexual Abuse." Report to Congressional Requesters, 2013. http://www.gao.gov/assets/660/659145.pdf Accessed March 21, 2016.
7. Bureau of Justice Statistics, "Sexual Victimization in Prisons and Jails Reported by Inmates, 2011–2012," Office of Justice Programs, U.S. Department of Justice, 2014. http://www.bjs.gov/content/pub/pdf/svpjri1112_st.pdf Accessed March 21, 2016.
8. The New York Times Editorial Board, "Prisons and Jails Put Transgender Inmates at Risk," November 9, 2015. Online at http://www.nytimes.com/2015/11/09/opinion/prisons-and-jails-put-transgender-inmates-at-risk.html?_r=0 Accessed March 21, 2016.
9. Craig Haney, "Mental Health Issues in Long-Term Solitary and 'Supermax' Confinement," *Crime and Delinquency* 49, no. 1 (2003): 124–56 http://www.supermaxed.com/NewSupermaxMaterials/Haney-MentalHealthIssues.pdf Accessed: March 21, 2016.
10. Craig Haney, and Mona Lynch, "Regulating Prisons of the Future: A Psychological Analysis of Supermax and Solitary Confinement," *New York University Review of Law & Social Change* 23 (1997): 477–558.
11. http://www.un.org/apps/news/story.asp?NewsID=40097#.VvC8OZMrKu5 Accessed: 3/21/16.
12. Varunee Faii Sangganjanavanich, and Javier Cavasos, Jr., "Workplace Aggression: Toward Social Justice and Advocacy in Counseling for Transgender Individuals," *Journal of LGBT Issues in Counseling* 4, no. 3–4 (2010): 187–201.

References

Janet E. Benson, "Undocumented Immigrants and the Meatpacking Industry in the Midwest," in *Illegal Immigration in America: A Reference Handbook*, ed. David W. Haines and Karen Elaine Rosenblum, 172–92 (Westport, CT: Greenwood Publishing Group, 1999).

Annette Bernhardt, Ruth Milkman, Nik Theodore, Douglas D. Heckathorn, Mirabai Auer, James Defilippis, et al., "Broken Laws, Unprotected Workers: Violations of Employment and Labor Laws in America's Cities," Institute for Research on Labor and Employment, University of California–Los Angeles, 2009. http://escholarship.org/uc/item/1vn389nh#page-1 Accessed: 3/21/16.

Bureau of Justice Statistics, "Sexual Victimization in Prisons and Jails Reported by Inmates, 2011–2012," Office of Justice Programs, U.S. Department of Justice, 2014. http://www.bjs.gov/content/pub/pdf/svpjri1112_st.pdf Accessed March 21, 2016.

Karma R. Chávez, "Identifying the Needs of LGBTQ Immigrants and Refugees in Southern Arizona." *Journal of Homosexuality* 58, no. 2 (2011): 189–218.

Craig Haney, "Mental Health Issues in Long-Term Solitary and 'Supermax' Confinement," *Crime and Delinquency* 49, no. 1 (2003): 124–56 http://www.supermaxed.com/NewSupermaxMaterials/Haney-MentalHealthIssues.pdf Accessed: March 21, 2016.

Craig Haney, and Mona Lynch, "Regulating Prisons of the Future: A Psychological Analysis of Supermax and Solitary Confinement," *New York University Review of Law & Social Change* 23 (1997): 477–558.

Immigration and Customs Enforcement, "Immigration Detention Overview and Recommendations," Department of Homeland Security, 2009. https://www.ice.gov/doclib/about/offices/odpp/pdf/ice-detention-rpt.pdf Accessed March 21, 2016.

Rogério M. Pinto, Rita M. Melendez, and Anya Y. Spector, "Male-to-Female Transgender Individuals Building Social Support and Capital From Within a Gender-Focused Network," *Journal of Gay & Lesbian Social Services* 20, no. 3 (2008): 203–20.

Varunee Faii Sangganjanavanich, and Javier Cavasos, Jr., "Workplace Aggression: Toward Social Justice and Advocacy in Counseling for Transgender Individuals," *Journal of LGBT Issues in Counseling* 4, no. 3–4 (2010): 187–201.

The New York Times Editorial Board, "Prisons and Jails Put Transgender Inmates at Risk," November 9, 2015. Online at http://www.nytimes.com/2015/11/09/opinion/prisons-and-jails-put-transgender-inmates-at-risk.html?_r=0 Accessed March 21, 2016.

United Nations News Centre, "Solitary confinement should be banned in most cases, UN expert says," October 18, 2011. Online at: http://www.un.org/apps/news/story.asp?NewsID=40097#.VvC8OZMrKu5 Accessed: March 21, 2016

United States Government Accountability Office. "Immigration Detention: Additional Actions Could Strengthen DHS Efforts to Address Sexual Abuse." Report to Congressional Requesters, 2013. http://www.gao.gov/assets/660/659145.pdf Accessed March 21, 2016.

PART 6

DEPORTING DREAMERS:
How Do "American" Youth Navigate Their Lives in Mexico after Deportation?

Undocumented immigrants in the United States often live in fear of deportation. They know their lives would be turned upside down if their American dreams are transformed into nightmares of deportation. Although deportation is upsetting and even traumatic for anyone who encounters this oppressive arm of the state, deportation is difficult in distinct ways for DREAMers—the moniker given to youths raised in the United States yet who lack legal status. As Roberto Gonzales (2015) explains, undocumented youth raised in the United States grow up feeling part of their communities and of this country. Although these youths face significant barriers to inclusion during adolescence, many DREAMers imagine that life as a deportee would be even worse.

The chapters in this section explore not only what life is like as a deportee in Mexico, but also the complex of laws and enforcement practices that can lead to deportation. These chapters reveal that DREAMers in Mexico continue to dream. Their youth, education, and English-language skills often translate into opportunities in Mexico. These opportunities, however, do not alleviate the pain they feel due to dreams deferred and families left behind. Juan Carlos Guevara, Angela Stuesse, and Mathew Coleman explain how deportation is not only emotionally painful, but can also involve an un-navigable web of endless bureaucracy. And, even though Juan Carlos is exactly the type of youth that DACA was designed to help, the process for applying was also unforgivable in the way bureaucracies often are: He missed the implementation date by two days and was thus ineligible.

Juan Carlos' story highlights many troublesome failings and dehumanizing incongruities that make up the patchwork immigration system in our country today. The 287(g) and successor programs that turn local law enforcement agencies into proxies for ICE—in addition to encouraging racial profiling and eroding local communities' trust in police—have turned the mundane act of driving to school, work, or even home from a celebratory graduation dinner into a dangerous activity for undocumented people. Meanwhile, the detention and deportation systems are poorly articulated, resulting in long wait times, unnecessary transfers, and confusion among detainees, staff, and legal professionals alike. Outrageously, these problems are so severe that they are leading to unwarranted and illegal deportations like Juan Carlos's. The fact that DHS recognized their egregious error and was willing to bring Juan Carlos back to the United States following his erroneous deportation is indicative of such incompetence that few would believe its authenticity had it not been documented. Finally, Juan Carlos's experience forces us to confront the reality that, while DACA provided relief to millions, it excluded many of those it was meant to help.

Alexis Silver's chapter shows how a minor traffic incident upended the life of Ezequiel, who was in his last year of high school in North Carolina. Ezequiel's second deportation, after he was questioned by police and asked for identification even though the officer had no reasonable suspicion that he had committed a crime, also shows how police officers may be over-reaching their mandate to enforce criminal laws. One wonders if an older white woman would be asked for identification as a passenger in a car during a routine traffic stop. Ezequiel faced stigmatization and profiling in North Carolina. In Mexico he found that his personal style also led to stigmatization. Nevertheless, in Mexico, Ezequiel, like Juan Carlos, was able to get a job in a call center—a theme that Jill Anderson explores in depth in her contribution.

As Anderson points out, the call center sector has more than doubled in Mexico during the same time period that millions of deportees have arrived in Mexico. Even though call centers feel like "home" to *los otros Dreamers*, as Anderson and Solis (2014) describe deported youth, and they experience a modicum of economic belonging, they also experience sociocultural exclusion in Mexico and physical exclusion from the United States. For many deported youth, the transnational call center serves as "an uncertain safe haven, a community of support and a temporary economic safety net" (Anderson 2015, 8). The presence of call centers in Latin America creates a labor market niche for some deportees. However, insofar as call centers are often deportees' only option for survival, they also have become yet another way that deportees are "fenced in."

References

Anderson, Jill. 2015. "'Tagged as a Criminal': Narratives of Deportation and Return Migration in a Mexico City Call Center." *Latino Studies* 13 (1): 8–27.

Anderson, Jill, and Nin Solis. 2014. *Los Otros Dreamers*. Mexico City: Jill Anderson & Nin Solis.

Gonzales, Roberto G. 2015. *Lives in Limbo: Undocumented and Coming of Age in America*. University of California Press.

17

I Used to Believe in Justice

Juan Carlos Guevara, Angela Stuesse, and Mathew Coleman

Juan Carlos Guevara grew up in Michoacán, Mexico, surrounded by family and close relatives. Following in the footsteps of millions, in 2000 his parents made the difficult decision to leave their home in search of a better future in the United States. Over time they brought their children, one by one, to join them. Because he was the oldest, Juan Carlos was the last to migrate to Atlanta, where he became a high schooler, quickly learned English, and excelled in school. As a result of the story detailed in this volume, today Juan Carlos holds a licenciatura degree in business administration from the Universidad Fray Luca Paccioli, Campus Iguala, in Guerrero, Mexico. In his free time, he enjoys cooking, martial arts, and poetry.

Angela Stuesse (PhD University of Texas, Austin 2008) is a cultural anthropologist who specializes in neoliberalism, migration, race, labor, social movements, and activist research. Her book, Scratching Out a Living: Latinos, Race, and Work in the Deep South (University of California Press 2016), explores how Latino migration has transformed the US South and impacted efforts to organize for workplace justice in the poultry industry. Her collaborative work with Mat Coleman focuses on the policing, detention, and deportation of Latino communities in the South, with an emphasis on racialized effects and community responses. An assistant professor of anthropology at the University of North Carolina–Chapel Hill, Stuesse serves on the editorial team of the American Anthropologist's "Public Anthropology" section and is a council member of the Latin American Studies Association's Otros Saberes, which promotes collaborative, transformative research and exchange between academics and civil society knowledge producers to further social justice. Her website is www.AngelaStuesse.com.

Dr. Mat Coleman (UCLA Geography, 2005) is associate professor in the department of geography at the Ohio State University. Dr. Coleman is a political and legal geographer who works in the areas of policing and race. Most recently he has worked with Dr. Angela Stuesse (UNC) on an NSF-funded project on sheriffing and new immigrant communities in Georgia. A major theme in Dr. Coleman's research concerns the need to ground complex theory in grounded fieldwork, focused on the 'everyday lives' of power and inequality. Dr. Coleman is editor of the Geographies of Justice and Social Transformation series at the University of Georgia Press. He is also an editorial board member for the Annals of the Association of American Geographers, Political Geography, *and* Geography Compass.

On August 15, 2012, Deferred Action for Childhood Arrivals (DACA) went into effect across the United States, enabling millions of undocumented young people to legalize their status. Juan Carlos Guevara, whose parents had brought him and his siblings to the United States nearly a decade prior in search of better opportunities, was not among them. As other DREAMers celebrated new beginnings, Juan Carlos, 22, huddled uncomfortably on a couch at his aunt's home in Acapulco, Mexico, wondering what his future might hold. Two days earlier he had been forced to "voluntarily" depart the United States for Mexico, his second removal that year.

Co-authors Angela Stuesse and Mat Coleman learned of Juan Carlos's story shortly before his departure to Mexico, when they were in Atlanta studying the genesis, logics, and effects of immigrant policing on local communities. His predicament was getting national attention as DREAMer organizations built public support in a call for prosecutorial discretion that would allow Juan Carlos to stay in the United States with his family. Confounded by his misfortune, Stuesse met with Juan Carlos and offered to help him share his story.[1] Told here in his own words with editing and limited legal background added by his coauthors for context, this chapter shares Juan Carlos's trials with US immigration enforcement leading up to and following the day of DACA's implementation, including his navigation of detention and deportation in Georgia, negotiation of reentry following an "illegal" deportation to Mexico, and the unfortunate timing that, rather than rendering him DACA-eligible, led to his life as one of *los otros Dreamers*.

It's been a nightmare I'll never forget. It all started close to midnight on Monday, June 4, 2011. I had just graduated from high school and was driving home after dinner at my girlfriend's house in Cobb County, Georgia, when my car was struck by a drunk driver. My "top ten" scholarly achievements and my blissful young relationship could do nothing to shield me from what was to come.

At the time, Cobb County was one of the country's earliest and most fervent partners in the 287(g) program, in which local sheriff's departments voluntarily agreed to collaborate with federal immigration officials in the enforcement of federal immigration laws.[2] Making this program even more dangerous for Georgia's half a million undocumented residents, we were ineligible for state driver's licenses, and the state had passed a law making driving without a license an arrestable offense.[3]

When the police arrived that night, I couldn't produce a license, so I was arrested along with the driver of the other car despite having no fault in the accident. My girlfriend and her mother came to the scene and spoke to the police officer there. "Well, it's not his fault," the officer explained to her. "He should be free to go, but because of these laws we have in Georgia, I'm supposed to take him." I spent the night in the Cobb County jail.

The next morning my family paid a bond of $400 for my release, but by then I had an "immigration hold"—my arrest had put me on the radar of federal immigration authorities—so the sheriff wouldn't let me go. Instead, I was transferred to another cell where I was held until immigration came for me on Wednesday. After spending the day in processing at the Department of Homeland Security's (DHS) Immigration and Customs Enforcement (ICE) office in Atlanta, that evening they dropped me at the Atlanta City Detention Center, more commonly referred to by its acronym, ACDC.

On Thursday my family paid a $7,500 bond for my release, but ACDC continued to hold me over the weekend. By Monday a friend of mine came and asked why I hadn't been released yet. They told him, "Oh, sorry, it was our mistake, we forgot to send the fax." So my problems with ICE began almost immediately.

Ten days after my arrest I was released and went home to my parents' house on bond. I was told a court date would be assigned in the future, and I was given a phone number to call to confirm the date. I knew it was very important to attend my court hearing, so I called regularly. Every time I was told a date had not yet been set. The new year came and went. By February I was very concerned, so I met with an attorney. She called immigration and confirmed there was no court date in the system.

Three days later, on February 24, 2012, immigration agents appeared at my doorstep. "Why didn't you attend your court hearing?" they asked. "Due to your failure to appear, the judge signed your deportation order." After a day at the Atlanta ICE office, they took me to my third jail, the Irwin County Detention Center.

Several days passed before I was able to speak with my family—for some reason their cell phones would not accept my collect calls. When we finally talked, I learned my family had hired an immigration lawyer. The lawyer explained that he had appealed the deportation order and that we would have to wait for the judge to consider the appeal and make a new judgment. In the meantime, he said, ICE was prohibited from transferring me to another facility or deporting me. I would have to wait at Irwin.

This gave me some hope, and I was relieved to know that at least for a little while longer I would be allowed to stay. But a few weeks later I was taken back to the Atlanta ICE office along with a bunch of other people, and the agents there told us we would be on a plane to Mexico the next day. We were left at ACDC to spend the night.

Panicked, I called my lawyer. He happened to be on vacation that week and was unreachable. His secretary tried to help. She called the Atlanta ICE office and was told, "According to our records he is not supposed to be deported. He's not on our list." She communicated this to me.

Meanwhile, at ACDC—which shares the same building as the Atlanta ICE office—I explained what my attorney had communicated to me, that I couldn't be deported until my appeal was heard. I told them that the ICE office had just confirmed that I was not scheduled for deportation, but the officers only replied, "Yeah, right. We checked your file and you have a final deportation order. You're leaving tomorrow." I couldn't believe it! ACDC and ICE were on two different floors *of the same building* and there was nothing I could do to get them to communicate with one another. And I was set to be on a flight to Mexico in a matter of hours.

So the next morning we were taken to the airport and put on a plane. We flew to Michigan, where we picked up more detainees. Then we flew to Texas. They loaded us into buses and drove us to the United States–Mexico border. We walked across the bridge and, just like that, I had been deported to Mexico.

The Mexican government's *Grupo Beta,* which aids migrants south of the border, offered to help. They explained, "Okay, guys, right now things are really dangerous here. The crime is so bad that there are no police officers in service. Only the army is in town. The best thing for you to do is to leave as soon as you can." And they took us to a bus terminal. That was the extent of their help.

What should I do? Where should I go? I had just left all my immediate family back in Atlanta. With a few dollars hidden in my shoe I purchased a phone card and called them. They wired me some money. To get back to my family's hometown in Michoacán, I would have to travel thirty hours by bus. But no one was left there. With whom would I stay? Instead, I opted to make the twenty-four-hour journey to Acapulco, where I had an aunt and a few cousins.

I was scared, angry, depressed. My family in Acapulco was kind and let me sleep on their couch even though I hadn't seen them in nearly eighteen years. On my second day there, I received a phone call from my lawyer in Atlanta.

He was back from vacation and shocked at the events that had taken place in his absence. He had been in touch with ICE and had news for me. "ICE made a mistake, Juan Carlos. You were illegally deported," he explained. "You shouldn't have been removed, and no one can explain to me why it happened, but they want to fix their mistake. At this point they are giving you two options. You can sign a form that will change your deportation into a voluntary departure; if you do this there will be no deportation on your record and your case will be closed. Or they will bring you back to Atlanta where you can wait to see if a judge will reopen your case. But if the judge doesn't agree to reopen, you will be deported again."

The choice was clear to me. This experience had already been far too wrenching. I would much rather accept voluntary departure than be put through the painful process anew. I told the lawyer of my decision, and he agreed to communicate it to ICE and have my case closed. But the next day, before he was able to take action, ICE called him and said, "We have decided to reopen the case." With this news, I decided to take the risk and go back.

That was around March. They told me that in order to return to the United States I would need to get a Mexican passport. I knew this would be a challenge, even more complicated since I had no documents in my name except one ID, but with the news that I might get a second chance in the United States, I was determined. So I traveled to my hometown in Michoacán to begin the process. I learned I would need my official birth certificate. Then I learned I needed both my parents' birth certificates. These were held at a different government office in Acapulco, so after a week or two of waiting I secured mine and went in search of theirs.

Acapulco was hard. Imposing on my aunt and her family was bad enough, but maneuvering in the city was even worse. People say the *narcos* on the border are bad, but in Acapulco it's on another level. It took me about a week to get my parents' birth certificates, and in the process I got robbed. My wallet was stolen, and with it, my only photo identification.

I returned to the government office in Michoacán and explained the whole thing. "I have everything you told me to get—my birth certificate, my parents' birth certificates—only now I'm missing the ID." They insisted they could not issue the passport without my photo identification. I was distraught. "I've been coming here for two weeks now, and every time I've shown you my ID. Why do you insist on seeing it again, now that it has been stolen?" They wouldn't budge.

So I sought out the offices of the Mexican election team and inquired about getting a voter registration card, which in Mexico serves as people's primary photo ID. There I was told that, because Mexico was in election season—national general elections would take place in July—they were not issuing voter registrations at that time. "You'll have to wait until August," the agent advised me. What more could I do? Did I really have no choice but to wait three months before getting a passport to return to Atlanta?

I shared all that had transpired with my lawyer. After communicating with ICE, he conveyed that they had instructed me to appear at the US embassy in Mexico City. We didn't know what was going to happen there, but I followed their instructions and took a bus to Mexico City. I showed up at the gates of the embassy and explained my case. The people there knew nothing about me, who I was, or why I was there. They refused me entry.

I spoke to my lawyer again, who inquired further and relayed, "Well, I talked to the ICE office and the embassy is supposed to give you a package with the documentation to travel back." Now here's a funny fact—the US Department of Homeland Security has an ICE officer at the embassy in Mexico City, and that office is only open on Mondays and Thursdays from 9:00 to 11:00, four hours a week. So by the time I had this additional information, the office was closed. I would have to return another day. Only the next Monday was a US holiday, so I was looking at an additional week's delay. I had nowhere to stay in the city, so I opted to travel the six hours back to Acapulco, wait a week, and return to try my luck.

The following Thursday I was back at the embassy. Again they knew nothing about my case. I said, "What's going on between all of you? Because ICE is telling me to come here to pick up something I need to travel back, and you have no idea who I am?!" The office hours ended and I embarked on another excruciating six-hour ride back to Acapulco. I was growing impatient and beginning to lose hope. The officers at the embassy probably thought I was crazy, insisting that I had been illegally deported and that ICE was sending documentation for my return to the United States!

When I showed up at the embassy for the third time, they miraculously welcomed me inside and gave me my documents to travel back. They explained that as soon as I signed the document I would have a maximum of seven days to board a flight. But upon examining the contents of the package more carefully, I noticed there was no plane ticket. They assured me that I should go to the Delta counter at the airport, where I would find a ticket waiting for me. I didn't think I could stomach much more of this roller coaster ride. Little did I know, it was only beginning.

At the airport in Mexico City, Delta confirmed that there was a reservation in my name to travel. But there was a small problem. Because I didn't have a passport, they said I needed to get a signed document from the Mexican immigration team in a different section of the airport permitting me to travel internationally. The immigration team was perplexed. "You're a Mexican. You don't need any kind of documentation to leave the country," they insisted. They sent me back to Delta. I crisscrossed the airport three times on my quest to get that piece of paper. Finally, exasperated, a Delta official accompanied me and we managed to secure the coveted immigration document.

My flight was scheduled for the morning of June 6, 2012. I left Acapulco the day before, arrived in Mexico City at 3:00 in the morning, waited through the night, and we departed for Atlanta at 10:00 am. Three hours later we landed. Still on the plane, taxiing toward the gate, I called my family to let them know I was back. I felt relief.

Reprieve quickly turned to humiliation when—before we had even arrived at the jetway—an ICE officer boarded the plane and, in front of all the passengers, escorted me down the rolling stairs and to a DHS van. The next twenty-four hours remain the most degrading day of my life.

They said they had to take my biometrics—my fingerprints, my picture, and everything—even though all this information was already in their system and they knew who I was. But their computers were down. It took at least five tries for the fingerprinting machine to finally work. Finally, around 11:00 pm, after more than twenty-four hours of travel, they took me to the Irwin County Detention Center. But I didn't sleep that night either.

They made me trade my clothes for inmate attire, and by midnight DHS came back for me. They insisted that I was required to check in with immigration officers at the airport and had bypassed this step in error, so they took me back to the airport in my orange jumpsuit. I was horrified and ashamed to appear in public like that. Like a criminal. As I imagined all the awful things people must have been thinking about me while they watched me pass by, it was the most distressing, disgraceful moment I've ever lived.

Then, to make matters even worse, when I was presented before the immigration authorities at the airport I overheard them say, "Didn't you guys know you could have done this at your office? Next time there is no need for you to come all the way here." My interactions with ICE were a story of incompetence and consternation at every single turn.

Back at Irwin, I awaited my court hearing. While I sat impatiently behind bars, my friends and thousands of other immigrant rights allies were marching on the Obama reelection campaign offices in Atlanta and across the country. "Education, Not Deportation!" they chanted, many of them cloaked in graduation caps and gowns. The president's advisors weighed how to respond to these DREAMers who demanded the "Deporter in Chief" provide them a path to legalization. Within twenty-four hours they announced Deferred Action for Childhood Arrivals (DACA), an administrative procedure that would legalize the presence of millions of undocumented young people like me who qualified for the program. My spirits lifted. I was proud of my friends and brave undocumented people everywhere, and I felt optimistic that my situation would soon improve.

I had hoped to be out on bond by now, but it was set unusually high at $40,000. My attorney requested a hearing to lower the amount. The day we walked into the hearing expecting to negotiate a more reasonable bond—and it was reduced to $20,000—to our surprise the immigration judge decided he wanted to decide my entire case that day too. He showed no mercy. My options were voluntary departure, which would allow me to get out on bond and leave the country on my own before a set date, or deportation. DACA was not yet an option, as its implementation wouldn't go into effect until August 15. So, with the help of a bond company, I opted for voluntary departure, put up $8,000, and was released. My final due date for leaving the country was set for August 13.

My friend Celia immediately involved me in Georgia DreamActivist. That organization had recently found success getting people's removal canceled by putting public pressure on ICE to live up to its 2011 "Morton Memo," which claimed it would focus its resources on deporting individuals with serious criminal backgrounds. In cases like mine, in which respectable members of the community with clear ties to the United States and no criminal convictions made public calls for leniency, ICE had been exercising prosecutorial discretion and allowing people to stay. It was my last, best hope.

I went to Washington, DC, and I told my story to every politician and news outlet that would listen. When I returned to Georgia, we held meetings all over Atlanta educating people and asking for their help. A public petition was created to raise awareness and implore ICE to use discretion in my case. My entire family was in Atlanta, including my twin brother, my younger US-citizen siblings, and my parents. Like many of my friends, I had dreams of attending college and making a difference in my community. I asked my attorney to file another appeal in my case that would allow me to stay until DACA's effective date. Perhaps then there would be some way for me to qualify and we could put this nightmare behind us. I didn't give up until my clock ran out.

But on August 13, 2012, two days before DACA took effect, my time was up. I had exhausted all options. I bade my family and friends farewell and returned to Mexico.

I used to believe in justice. Now, I'm not so sure it exists.

I have lived four long and difficult years since that day. I lament not being present for my younger siblings as they grow older. My grandmother's diabetes resulted in an amputation, and I was unable to be there to care for her. I also regret the tragic end of a genuine relationship with my girlfriend and her family. Like Ezequiel (see Silver, this volume) and Sergio (see Gonzalez, this volume) I have often felt lonely as I've worked to reestablish ties with family in Mexico and build new friendships while struggling to maintain ever-weakening relationships with my loved ones in the United States.

I moved to Iguala, Guerrero, and I enrolled in college. Not long after, forty-three students disappeared in Iguala at the hands of local politicians in what has become known as the Ayotzinapa massacre. People and businesses left in fear. The local economy tanked. Walking alone at night became impossible, and when I traveled beyond the area I felt stigmatized. It was a terrible time.

But things are getting better. I found liberation in poetry, culinary arts, and martial arts. I got a puppy. And I am graduating from college next week with a degree in business administration. As in Georgia, I became one of the top students in my class, receiving high marks and tutoring others along the way. I have collaborated with local government officials to help bring tourism back to Iguala. I am now planning my next moves for my career, my health, and my future. My greatest hope is that one day I will see my family again.

Yes, it's been a nightmare I'll never forget. The story of how I became one of *los otros Dreamers* is so fantastical it's hard to believe it happened. But it did.

It's true what they say. Life is full of highs and lows. But I have persevered. Today I feel there's no obstacle I cannot overcome. And in time, I have no doubt, I will thrive.

Notes

1. Stuesse was accompanied during this visit by research assistant Nolan Kline, who participated in the joint interview with Juan Carlos.
2. (Shahshahani 2009, Coleman and Stuesse 2014, 2016). For more in this volume on 287(g) and the collaboration between local and federal law enforcement agencies in immigrant policing, see the chapters by Garcia, Kline, and Silver.
3. (Stuesse and Coleman 2014).

References

Coleman, Mathew, and Angela Stuesse. 2014. "Policing Borders, Policing Bodies: The Territorial and Biopolitical Roots of U.S. Immigration Control." In *Placing the Border in Everyday Life*, ed. R. Jones and C. Johnson, Farnham: Ashgate, 33–63.

Coleman, Mathew, and Angela Stuesse. 2016. "The Disappearing State and the Quasi-Event of Immigration Control." *Antipode* 48 (3): 524–43.

Shahshahani, Azadeh. 2009. *Terror and Isolation in Cobb: How Unchecked Police Power Under 287(g) Has Torn Families Apart and Threatened Public Safety*. Atlanta: American Civil Liberties Union. http://www.aclu.org/files/intlhumanrights/immigrantsrights/asset_upload_file306_41281.pdf, accessed July 29, 2013.

18

No Place Like Home:

From High School Graduation to Deportation

Alexis M. Silver

Alexis M. Silver is an assistant professor in the sociology department and Latin American studies program at Purchase College, State University of New York (SUNY–Purchase). Her research focuses on immigration and youth, new immigrant destinations, 1.5-generation return migration and deportation, and transnational families.

The first two decades of the 2000s saw a marked increase in local and state level immigration enforcement in the United States, with a disproportionate number of anti-immigrant ordinances and policies implemented in states with conservative governments and new immigrant destinations (Olivas 2007; Ramakrishnan and Wong 2010; Varsanyi 2010; Varsanyi et al. 2012). The US South emerged as a primary new immigrant destination in the 1990s, where the population of Latinos increased by over 300 percent between 1990 and 2000 (Kochhar, Suro, and Tafoya 2005). Because many of the recent Latino immigrants to the South lacked immigration authorization, they were both conspicuous and susceptible to targeted immigration enforcement efforts. In addition to placing unauthorized immigrants at heightened risk of deportation, anti-immigrant policies also isolated and criminalized immigrant populations (Dreby 2015; Flores 2014; Golash-Boza 2014 and 2015; Kanstroom 2007). Indeed, increased enforcement led to dramatic rises in deportations in the early 2000s, peaking with a record 438,421 deportations in 2013 (Gonzalez-Barrera and Krogstad 2014). Because immigration enforcement efforts tend to rely, in part, on racial profiling, Latinos were particularly vulnerable to deportation (Golash-Boza and Hondagnue Sotelo 2013; Golash-Boza 2015; Weissman, Headen, and Parker 2009).

Scholars have argued that the ever-present threat of deportation in the United States creates a climate of "legal violence," wherein migrants are marginalized and criminalized (Menjívar and Abrego 2012). Though analyses of the threat of deportation tend to center on migrants' experiences in host countries, the hostility of "legal violence" can extend beyond national boundaries. Despite returning to their countries of citizenship, deportees often find that they cannot escape the stigma of criminalizing narratives surrounding illegality (Anderson, this volume; Coutin 2007).

Indeed, deportation records can continue to marginalize deportees and impede their opportunities in their countries of birth.

For foreign-born young adults who grew up in the United States, deportation marks a violent separation from the only adolescent and adult life that they have ever known. As deportation often coincides with separation from family, the pain of isolation upon return to origin countries can feel even more acute than the anxiety of exclusion in the United States. Although young adult immigrants can struggle to adapt to their illegality and exclusion as they enter into adulthood in the United States (Gonzalez 2011; Silver 2012), they also often lack the linguistic, cultural, and social capital to successfully adapt to their countries of origin. Moreover, the trauma of deportation, coupled with weak infrastructures to reintegrate deportees back into origin countries, may further limit their ability to thrive in their countries of birth (Hagan, Rodriguez, and Castro 2011). Thus, even as young deportees can use their English language skills to obtain work and steady income, they continue to lack social membership in their countries of origin in spite of their citizenship status.

This chapter tells the story of one young man, Ezequiel,[1] who was deported twice from Charlotte, North Carolina, once in 2007 and again in 2010. I interviewed him in 2015 in Mexico City while conducting (ongoing) research about migrants who had grown up in the United States and since returned to Mexico, either as a result of their own or their parents' deportations, or by choice. His story reflects themes of isolation, loss, powerlessness, and social stigma that were echoed by many of the respondents that I interviewed, regardless of the circumstances of their return migrations.

Although youth in new immigrant destination states were aware of the anti-immigrant policies implemented during the first decades of the 2000s, many felt comfortable in their surroundings, at least while enrolled in high school (Silver 2015). They were institutionally and socially integrated in their communities, and yet, outside of the protective walls of high school, they were increasingly vulnerable to surveillance and deportation. Indeed, Latinos in North Carolina were disproportionately targeted in traffic stops, which ultimately made them vulnerable to deportation due to the 287(g) program (Weissman, Headen, and Parker 2009). This program authorized the US Immigration and Customs and Enforcement (ICE) to train local police officers to enforce immigration laws (US Immigration and Customs Enforcement 2011). North Carolina rapidly emerged as a national leader in establishing memorandums of agreement allowing police in various counties throughout the state to begin deportation proceedings.

North Carolina's focus on immigration enforcement was, in part, a response to the rapid rate of growth of the Latino population in the state. According to US Census estimates, North Carolina experienced the fastest rate of Latino population growth in the country between 1990 and 2000, with nearly a 400 percent increase. Growth continued into the next decade, though at a considerably slower rate (111 percent). As of 2011, roughly half of the state's Hispanic residents, like Ezequiel, were born outside of the United States. These quick-changing demographics were met with a social and legislative backlash as long-term residents of North Carolina struggled to adapt to their new neighbors (Marrow 2011; Silver 2012).

Ezequiel had come with his parents from Mexico to North Carolina in 2000 when he was eleven years old. Although Ezequiel was conscious of growing anti-immigrant sentiment in the state of North Carolina, he had never felt personally threatened prior to the day he was pulled over after school. His encounter with the police that day in June 2006 started the long process of his removal. Additionally, that afternoon marked the beginning of a new sense of powerlessness that would come to dictate his future.

Ezequiel was still a teenager in 2006, and he had no idea of the magnitude of his mistake when he accidentally ran a red light turning onto Main Avenue in Charlotte. He pulled over when he saw the flashing lights in his rearview mirror. With no license to show the police officer, Ezequiel offered him his high school ID card. When the officer informed him that he would have to take him to the police station, he went along willingly. Nine years later, when recalling the incident, he told me that he was completely unaware that the police department was integrated with ICE, and he had no idea he would be processed for deportation. Mecklenburg County had joined the 287(g) program only four months prior, so it was unsurprising that he did not expect the traffic violation to result in deportation.

Ezequiel blamed himself for his deportation, pointing to his lack of knowledge as the catalyst in "destroy[ing]" his life. In contrast, he placed very little blame on the officer who processed him, even as he recounted threats made toward his mother. He described how he negotiated the terms of his deportation, saying,

> I honestly begged and begged him . . ., "just let me finish high school". . . And he was actually very cool. He said, "You know what, I'm going to give you six months . . . after that date I don't want to see you here. If I go and look for you at your mom's house, because I know where you guys live at, you and your mom is going to be gone. . . . I really don't want to get you into a worse situation." Meaning, get my mom out also. . . . But I mean he was actually cool about it, and he let me go that same day.

Ezequiel felt relieved that he was given a grace period to finish high school and say goodbye. Not wanting to jeopardize the safety of his mother, he made no attempt to evade the authorities. Six months later, on December 24, 2006, Christmas Eve, he turned himself in.

Before returning to Mexico, he spent "about three weeks" in a detention facility in Atlanta that he described as "really, really bad." He was afraid of the other detainees, who yelled and made violent threats toward one another, he was uneasy around the guards who seemed indifferent, and he was distressed about his deportation. From Atlanta, he flew to Texas, and from Texas, he was bused to Mexico. He joked that the one opportunity he had to ride in an airplane was the day he got deported. And though he used humor to cope, he remembered well how that flight began the most frightening day of his life.

He recalled feeling panicked when the bus from Texas crossed the border and dropped off the deportees in Matamoros. Terrified that he would get "robbed," "kidnapped," "killed," or "picked up" only to be murdered and have his body "discovered" elsewhere days later, Ezequiel focused on finding his way from Matamoros to Mexico City without delay. Lacking money and an official ID, however, he could not pay for bus fare. Fortunately, his mother could wire money to another deportee who had an ID, and could therefore receive the wire transfer. Offering his helper half of the money, Ezequiel bought a ticket to Mexico City and traveled to an unfinished house that his mother owned in the poor outskirts of the city.

Ezequiel was in a state of shock. He had very little money to buy food and no idea how to search for a job. He saw people shining shoes, and figured he would do that until he found something better. After approximately one month, Ezequiel met a cousin who told Ezequiel that he could make better money working in a call center using English. Soon after, Ezequiel applied to work at TeleTech, a customer-service call center that partnered with Bank of America and T-Mobile among many other US companies. In spite of his improved circumstances, Ezequiel continued to feel out of place in Mexico.

He described the first months after his deportation as almost unbearable, saying, "I only lasted eight months. I couldn't do more." He had saved up about $3,000 to pay for his trip back to the United States, and although he managed to cross over, his journey was harrowing. He explained,

> I had to try three times. The first time I tried I couldn't make it 'cause the *coyote* left us. He left us in the desert, just like that. . . . I didn't move from where I was. I stayed in the road and just waited for immigration to come by, which took about 15 hours. . . . And then I tried a second time. I did it with a cousin . . . and we actually got to the border. We walked for about three days . . . We got caught in the process, so we had to come back again. Then on the third time, he didn't want to try again. . . . So, by myself, I made it. It took me another two weeks of walking.

Being abandoned in the desert and walking for weeks traumatized Ezequiel. He tried to put the experience out of his mind and focus on being together with his family, but the reunion was short-lived. A year and half later, Ezequiel got pulled over again, on the same busy avenue.

DEPORTED AGAIN

Ezequiel's second encounter with the police began before he entered the car, when he was walking down the stairs from a department store. He spotted the police car in the parking lot and was immediately aware of his "baggy jeans and baggy clothes." Although Ezequiel felt anxious that he was "looking bad," he knew his friend, who was driving, had a license. He did not know, however, that his friend did not have car insurance or a registration sticker. Conjuring a sense of déjà vu, he described how the police car followed them back to Main Avenue where he had gotten pulled over in 2006, saying, "That's street's just bad luck for me!" He described what followed, saying,

> I'm sitting in the seat behind the driver, and there shouldn't be a reason for the cop to ask me for something. So, he asks the driver for his license, and he gives it to him, and I came to find out that he was owing some tickets so they took him in. Then the cop comes to me, and asks me for an ID. So for the second time I didn't have a wallet. Same drill . . . as soon as he told me they were taking me, I already knew that I wasn't going to come out. Because as soon as my fingerprints are going . . . into the system . . . it was going to show that I had already been deported. And I knew they weren't going to give me another chance. So the same thing happened. I got deported.

Ezequiel was not driving, nor did he own the car. The young men, who were all Latino, had no drugs or alcohol in the car, nor were they intoxicated. None of this stopped the police officer from asking Ezequiel for his identification. Ezequiel felt that their clothes, their ethnicity, or perhaps a combination of the two had prompted the police officer to run the license plates of the car. Now classified as a repeat violator of US immigration law, he was deported again in January of 2010. Not wanting to risk the journey back after his last experience, he decided to accept his fate. He was better prepared this time, but he continued to struggle as he searched for a sense of home away from his family and the country he knew best.

UNWELCOME AT HOME

Even after five years in Mexico, Ezequiel noticed stares and whispers. He knows he stands out. He chalked this up to his American upbringing, and he aligned himself with other deportees and return migrants as he described the social isolation that he felt. Transitioning seamlessly from first person singular to first person plural while talking about himself and others like him, he explained,

> I'm different. . . . I wear different clothes. We carry ourselves very differently. One day I was on the metro when I was coming out of work with my coworkers, and we're loud, very loud. As immigrants, people that grew up over there, we're different. We have this freedom of speech, that we just say what is on our minds. We don't hold it back and people here, they have a problem with that. . . . So they hear you talking English, and like one friend told me, "What if I feel more comfortable communicating with you in English? There's nothing wrong with that. It's not a problem." But other people don't understand. . . . They just give you that look.

Tattooed, loud, and almost always wearing a baseball cap angled to the side, Ezequiel regularly feels judged as a nuisance or a criminal. He attributed this reaction to his perceived American traits, even calling upon patriotic language like "freedom of speech" to explain his behavior. Ezequiel had a difficult time blending into his surroundings, but he had no desire to give up his style or mannerisms to assimilate.

While the social stigma he faced on a daily basis was stressful, Ezekiel was more angered by perceived discrimination from people in positions of authority. Even though he was legally a Mexican citizen, Ezequiel lacked the necessary documents to apply to college. Having lost his birth certificate, he struggled to get the necessary paperwork to prove his identity and obtain his school records. He explained, incredulously, how an agent in a government office once tried to bribe him after hearing him speak English. The agent helping him had been cooperative until he heard Ezequiel on the phone. Ezequiel thus attributed his change of heart to the agent's assumption that Ezequiel had money, because, as he explained, "You either went to school to learn English, or you learned it in the United States." He continued,

> People just think you don't know. . . . I asked, "How much is it [to get my birth certificate], 200 pesos? 300 pesos?" And he said, "No, that's not enough." So I asked him, "How much do you want?" And he said, "$2,000." But he told me with a smile, "A couple thousand."

Ezequiel recalled the incident with frustration, as he felt that exploitation was preventing him from reaching his full potential. Nonetheless, he was satisfied with his job at a call center. In many ways, he had overcome the acute pain of deportation, even as he struggled to find a sense of membership in his country of origin. Still, he continued to lament the separation from his family.

EXILED FROM FAMILY

Ezequiel kept in touch with his mother and brother who remained in the United States, but he was quick to point out that the relationship suffered under the stress of separation. He explained how he thought he might never get over the trauma of being forced to live apart from his family, saying,

> It's not going to heal. For me at least it hasn't healed. I understand everything that has happened, and I want to think that there's a reason for it, but growing up away from my mom and my brother, and we were super-close, and now we're [motions with his hands] *far* apart. That's what I really regret. Because I'm not going to have a second chance, or a second mom, or a second brother. So talking to them on the phone, texting them, it's not the same. They're home. And I just miss even like her calling me out and telling me I didn't do my laundry last night. I even miss that.

Ezequiel could not adjust to life without his family. Moreover, when he heard that his brother was cutting class and smoking marijuana, he blamed his own absence. Had he not been deported, he felt like he could have been there as a "father figure" and steered him in a better direction.

As vividly as he felt the pain of family separation, Ezequiel knew his experiences were not unique. He linked his own suffering to the widespread suffering of other deportees, saying, "I just try to not think about it, because it's such a tough situation, not just for me, but for all of us. And especially for all of us . . . that haven't done anything wrong." Cognizant of the collective losses of other deportees and their families, Ezequiel related his own story to theirs. Dreaming that North Carolina would one day recognize the repercussions of its hostile strategies, he wished out loud, "I have hopes that they say, 'You know what? We do apologize for the ones that were deported for no reason,' which I don't think is going to happen, but I still have my hopes. I just think they don't know what they have done. . . . They've deported a lot of people, and they've hurt a lot of people." Although Ezequiel blamed his own carelessness for his deportation earlier, he also blamed the government for hurting thousands of individuals and families who, in his eyes, had done nothing wrong.

Ezequiel knew that his life would never be the same after his second deportation. Although he had not been involved in any criminal activity, Ezequiel found himself entangled in the machinery of immigration enforcement. Much to his dismay, the suspicion that he faced in the United States continued to haunt him in Mexico. And while the consequences of social stigma in Mexico were not as grave as the legal consequences he faced in the United States, he nonetheless felt criminalized in both countries. As a deportee living in Mexico, he retained a sense of "liminality," or "in-betweenness" (Menjívar 2006; Cebulko 2013, 2014), and he could not find a full sense of belonging.

Ezequiel's story poignantly illustrates the extreme inequality of power between the state and the individual under a "deportation regime" (De Genova, 2010). Ezequiel felt powerless to dictate his own movements or maintain control over his own family arrangements. Even in Mexico, Ezequiel continued to feel imprisoned by his illegality. Though Ezequiel believed that the immigration enforcement tactics that led to his deportations were unjust, he also blamed himself for not knowing more about immigration laws. Like the deportees described in Anderson's chapter, Ezequiel had adopted the neoliberal ideal of personal responsibility, and he felt compelled to accept his life circumstances as a result of his own actions. Though Ezequiel had experienced tremendous hardship, he tried not to dwell on his losses. He knew that his story was one among thousands. And while the ability to connect his own losses to the losses of other deportees gave him a sense of community, he knew that membership in a community of migrants and deportees was membership in a community intimately marked by exclusion from two nations.

Note

1. To protect respondents, all names, including street names, have been changed.

References

Cebulko, Kara B. 2013. *Documented, Undocumented, and Something Else: The Incorporation of Children of Brazilian Immigrants.* El Paso: LFB Scholarly Publishing LLC.

Cebulko, Kara. B. 2014. "Documented, Undocumented, and Liminally Legal: Legal Status During the Transition to Adulthood for 1.5-Generation Brazilian Immigrants." *Sociological Quarterly* 55 (1): 143–67.

Coutin, Susan Bibler. 2007. *Nations of Emigrants: Shifting Boundaries of Citizenship in El Salvador and the United States.* Ithaca, NY: Cornell University Press.

De Genova, Nicholas. 2010. "The Deportation Regime: Sovereignty, Space, and the Freedom of Movement." In *The Deportation Regime: Sovereignty, Space, and the Freedom of Movement*, ed. Nicholas De Genova and Nathalie M. Peutz, 33–68. Durham, NC: Duke University Press.

Dreby, Joanna. 2015. *Everyday Illegal: When Policies Undermine Immigrant Families.* Oakland: University of California Press.

Flores, René D. 2014. "In the Eye of the Storm: How Did Hazleton's Restrictive Immigration Ordinance Affect Local Interethnic Relations?" *American Behavioral Scientist* 58 (13): 1743–63.

Golash-Boza, Tanya and Pierrette Hondagneu-Sotelo. 2013. "Latino Immigrant Men and the Deportation Crisis: A Gendered Racial Removal Program." *Latino Studies* 11 (3): 271–92.

Golash-Boza, Tanya. 2015. *Deported: Immigrant Policing, Disposable Labor, and Global Capitalism.* New York: New York University Press.

Gonzales, Roberto. 2011. "Learning to Be Illegal: Undocumented Youth and Shifting Legal Contexts in the Transition to Adulthood." *American Sociological Review* 76 (4): 602–19.

Gonzalez-Barrera, Ana and Jens M. Krogstad. 2014. "U.S. Deportations of Immigrants Reach Record High in 2013." Pew Research Center, October 2. Retrieved March 7, 2016 at http://pewrsr.ch/Zx2c6E

Hagan, Jacqueline M., Nestor Rodriguez, and Brianna Castro. 2011. "Social Effects of Mass Deportations by the United States Government, 2000–10." *Ethnic and Racial Studies* 34 (8): 1374–91

Kanstroom, Daniel. 2007. *Deportation Nation: Outsiders in American History.* Cambridge, MA: Harvard University Press.

Kochhar R., Robert Suro, and Sonya Tafoya. 2005. "The New Latino South: The Context and Consequence of Rapid Population Growth." Paper presented at the *Immigration to New Settlement Areas Conference.* Washington, DC: Pew Hispanic Research Center, July 26. http://www.pewhispanic.org/2005/07/26/the-new-latino-south/

Marrow, Helen B. 2011. *New Destination Dreaming: Immigration, Race, and Legal Status in the Rural American South.* Stanford, CA: Stanford University Press.

Menjívar, Cecilia. 2006. "Liminal Legality: Salvadoran and Guatemalan Immigrants' Lives in the United States." *American Journal of Sociology* 111 (4): 999–1037.

Menjívar, Cecilia and Leisy J. Abrego. 2012. "Legal Violence: Immigration Law and the Lives of Central American Immigrants." *American Journal of Sociology* 117 (5): 1380–421.

Olivas, Michael A. 2007. "Immigration-Related State and Local Ordinances: Preemption, Prejudice, and the Proper Role for Enforcement." *University of Chicago Legal Forum,* 2007-A-52, 27–56. Retrieved on March 7, 2016. Online at http://papers.ssrn.com/sol3/papers.cfm?abstract_id=1069121

Ramakrishnan, S. Karthick and Tom Wong. 2010. "Partisanship, Not Spanish: Explaining Municipal Ordinances Affecting Undocumented Immigrants." In *Taking Local Control: Immigration Policy Activism in U.S. Cities and States,* ed. Monica W. Varsanyi, 73–96. Stanford, CA: Stanford University Press.

Silver, Alexis. 2012. "Aging into Exclusion and Social Transparency: Undocumented Immigrant Youth and the Transition to Adulthood." *Latino Studies* 10 (4): 499–522.

Silver, Alexis M. 2015. "Clubs of Culture and Capital: Immigrant and Second-Generation Incorporation in a New Destination School." *Ethnic and Racial Studies* 38 (5): 824.

US Immigration and Customs Enforcement. "Delegation of Immigration Authority Section 287(g) Immigration and Nationality Act Fact Sheet." Retrieved on March 7, 2016. https://www.ice.gov/factsheets/287g#wcm-survey-target-id

Varsanyi, Monica W. 2010. *Taking Local Control: Immigration Policy Activism in U.S. Cities and States.* Stanford, CA: Stanford University Press.

Varsanyi, Monica W., Paul G. Lewis, Doris M. Provine, and Scott Decker. 2012. "A Multilayered Jurisdictional Patchwork: Immigration Federalism in the United States." *Law & Policy* 34 (2): 138–58.

Weissman, Deborah., Rebecca C. Headen and Katherine L. Parker. 2009. *The Policies and Politics of Local Immigration Enforcement Laws: 287(g) Program in North Carolina.* Immigration and Human Rights Policy Clinic, University of North Carolina at Chapel Hill. Retrieved on March 7, 2016 from www.acluofnorthcarolina.org/files/287gpolicyreview_0.pdf

19

Call Centers, Transnational Mobility, and (Neoliberal) Citizenship

Jill Anderson

As a bi-national interdisciplinary scholar based in Mexico City, Jill Anderson is the director of Otros Dreams en Acción *(ODA). She is the co-author of the book* Los Otros Dreamers *(2014), and author of articles about transnationalism, bi-national youth, and post-deportation/return migration in Mexico.*

One day in 2012, a homeless man overheard Peter speaking English at a car dealership where he was making 1,000 pesos a month.[1] The man called Peter over and said, "Hey, come here. You speak English. Go to TeleTech in León and tell them you want to work for Dish Satellite." Although he thought the tip sounded like a possible setup, Peter decided to find out more. When he visited the call center, the response took him by surprise: "You're hired. You start tomorrow." They were looking for English-language fluency and Peter was a perfect match because he had grown up in the United States. In fact, at the time, he spoke little Spanish. Peter's brother, Luis, started working at the call center about three months later.

Both recall this event as the moment "when everything changed." In 2011, Luis had been detained in their Denver, Colorado, home and deported.[2] Peter, also undocumented, decided to join him in Mexico a few months later. Upon finding jobs at the call center, their outlook and opportunities shifted. TeleTech paid them about 42 pesos an hour, a rate equivalent to that of nurses and teachers in the area. They were able to purchase a small home on the outskirts of León, where they still live. For the first time, they met other people living in Mexico who had grown up in the United States. According to Peter's calculations, about 95 percent of his fellow workers had returned or been deported from the United States. To this day, they are grateful for the call center's presence in their state. The brothers proudly told me about a plaque inside of TeleTech that commemorates the presence of the former president of Mexico and champion of the North American Free Trade Agreement, Vicente Fox, at the company's inauguration.

Between 2000 and 2010, call centers based in Mexico and dedicated to foreign markets grew from 8,631 to 18,701 locations—a 116 percent increase (Thirión 2012, 163). Due to the deregulation of long distance telephone services as part of economic restructuring in Mexico during the 1980s and 1990s and technological advances that allow for increased telephone-computer integration, outsourced call centers have grown exponentially (Arteaga García 2005; Thirión 2012). According to an international survey of 2,500 call centers in seventeen countries, the geography of transnational call centers closely follows "cultural ties and postcolonial relationships" between nations (Batt, Holman, and Holtgrewe 2007, 21). Whereas India's well-known outsourced call center industry is a consequence of the British occupation of India, the current growth of English-language call centers in Latin America is directly related to US military and economic interventions that have also led to mass migration.

In the ten-year span in which the number of outsourced call centers ballooned across Mexico, removals by the US Department of Homeland Security increased by 105.5 percent, from 188,476 in 2000 to 387,242, in 2010. Mexican nationals accounted for more than seven of every ten removals in 2010 (Elmi and McCabe 2011).[3] As the number of deportations increased, so did the number of entire families returning to Mexico alongside a deported family member, including US citizen children (Gonzalez-Barrera 2015). The number of undocumented young people returning to Mexico (semi-)voluntarily has also increased in the face of entrenched obstacles and the increasing threat of deportation (Gandini, Lozano-Ascencio and Gaspar Olvera 2015; Anderson 2015). The expansion of the call centers is not a coincidence. The industry actively pursues employees who offer their customers "native" cultural and linguistic cues while their location in Mexico means they can pay workers substantially less than the US minimum wage.

In Mexico, El Salvador, Guatemala, Honduras, and the Dominican Republic (to name a few key countries), the deportation system benefits the global call center industry at extraordinary financial, social, and personal cost to its employees (Brotherton and Barrios 2011; Coutin 2007; Golash-Boza 2014; Golash-Boza 2006; Hernandez and Coutin 2006). In this essay, I share the personal stories of Peter, Luis, Sybil, and Chris. They are each Mexican-born, US-raised young adults who experienced deportation in their early twenties and are now working in call centers in León, Nogales, and Mexico City. Based on their ways of mapping survival and making sense of life after deportation, I suggest that current economic, political, and social control policies in the United States and Mexico criminalize immigrants and offer them the limited terms of neoliberal citizenship in return.

Neoliberalism refers to twentieth-century innovations on nineteenth-century political and economic ideals of free trade—innovations that include privatization, deregulation, free trade agreements and austerity budget measures in order to increase the role of transnational private enterprise in national economies.[4] Emerging ideas around neoliberal citizenship explore ways that neoliberalism influences the participation of individuals in democratic societies. As many scholars have observed in diverse contexts around the globe, the actions, agency, and rights of neoliberal citizens increasingly supersede the national political economies upon which our historical concepts of citizenship are based (Arteaga García 2005; Coutin 2007; McNevin 2007; Sassen 2008; Ong 2005).

Furthermore, deportation and transnational call centers are both aspects of the "neoliberal cycle" that Tanya Golash-Boza (2015) delineates in her book *Deported: Immigrant Policing, Disposable Labor, and Global Capitalism*. The neoliberal cycle regulates the movement of people, capital, and products via "privatization, global inequality and outsourcing, low-wage work, cutbacks in social services, and enhanced enforcement" within and across national borders (2015, 3).[5] The threat of deportation maintains a shadow economy where wages are suppressed and work conditions are not regulated. This is as true in the United States as it is in other countries with expansive deportation regimes like Mexico and the Dominican Republic. However, young people who experience deportation or make the decision to leave behind the threat of deportation, find themselves caught in the cycle in their countries of origin upon return. Transnational call centers are proving to be yet another temporary stop along the vicious circle of displacement from local systems of employment, education, and culture that began with the parents of today's immigrant youth.

Peter, Luis, Sybil, and Chris have been directly affected by the racially-organized economic disparities of the neoliberal cycle at many key points in their lives, and are now working in call centers that serve US populations (English- and Spanish-speaking) from locations across Mexico. Together, their stories bear witness to the turbulent mix of opportunity and desperation that characterizes the neoliberal deportation to call center pipeline.

Sybil is a supervisor at a call center that employs about 260 people on the border of the Mexican state of Sonora and Arizona. Like Peter and Luis, she estimates that about 90 percent of her fellow employees lived in the United States for a significant period of time. As a leader of the team that takes the customer service calls for a local newspaper in the United States, she describes calls from newspaper subscribers who are "angry and irate about newspapers not arriving on time." While the job pays a decent wage compared to other opportunities in Nogales, Sybil noted with a combination of disappointment and clarity: "My vocation is in the medical field."

Before her deportation in 2013, she worked as an in-home caregiver in Nogales, Arizona. She earned a caregiver's certificate and a nursing assistant degree, although she could not complete the certification process due to her undocumented status. In 2009, Sybil was pulled over by local police for speeding and was immediately detained. After two weeks in an ICE detention center, Sybil insisted on speaking to an immigration judge and was released to "fight her case." She spent four years arguing for her right to stay in the United States, but in 2013 her appeal was denied. Having grown up in Arizona since she was three years old, she observes that those "twenty years did not count for much." Her two US-citizen children, adolescents at the time, stayed behind with family members. Sybil laments that her deportation has been much harder on them. They were forced to change schools, move to more precarious living situations, and see her only on the occasional weekends when someone could accompany them across the international border for a visit.

Sybil currently oversees forty-two agents whose "lives have been rough. They tend to act up." In order to keep their jobs, the agents must arrive on time, adhere to strict quality control guidelines, work long hours with regulated breaks, and offer impeccable service when faced with irate, impatient, or abusive customers. In over four years of interviews and fieldwork, I have heard the call center environment compared to high school by many, and to prison by others. Reflecting on the tension in the atmosphere inside the call center, Sybil describes moments where she wondered to herself, "What if everyone gets into a big brawl?"

Even if they meet all of the expectations for good behavior, the job is inherently precarious. When the call center's agreement with a client company ends, the call center suddenly fires the employees "for little things." Since there is no alternative that pays an equivalent wage, many struggle after being abruptly dismissed. They become desperate, looking for ways to cross the border back to their families, returning to self-destructive alcohol and drug habits, or finding financial income via underground markets connected to organized crime.

The call center where Sybil works pays a new "agent" about 4,400 pesos a month. In contrast, when she first arrived in Sonora, Sybil worked as a dental assistant for 1,000 pesos each month. As a supervisor, Sybil now earns a salary that is significantly higher than almost any other legal employment opportunities in Nogales. Similar to Golash-Boza's findings in her research with Guatemalan deportees, "the integration process of deportees is highly skewed by the presence of call centers" (2016, 14). Employment in the fields in which these young people may have considerable skills (construction, business administration, or in the case of Sybil, medical care), pays considerably less and/or depends upon requirements that returning and deported youth cannot meet: previous experience in Mexico, networking, and a Mexican-based education and/or the complicated revalidation of a US-based education.

Transnational call centers throughout Mexico actively recruit English-speaking deportees and facilitate their employment in ways that other industries and institutions do not. Unlike many businesses and organizations, outsourcing call centers in Mexico typically do not demand the complicated revalidation of US education documents by the Mexican Department of Education, accept employees with tattoos, and waive the otherwise debilitating lack of experience and contacts in Mexico.

While there are many theories we can use to understand the causes and consequences of mass emigration, the "escape valve" theory posits that governments and elites in countries of origin have "exported" their citizens who would otherwise demand access to land, employment, and education. Thus, the government escapes the domestic consequences of privatization and neoliberal reforms that have proven to increase national wealth disparity as well as human rights violations. In Mexico, the call centers suggest a new circularity to this "escape valve" where deportees are tracked into the transnational economy of the call centers with such efficiency that it limits their integration into local and national communities and allows the Mexican government to continue to evade its responsibilities for the safe and stable integration of its returning citizens.

The call center is a frustrating place to work, and Sybil hopes to save enough to go back to school in Mexico. Because nursing and caregiving do not promise a living wage in Nogales, Sonora, she is considering business administration or real estate, shifting her employment interests from one based on her sense of vocation in public health to one based on the ability to more effectively participate in the private sector. She remembers how for the first several months she "didn't eat" and battled depression, but now she is doing better. Her US-citizen kids, however, still call from Nogales, Arizona, to say things like, "Mom, we need you over here, we want you over here, just cross, just jump the border, or something."

While Sybil was deported due to a minor traffic violation, Luis was deported in 2011 after having been arrested for illegal distribution of a pharmaceutical drug. A few weeks later, Peter, who had little recollection of Mexico despite having been born there, followed his younger brother to Guanajuato. Peter was also unable to regularize his immigration status in the United States. He had been an active member of the Junior ROTC in high school and had only recently stopped studying at a local college due to the high costs of paying out-of-state tuition as an undocumented student. He made his decision to return in solidarity with his brother, but also with the recognition that his undocumented status was limiting his options. If he had stayed, Peter would have likely qualified for DACA in 2012.

After about a year and half working at TeleTech in León, the brothers decided to leave the company. Over an abundant meal at the Sirloin Stockade buffet, they talked about their place in the global supply chain, observing how TeleTech and other call centers are making a profit on outsourced labor in Mexico, while offering opportunity where there are few better options. The initial pay was quite satisfactory, but as the brothers moved up in the company they became disillusioned. Peter remembers, "Since I was a Loyalty Agent, the ones that actually retain the customers, we were getting underpaid severely . . . compared to US workers. I got a .10 peso raise. It was like a slap in the face." Both remember excruciating calls where they were not allowed to hang up (if the call agent hangs up on the customer for any reason, it is grounds for dismissal). When the company refused to give them time off or adjust their hours so that they could care for their ailing grandmother, they quit.

However, a few years later, in early 2016, both have found better positions at other call centers. This is typical worldwide within the call center industry. Companies like TeleTech that provide a variety of clients with their customer service needs (such as Dish Satellite, Time Warner Cable, and the US Embassy) are often more surveillance-oriented, pay their agents less money, give them less autonomy and authority, and cut costs whenever possible. Companies that hire agents for in-house customer service generally pay their agents higher wages, give them more autonomy and protections on the calls, and provide more stable and humane work environments.

Luis feels particularly satisfied that his current position combines his knowledge about construction that he learned "on the job" in Colorado with the customer service expertise he gained from working at TeleTech. In addition, he has direct communication with the owner and other employees of the company, works from home, and is paid about $7 USD an hour. He says, "I honestly have respect and authority here. If they are disrespecting me, I don't have to take that abuse." Luis found the job by answering a Craigslist ad, a platform that many small business owners are using to connect directly with deportees and returning people in Mexico.

Peter has also found a working environment that is more promising. He works for a US-based company that offers low-interest micro-loans to Spanish-speaking and English-speaking individuals in the United States. In addition to the better work conditions and slightly higher wages, he is hoping to be promoted to manager "because they have the ability to go back and forth to the United States. Once you get to be a manager, they get their trips paid for by the company." Understandably rejecting the low wages and poor working conditions of local jobs in Mexico, Peter has found work with a US-based loan company that has outsourced their customer service to Mexico. The remote possibility of legal, international mobility is one of the principal incentives to go to the office every day.

In addition to economic stability, family reunification and the ability to visit the United States legally are top priorities for returning and deported young people in Mexico. Peter's hopes are not unfounded. Moving up in the call center employment hierarchy has been a positive factor for some. By "proving" to a US embassy officer that they have established ties to Mexico, I have met several young people throughout Mexico who have successfully applied for a B1/B2 visa, the non-immigrant tourist/business visa that all Mexicans must receive in order to visit the United States.

Applying for a "tourist visa" is risky endeavor, but the possibility of a visa that is valid for up ten years for visits up to six months at a time to visit one's family and home has inspired many to try. Regardless of the outcome, the application and interview process costs a nonrefundable $160 USD and requires the applicant to file their photo and fingerprints with the US government. Depending upon the opinion of the embassy officer who reviews the case, people with a registered or admitted "unlawful presence" (180 days or more in the United States without a valid legal visa after having turned eighteen) have met with one of three possible outcomes. First, a person may be denied their visa and assigned a ten-year ban from returning to the United States, starting from the date of their voluntary return. Second, a person may be denied but not be assigned a ban, a decision that is at the discretion of the embassy officer. Third, the person may receive a visa for up to ten years.[6]

It is a costly, obscure process. The ramifications of the visa application outcome on a person's life and the lives of their families are startling. In his field research since 2012, Michaël Da Cruz has found that many returning and deported Mexicans are reconfiguring their expectations and identities to include long-term plans in Mexico based on their call center employment (2014). Established ties in Mexico are the "burden of proof" that the US government demands in order to grant a non-immigrant visa. A ban can be devastating. A positive response, however, almost instantly transforms vulnerability into opportunity.

Young people who have been deported, unlike those who returned voluntarily (at least in the eyes of the US government), have already been assigned a three-year, ten-year, or lifetime ban from returning to the United States. These are automatic penalties proscribed by the 1996 IIRIRA law. Those who experienced deportation, or received a ban upon applying for a visa, can apply for a waiver. The waiver costs $560, and in most cases, the applicant must demonstrate great hardship to a US-citizen family member. For deported young people, rebuilding their lives in Mexico is a practical necessity at great personal and familial cost, and the call centers are often the thin ice between a modicum of stability and debilitating un/under-employment. Luis and Sybil have ten-year bans, and Peter does not yet know if he will be assigned a ban for his years of "unlawful presence." One of his primary motivations for continuing to work in the call center is pinned on the uncertain but determined struggle to establish a legal route back home.

Chris, a working father of twins, grew up in Los Angeles and now lives in Mexico City after his deportation in 2009 following criminal charges and time served in a county prison. His mother and US-citizen siblings are still in Huntington Beach, California, where he grew up. Due to the "violent crime" that prompted his deportation, he is banned for life from the country where he lived for eighteen of his twenty-six years. He describes his return to Mexico in 2009 with a well-rehearsed turn of phrase and a charming smile, "I came back due to some poor choices I made when I was younger."

Arrested for a particularly violent fist-fight with a young man who lived in the same apartment complex as his mother in Huntington Beach, the eighteen-year-old Chris was accused of multiple felonies. He recalls, "It wasn't gang-related but since we were known as gang-affiliated, the gang unit was trying to throw gang charges on us as well. I ended up having three felonies with a strike." Although the other young man dropped the charges, the State of California pursued the case because it was considered violent. Chris, with his mother's support, fought the accusations from county jail for a year and a half. He eventually accepted a plea agreement for "365 days of time served" and immediate deportation with a lifetime ban.

For the first year in Mexico, Chris lived in Ensenada and worked at a *maquila* making shirts for brands like Randy Couture. He made about 1,200 pesos a week working twelve-hour shifts. After about a year, he decided to move to Mexico City, where he has extended family. After working at Leer Inc., making auto parts from scratch for similar pay, a friend told Chris about a call center, Telvista. Located in the historic center of Mexico City, AT&T had employed Telvista to handle all its customer service calls. Chris began to make more money: 7,200 pesos a month, plus bonuses for completing customer surveys. He remembers how "the environment of Telvista had me hooked. I felt like I was settled. I felt like I was finally part of something. Being in Mexico, I didn't know anybody who spoke English, and it was very difficult for me to carry a conversation in Spanish, so when I got to Telvista, it kinda felt like home, in a sense."

When the AT&T campaign ended, Chris's contract was immediately terminated. He worked for another client campaign, but the money was never as good. Eventually, like Peter and Luis, he was able to use the technical support and customer service skills learned at Telvista to find a better job at CompuCom, a call center dedicated exclusively to technical support. Working on the team providing customer service for supermarket chain Winn-Dixie, Chris remembers it as a "good experience. . . . I had my own little office. It wasn't like a lot of other ones, where they didn't allow you to bring pictures to personalize your desk." When we spoke, he had found another job that "builds on" his sales and customer service expertise from other call centers. He makes 9,300 pesos a month plus commissions and bonuses paid in dollars.

Chris observed how working in an English-speaking call center in Mexico can feel like "home." Many of the young people I have interviewed since 2012 allude to a sense of belonging in call centers that paradoxically but directly results from the denial of belonging in the United States *and* in Mexico. Deportees employed by call centers and other transnational companies find that their realm of action, agency, and rights is seemingly limited to the transnational company, as opposed to either of the national communities in which they were born or grew up. Chris has become a neoliberal citizen whose mobility across borders is restricted, even as his participation in his local community is more transnational than national.

Another key feature of the neoliberal citizen is a hyper-individualized sense of personal responsibility for one's well-being, as opposed to the expectation of responsibility on the part of the government or one's community to protect rights and ensure equal opportunity for youth. For example, as Chris explained to me in the interview, his deportation was due to "poor choices" and not the systemic, legalized fabrication of criminal/illegal-immigrant status that disproportionately affects brown and black men in the United States. The logic of neoliberal citizenship can be deeply internalized in our own autobiographies, family dynamics, and classroom experiences.

Young people like Peter, Luis, Sybil, and Chris are not integrated as national citizens upon return to their birth country, and instead, must exploit the precarious agency made available to them via the neoliberal cycles that have directly affected the course of their lives. In many ways, they are the privileged ones in the aftermath of deportation. Deported and returning Mexicans who are not able to find jobs in call centers are more likely to face desperate economic challenges, potentially violent contexts, and alienation. With the support of their bi-national families and communities, others have insisted on educational opportunity and entrepreneurial projects as alternatives to call center employment.

Around the same time that Peter heard about the call center in 2012, I was sitting around a table with a small group of returning and deported youth working at TeleTech in Mexico City. We coined the term *los otros Dreamers*," as referred to in Chapter 14, to name our new Facebook group. We wanted to describe the overlooked experience of young people who had grown up in the shadows of the failed DREAM Act, who did not or would not qualify for DACA, and who now lived in Mexico. We did not know the Facebook group would grow to include over 1,000 people, that we would all be involved in a bi-national book project of the same name, or that so many others would feel themselves heard and recognized by the term. Perhaps transnational community organizing and the mutual recognition of belonging and agency in a post-deportation community are aspects of neoliberal citizenship also?

Notes

1. Each of the young people I interviewed for this article expressed their wish to appear with their own first names. In all cases, I have changed or omitted the identifying details of current employment.
2. Luis wrote about his detention and deportation for the book *Los Otros Dreamers* (Anderson and Solis 2014). The young people I interviewed for this article are friends and family members of the contributors to the book with whom I continue to collaborate as part of the organization Otros Dreams en Acción (ODA).
3. The DHS differentiates between "removals" and "returns," although both are considered deportations in a practical sense. DHS oversees "removals" as "compulsory and confirmed" deportations via transportation to the international border in handcuffs and a supervised exit of the country. "Returns" result from the signing of a "voluntary departure" order where the person has a defined period of time to leave the country. As we read in the chapters of this book, immigrants are often told about a significant distinction between the removal and return/voluntary departure. Unfortunately, in practice the penalties can result in legal penalties under all circumstances of return.

4. Originally taken up in the 1930s, "neoliberalism" was used to name a middle road that advocated for the more regulatory intervention of a strong state in market economies from the other two perceived extremes in capitalist governance: a purist model of "free market" classical liberalism versus the reallocation of national resources via central planning under social liberalism. In the 1960s, critics of the US-supported overthrow of Ignacio Allende (a social liberal) in favor of Augusto Pinochet's coup took up the term to critique Pinochet's economic policies informed by economic advisors closely associated the University of Chicago. Today, "neoliberalism" continues to retain a connotation of critique, in so far as it is a term that seeks to name the totality and interconnection of economic policies across international borders that are more widely but obscurely referred to as distinct in terms such as "globalization," "free trade," and "national debt."
5. Although the focus of this essay is on US government deportations of Mexican-born citizens, it is of vital importance to note that between 2015 and 2016 detentions and deportations of Central American migrants in Mexico more than doubled with financial and military support from the United States under a bilateral program named Frontera Sur. For more information, see the detailed report, "Programa Frontera Sur: Una Cacería de Migrantes," in *Animal Político.*
6. In *Aftermath: Deportation Law and the New American Diaspora* (2012), Daniel Kanstroom details the history, the constitutionality, and the effects of deportation and deportation bans on what he in turn describes as "the new American diaspora" and as "noncitizens abroad" (175). In compelling legal arguments that demonstrate how "the roots of the modern deportation system are deeply intertwined with the history of slavery" in the United States, Kanstroom contributes to growing arguments for the human rights violations inherent in the automatic deportations and legal bans under the 1996 Illegal Immigration Reform and Immigrant Responsibility Act.

References

Anderson, Jill. 2015. "'Tagged as a Criminal': Narratives of Deportation and Return Migration in a Mexico City Call Center." *Latino Studies* 13 (1): 8–27.

Anderson, Jill and Nin Solis. 2014. *Los Otros Dreamers*. Mexico City: Jill Anderson and Nin Solis.

Arteaga García, Arnulfo. 2005. "Work and Citizenship in Mexico in the Era of Globalization." *Relations Industrielles/Industrial Relations* 60 (4): 737–61.

Batt, Rosemary, David Holman, and Ursula Holtgrewe. 2007. "Call Center Workers in International Perspective." *Perspectives on Work* 10 (2): 21–23.

Brotherton D. C. and L. Barrios. 2011. *Banished to the Homeland: Dominican Deportees and Their Stories of Exile*. New York: Columbia University Press.

Coutin, Susan Bibler. 2007. *Nations of Emigrants: Shifting Boundaries of Citizenship in El Salvador and the United States*. New York: Cornell University Press.

Da Cruz, Michaël, 2014. *«Back to Tenochtitlan»: Migration de retour et nouvelles maquiladoras de la communication: Le cas des jeunes migrants employés dans les centres d'appel bilingues de la ville de Mexico,* (doctoral thesis) Université Aix-Marseille.

Gandini, Luciana, Fernando Lozano-Ascencio and Selene Gaspar Olvera. 2015. *El Retorno en el nuevo scenario de la migración entre México y Estados Unidos*, México DF: Consejo Nacional de la Población (CONAPO).
Golash-Boza, Tanya. 2015. *Deported: Immigrant Policing, Disposable Labor, and Global Capitalism*. New York: New York University Press.
Golash-Boza, Tanya. 2016. "'Negative Credentials,' 'Foreign-Earned' Capital, and Call Centers: Guatemalan Deportees' Precarious Reintegration." *Citizenship Studies* 20 (3–4). Retrieved March 11, 2016 from http://dx.doi.org/10.1080/13621025.2016.1158357
Gonzalez-Barrera, Ana. 2015. "More Mexicans Leaving Than Coming to the U.S." Washington DC: Pew Research Center. Retrieved March 11, 2016 from http://www.pewhispanic.org/2015/11/19/more-mexicans-leaving-than-coming-to-the-u-s/
Hernandez, Ester and Susan Bibler Coutin. 2006. "Remitting Subjects: Migrants, Money and States." *Economy and Society* 35 (2): 185–208.
Elmi, Sheida and Kristen McCabe. 2011. "Immigration Enforcement in the United States." Migration Information Source. Washington DC: Migration Policy Institute. Retrieved March 9, 2016 from http://www.migrationpolicy.org/article/immigration-enforcement-united-states#19
Kanstroom, Daniel. 2012. *Aftermath: Deportation Law and the New American Diaspora*. Oxford: Oxford University Press.
McNevin, Anne. 2007. "Irregular Migrants, Neoliberal Geographies and Spatial Frontiers of 'The Political.'" *Review of International Studies* 33 (4): 655–74.
Ong, Aihwa. 2005. "(Re)Articulations of Citizenship." *PS: Political Science and Politics* 38 (4): 697–99.
Animal Político and the Department of International Studies and the Masters Program in Journalism and Public Affairs of CIDE. "Programa Frontera Sur: Una cacería de migrantes." 2016. Mexico City: *Animal Político*. Retrieved March 15, 2016 from http://www.animalpolitico.com/caceriademigrantes/reportaje01.html
Sassen, Saskia. 2008. *Territory, Authority, Rights: From Medieval to Global Assemblages*. Princeton, NJ: Princeton University Press.
Thirión, Jordy Micheli. 2012. "El sector de call centers: Estructura y tendencias. Apuntes sobre la situación de México." *Frontera Norte* 24 (47): 163.

PART 7

RETURNING "HOME": What Happens to Migrants Who Return to the United States After Being Deported?

In a 2012 article, Cecilia Menjívar and Leisy Abrego delineate the concept of "legal violence," which refers to "the harmful consequences of implementing a restrictive body of law that criminalizes individuals" (1413). They use this concept to argue that laws shape the lives of immigrants in pernicious ways. The contributions in this section render this legal violence evident and show how immigration law can narrowly circumscribe the lives of migrants who are legally vulnerable. They also shed light on structural violence—the poverty and exclusion which often forces people to migrate—as well as on actual violence that migrants face both while crossing the border as well as at the hand of the state in immigration detention facilities.

The first contribution in this section is by Nancy Hiemstra, who explains the structural violence that led Santiago to leave his home country of Ecuador in search of opportunities in the United States. Although it cost Santiago $15,000 to get to the United States, he was unsuccessful in his first two attempts. Because he took out a loan for that $15,000 and cannot afford to pay it back on what he can earn in Ecuador, he feels compelled to try again, even though he and his wife fear he may never make it back to Ecuador alive. Santiago believes he has no option other than to risk imprisonment, injury, and possibly even death because emigration to the United States is the only way he will be able to pay back the $15,000 loan plus thousands of dollars in compounded interest that he borrowed to travel to the United States. If Santiago makes it to the United States, he will work in the shadows until he repays his debt and then work some more to save up money to bring home. The tremendous debt associated with the cost of his illegal migration will render Santiago even more vulnerable to exploitation than other undocumented workers who are not indebted. Many undocumented migrants, like Santiago, travel to the United States as target earners, hoping to earn enough money to improve their situation in their home country. Many of these migrants end up staying in the United States, and find it increasingly difficult to return home as they settle in their new homes.

San Juanita Garcia introduces us to María Inez, who has gradually made the United States her home over the past sixteen years. Her husband, Jesús, first traveled to the United States in 1990. After traveling back and forth for many years, they finally decided that María Inez and the children should also travel to the United States. Jesús had arrived too late to qualify for legalization through IRCA and thus the other family members also had to travel as undocumented migrants. María Inez also traveled back home several times during her stay in the United States. On one occasion she was caught and deported, which now means that she is extremely unlikely to ever have the opportunity to legalize her status. She is now "fenced in" the United States as the risks of returning to Mexico are too high. María Inez is in her fifties and her ability to get by without health care is increasingly difficult. This essay sheds light on the travails of undocumented status for older migrants.

Roberto Gonzales introduces us to Sergio who is much younger yet whose life is similarly circumscribed by legal violence and the ever-present threat of deportation. Sergio was deported on criminal grounds and thus will never be able to become a legal resident or a citizen of the United States. Despite this, he chooses to live in the United States, as inconspicuously as possible because he has no family in Mexico and feels at home in the United States, where he has lived since he was three years old.

All undocumented migrants are at risk of deportation. However, those migrants who have been previously deported can face even graver consequences. First of all, their fingerprints have already been recorded into government databases. Thus, any law enforcement officer with access to this database can easily identify them as a deportable person. Moreover, if apprehended, they can face criminal charges for illegal entry, which carries a federal prison sentence of up to twenty years. These extreme consequences, however, do not keep deported migrants from attempting to return—especially in those cases where their families live in the United States and when, like Santiago, they have debts that can only be repaid if they work in the United States. As you read these contributions, think about the various forms of violence these immigrants confront: structural, legal, and physical—both in their countries of origin and in the United States.

20

No hay otro:
An Ecuadorian Tale of Repeated US Immigration

Nancy Hiemstra

Nancy Hiemstra is a political geographer and Assistant Professor of Migration Studies in the Department of Women's, Gender, and Sexuality Studies at Stony Brook University in New York, USA. Her research analyzes political and sociocultural reverberations of detention and deportation policies in the United States and Latin America. She has published related work in Annals of the Association of American Geographers, Antipode, Environment and Planning D, Geographica Helvetica, *and* Geopolitics. *She is co-editor (with Deirdre Conlon) of* Intimate Economies of Immigration Detention: Critical Perspectives *(Routledge, 2016).*

In the spring of 2009, I was in the southern Andean city of Cuenca, Ecuador, volunteering at the *Casa del Migrante*, a local government agency that offers a variety of services to migrants and their families. When I had first started there a few months earlier, Carmen, the lawyer charged with providing legal assistance and advice, immediately handed me a bulging binder of forms. Each form had been filled out when a family member of someone detained in the United States came in seeking information: *Where was he? Would she be deported? When was he coming?* Once detained, Carmen explained, migrants often just disappeared for months to family members in Ecuador. Since she did not speak English, Carmen's efforts to help relatives had been limited to rarely-answered emails and faxes to the Ecuadorian Ministry of Foreign Affairs. "Could you try to help the families?" she asked me.

Over the coming months, I figured out how to answer family members' questions. With my own laptop, Skype account, and the Casa's wireless Internet connection, I called dozens of US detention facilities, Immigration and Customs Enforcement (ICE) offices, Border Patrol offices, and organizations attempting to assist detained migrants. I gradually learned how to navigate the detention system and what pieces of information to gather from family members in order to find and trace detained migrants from apprehension to deportation. Then, I interviewed forty deportees after their return to Ecuador.

In March, a woman named Rosa from a rural, agricultural sector southeast of Cuenca came in to the Casa del Migrante with questions about her detained husband Santiago. Rosa and Santiago's story encapsulates why so many Ecuadorians migrate to the United States, and why they are not deterred by increasingly harsh US immigration and border enforcement policies. These policies include intensified patrolling and apprehension initiatives, expanded detention capacity, criminalization of immigrants, elimination of provisions to protect migrants' rights, and deportation to migrants' countries of origin. While this multi-pronged approach does make it more difficult for migrants to reach the United States, it does not stop undocumented migration. Instead, these policies collectively contribute to the development of a robust human smuggling industry, which in itself ensures continued illicit migration. Many Ecuadorians, driven by profound poverty and lack of opportunity in Ecuador, take out substantial loans to enlist human smugglers in facilitating their journey. Once thus ensnared by debt, Ecuadorians have no choice but to make repeated migration attempts, whatever they may encounter.

Rosa was accompanied by another woman, Linda. Santiago had been traveling from Ecuador to the United States with his brother-in-law Jorge, Linda's husband, when they were detained somewhere near the United States–Mexico border. This was the second attempt for both Santiago and Jorge; their first had been one year earlier, also ending in detention and then deportation. Rosa and Linda were concerned because they had not heard from either of the men since a short call over two weeks earlier reporting that they had been caught again.

I recorded key identification information for each man, such as full names, birthdates, and parents' names, then the women gave me their cell phone numbers and left. Through a series of Skype calls over the next few hours, I learned that Santiago and Jorge were in an immigration detention center near the United States–Mexico border, in Florence, Arizona. Every day, ICE has about 34,000 migrants detained in its custody, held in over 200 facilities around the United States: an assortment of dedicated detention centers, county jails, and prisons, some run by ICE but many contracted out to private companies or state and local governments. From previous searches for detainees, I knew that how long Santiago and Jorge were to be detained depended on a number of factors that were difficult to predict, including their particular immigration history, how long it took ICE to acquire travel documents for them, space availability on deportation flights to Ecuador, and luck.

I called Rosa and Linda to let them know. They seemed sad that their husbands would definitely be deported, but anxious to know when they would arrive back in Ecuador. After that, Rosa returned to the Casa several times to check in. Santiago returned to Ecuador on an ICE flight, five weeks after being detained. Jorge's paperwork had been delayed for some unexplained reason, and he returned two weeks after Santiago.

Santiago was one of thousands of Ecuadorians journeying to the United States in 2009. The total number of migrants deported that year was nearly

400,000, and Ecuador was eighth on the US list of origin countries receiving deportees (in 2015 Ecuador was sixth on the list) (US ICE 2010, 2015). Approximately 10 percent of Ecuador's population of 16 million lives abroad, with perhaps as many as one million living in the United States.

International migration out of Ecuador to the United States has always been linked to US policies. Though migration to the United States did not begin until the 1950s, its early foundations were laid in the country's post-independence period in the 1800s, when Ecuador—heeding United States and European advisors—developed an export-based economy. When Ecuadorian exports plummeted during the United States' Great Depression, economic instability increased country-wide. Cuenca and the surrounding region was particularly hard-hit by the collapse of its "panama" hat industry, and some hat exporters drew on their international trade connections to migrate to the United States. Over the next several decades, migration became an increasingly popular strategy for dealing with continued economic hardship in the region (Kyle 2000; Jokisch 2001).

Then, Ecuador was among the many countries sucked into the Latin American debt crisis of the 1980s. Tempted by easy credit amidst the high oil prices of the 1970s, again following the advice of the United States and other countries, Ecuador borrowed heavily from international lenders. When oil prices crashed and interest rates on loans skyrocketed, Ecuador fell deeper and deeper in debt to US-backed international financial organizations such as the World Bank and International Monetary Fund. Consequently, successive Ecuadorian governments entered into a cycle of imposed austerity measures, rising inflation, and growing poverty—a cycle that critically shaped everyday realities (Carriére 2001; Acosta, López, and Villamar 2004).

The situation culminated in *la crisis* of 1999–2001. The proportion of the population living in poverty grew to over 70 percent, and the government was plagued by instability (Acosta, López, and Villamar 2004). In this context, migration out of Ecuador exploded, from all regions and socioeconomic classes. Europe (primarily Spain, secondarily Italy) came to rival the United States as a destination. But the majority of migrants leaving the area around Cuenca drew on and expanded existing networks to reach the United States (Jokisch and Pribilsky 2002).

The overwhelming sense of crisis in Ecuador had dissipated by the late 2000s when I conducted research, but the reality of pervasive poverty, lack of opportunity, and daily hardship remains for many. And migration is now firmly entrenched as a possible way out.

I called Santiago on Rosa's cell phone two weeks after he returned, and he agreed to an interview about his experience of detention and deportation. Since he had no immediate plans to come into Cuenca, Santiago suggested that I come out to his home, and gave me directions. The next day, I took a taxi to a small market at the edge of the city, and boarded a bus—not a relatively sleek city bus, but the kind that goes to rural areas:

smaller, older, with racks on top for strapping down all types of cargo, and colorfully decorated with decals, tassels, and small homages to patron saints. Over the next hour and a half, the bus plodded deeper and deeper into the lush green hills southeast of Cuenca. The road went from asphalt to dirt shortly outside of the city, the bus kicking up a haze of dust wherever it went, except in places where home and business owners hosed down the road.

When I told the driver the name of the crossroads Santiago had given me, he did not know it, but his assistant said he thought he knew the place.

"Who are you going to see?" asked the young man. When I said Santiago's name, he replied, "The one who was in jail in the United States?" In Ecuadorian communities where international migration is a common household strategy, stories of failed journeys stand out. Detention and forced return are attributed to personal bad luck or mistakes, and seen as exceptions to the norm of successful migration.

After the road became one lane and surprisingly steep, the assistant directed me to get off at an unmarked bend. He gestured to a single track path twisting up and out of sight over the crest of a hill, and said the house I wanted was up that way. The bus continued on down the road, leaving me standing alone. I was surrounded by green terraced farmlands, the landscape marked by stands of trees, spotted with occasional cows, and a few houses spread out in the distance.

A smiling, elderly woman in a colorful *pollera* skirt and bowler-type hat—dress typical of indigenous women in the area—soon appeared on the path; the family must have been watching for the bus. She greeted me kindly, introducing herself as Rosa's mother, then I followed her up the path for about ten minutes.

Santiago and Rosa's house sat atop a hill, with a beautiful view all around. Corn grew down all sides of their hill in carefully terraced fields beginning just beyond the neat dirt yard. The house was two stories, walls of mud and straw mixed together and a zinc sheet roof, with a wood railing around a porch on the second level. There were a few smaller structures around the house, and an area for washing clothes by hand.

Rosa greeted me shyly, and introduced Santiago. He seemed older than thirty-eight to me, with the leathered skin and hands of a man who had worked outside his whole life and a lined, tired face. After introductions, we settled on benches in the shade of the house—Santiago, Rosa, her mother, me—and I pulled out the list of questions I had prepared for my interviews of deportees. While we talked, their smaller children played at our feet and older ones passed in and out of the yard, puppies yelped, and chickens pecked about.

Though neither Santiago nor Rosa dressed in traditional indigenous clothing as Rosa's mother did, their lives were shaped by the systemic marginalization and impoverishment of indigenous peoples all over the country, and compounded by *la crisis*. Santiago had reached sixth grade before leaving school to farm full-time with his own father, on the land where we now sat, which had been in his family for years. He and Rosa married as teenagers and eventually had nine children. Santiago frequently worked as a day laborer in the countryside or in Cuenca to supplement their farm income, but they still struggled to get by.

One day, a woman who lived up the road paid them a visit. She was a *coyota*, a human smuggler, and she painted a pretty picture of how Santiago would easily make a lot of money if he simply went to the United States. She assured him she had the contacts and experience to get him there safely and quickly, for just $15,000.

Santiago and Rosa talked it over, together with his brother-in-law Jorge and Jorge's wife Linda. In Cuenca and the surrounding areas, evidence of previous successful migration abounds, such as flashy four-wheel drive trucks and big new homes paid for with remittance money. They decided it would be worth the investment.

"I decided to go," said Santiago, "because of the economy here. To see if we could help our children get a better education. Also to save for our old age."

Rosa added, quietly, "Because of poverty."

So they borrowed against their land through a local moneylender, a *chulquero*, and gave the money to the *coyota*.

Human smuggling operations in Ecuador have developed in direct correlation with hardening US immigration and border enforcement policies. Early Ecuadorian migrants, whatever their legal status, flew directly to the United States. As the United States gradually restricted entry requirements in the 1970s, undocumented migrants began to fly instead to Mexico, then cross the United States–Mexico border by land. A human smuggling system was born. Individuals, then called *pasadores*, helped with travel arrangements—a plane ticket, a visa to Mexico, a false US passport—in exchange for a fee. If the migrants did not have the money, which was about $1,200 in the 1970s and early 1980s, then the *pasadores* could connect them with a *chulquero* who granted cash loans at high interest rates (Jokisch 1997; Kyle and Liang 2001).

More and more Ecuadorians were driven to migrate in the late 1990s and early 2000s, which coincided with a US crackdown on undocumented immigration, spurred by racialized fears of growing numbers of nonwhite immigrants, a prolonged economic downturn, and then, particularly in the aftermath of the attacks of September 11, 2001, the conflation of immigration and terrorism. Largely steered by goals of deterrence, US border enforcement efforts entailed escalating militarization of the United States–Mexico border, more Border Patrol officers, and targeted operations to force migrants to more remote and dangerous crossings. The contemporary legal framework funneling migrants toward deportation took shape, and detention capacity ballooned (Meissner et al. 2013). The United States expanded activities to try to intercept migrants before they ever reached US borders, including increased policing at sea. It also enlisted transit countries, particularly Mexico and Central American countries, to apprehend, detain, and deport US-bound migrants, through offers of aid and the formation of regional organizations (Kyle and Liang 2001; Coleman 2007).

As Ecuadorians continued to migrate in the face of escalating US border enforcement activities, human smuggling operations from Ecuador grew at one of the fastest rates in the world (Thompson and Ochoa 2004). Geographical routes became more convoluted, typically entailing some combination of boats or planes from Ecuador to Central America, then buses, trucks, and cars from there to the United States–Mexico border (Ramírez and Álvarez 2009). The risk of assault, robbery, and death increased, as did cost—to the $15,000 that Santiago paid. Smugglers even incorporate the risk of apprehension en route into their business model by including multiple attempts in their price. They also came to play an important role in instigating new migration attempts through active recruiting, in efforts to maintain and grow their business (Kyle and Liang 2001; Jokisch and Kyle 2008).

Santiago's and Jorge's first attempt in March of 2008 ended in Texas, where they were detained for a month. After that, Santiago tried to negotiate with the *coyota* to recoup the smuggling fee. She said, however, that that was not possible, insisting she had already spent most of it to pay for the first trip—the flights, guides, bribes—but, she assured him, he could try three times for the original fee.

So, in February of 2009, Santiago and Jorge left again, flying from Quito to Panama, then from Panama to Honduras. The rest of the trip was by land from Honduras to a town just south of the United States–Mexico border. There, they were placed in a group of twenty-five people, with four guides. Their guides told them they would walk through the desert for several nights, and gave each a small bag of food and a gallon of water, "Not enough of either," said Santiago. On the second night, they spotted a Border Patrol vehicle in the distance, and the guides led them to a canyon to hide. Suddenly, there were helicopters overhead, and then agents chasing them. Santiago tried to hide in a cave, but an agent grabbed his leg to pull him out. He saw them kick Jorge after he had been caught, too.

Twelve of the migrants in his group were apprehended. They were taken to Nogales for one night, where they had to sleep on the floor "like dogs." They were given little food, and the room was painfully cold—one of the often-reported *hieleras,* iceboxes, many migrants caught on the border endure. After Nogales, he was in the Florence, Texas, detention facility for three weeks, then transferred to another detention center in Otero, New Mexico, for ten days, then to Oakdale, Louisiana, from where he was deported. During every transfer, Santiago was chained hands, feet, and waist.

Santiago's detention experience illustrates the chaos, confusion, and degradation recounted by so many of the Ecuadorian deportees I interviewed (Hiemstra 2012, 2013, 2014). While detained, Santiago was unclear about exactly why he was detained, how long he would be in each place, and when (and even if) he would be deported. Though he was not informed of this, I discerned that Santiago had been deported through "Expedited Removal." Through this process, migrants apprehended within 100 miles of the US border, and in the United States less than fourteen days, are ordered removed without a hearing before an immigration judge.

Santiago found detention difficult to bear. After the brief call when he was first caught, he was not able to call his family in Ecuador because he had no money. "I begged one official to let me call, but he said only if I had someone to call in the United States." There was not much to do to pass the time and, Santiago said, "many want to kill themselves waiting." One Ecuadorian, Santiago told me, was desperate and did not know how much longer he could endure being locked up. When an ICE official told him he had four more months, the man tried to hang himself with a towel, after which he was put in solitary confinement for six days. Santiago suffered from two hernias that caused him constant pain, but to visit a facility's medical office, he had to make a request that took at least three days, then medical personnel responded by giving him some Tylenol and telling him to drink more water. The food was sparse and tasteless, and the water did not taste clean.

Santiago was finally deported after five weeks. Despite his frustration at the duration of his detention, many deportees I interviewed were held considerably longer, the time for some stretching months. Two days before Santiago's deportation, ICE had him call the Ecuadorian consulate to give personal identification details, and that was when Santiago knew he might be deported soon. "But still you can't be sure. Sometimes they say, 'You're leaving soon,' but it's a lie, and they're just sending you to a different place." The fact that his brother-in-law Jorge, with an identical migration history and record with ICE, was deported two weeks later illustrates the unpredictability and uncertainty inherent to the US detention and deportation process. ICE officials told Santiago that if he was caught again, he could be in jail for a year. In accordance with stated goals of deterrence, the penalties for "illegal entry" have been progressively expanded. Consequently, more migrants are spending more time in detention prior to deportation.

Santiago experienced the deportation flight as one more humiliation. He was chained on the plane, given minimal food and water, and treated poorly by the guards. His flight arrived to Guayaquil, a city on the coast. After processing by Ecuadorian Migration, Santiago took a bus four hours to Cuenca, and from there another bus to his home.

I asked Santiago how he felt when he arrived. "The kids were happy," he said, smiling. Then, after a pause, "To get out of detention, happy. Because of the debt, sad."

While some migrants' journeys are paid by family already in the United States, most—like Santiago—fund all or part of the trip by taking out loans. High interest rates mean that migrants and their families can quickly owe more than the original loan. Migrants who are deported before they can repay their migration debt typically feel that they have no option but to migrate again (Jokisch 2001; Stoll 2013; Hiemstra 2012). By driving up smuggling fees, then, escalating US enforcement leads to increased indebtedness for migrants and their families. Because of smuggling debt, despite dangerous journeys to the United States, dehumanizing experiences in detention, and the threat of extended incarceration, migrants are not deterred. Instead, policies supposedly enacted to deter actually contribute to continued migration.

Before Santiago's return, Rosa had asked Carmen at the Casa del Migrante if there were any ways to recover the smuggling fee in order to pay back the *chulquero*. Carmen explained that the only avenue was to file charges against the smuggler.

"Did you get the *coyota* to sign anything when you gave her the money, verifying the deal?" Carmen asked.

Rosa shook her head, and looked down. "No, we just talked about it."

Carmen had sighed, familiar with this answer. She had been doing this work for years, and she knew it was practically unheard of for smugglers to return the money. Often migrants did not have an address or even the full name of the *coyote*. If someone had paperwork—and few did—to prove the exchange of money, that was a positive first step. But it would still be an uphill battle. They would have to hire a lawyer to pursue the case, and if charges were filed against a *coyote*, he or she usually disappeared for a while, either hiding out in Ecuador or going to the United States.

When I was at their home, Rosa expressed that she did not want Santiago to make a third attempt. She worried that he could die on the trip there due to his already poor health or other dangers during the journey—there were increasing tales of kidnapping and gang activity in Central America and Mexico. But the lender to whom they had mortgaged their land kept returning, asking for repayment. They had asked him if they could pay it back more slowly than the original agreement, to try to do it from what the family could earn in Ecuador, but he would not agree to that idea. What's more, they were being charged 4 percent interest per month, so the amount they owed was steadily growing.

"We could lose our land," Rosa said tearfully.

Rosa's mother added quietly, "That is why I cry now. What will happen with my daughter and the children?"

"I don't want to go again either," Santiago told me. "But I don't know what to do about the debt."

Santiago looked around, seeming to survey his family, his house, his land—all that he was now at risk of losing because of his migration debt.

Then he looked down at his hands. "But if I can't get the money back," Santiago said slowly, sadly, "*No hay otro—tengo que intentar otra vez*. There is no other way—I have to try again."

Santiago and Rosa's predicament exemplifies the impossible situation in which many migrants and their families find themselves. US policies aimed at deterring undocumented migration certainly do make it more difficult to reach, enter, and remain in the United States: more dangerous, expense, and circuitous routes; the criminalization of apprehended migrants; abysmal conditions of detention; and a massive deportation program. These policies, however, simultaneously assure that migrants must keep trying to migrate—that they will not be deterred—by fueling a thriving human smuggling industry. More difficult journeys translate to the increased necessity of enlisting human smugglers, and to pay a smuggler migrants and their families often leverage critical household assets. Once a migrant makes that initial financial commitment to migrate, therefore, there is no turning back. Debt works as a powerful counter to US goals of deterrence. The thriving smuggling industry also pulls in new migrants through recruitment efforts.

The continued failure to recognize this mismatch between policy objectives and outcomes points to fundamental flaws in the US approach to controlling immigration. Policymakers continue to overlook—or intentionally make invisible—the critical role of agencies, individuals, and private entities that benefit in various ways, financially and otherwise, from increased immigration policing and incarceration (Golash-Boza 2009; Conlon and Hiemstra 2014; Hiemstra and Conlon 2016). Instead of addressing the underlying causes of illicit human mobility across borders, and assessing the actual consequences of dominant policy initiatives in countries of migrant origin and transit, they implement approaches that are not just inhumane but also ineffective. What's more, policies supposedly intended to deter migration do the opposite, effectively playing an important role in continued undocumented migration to the United States.

Acknowledgements:

I would like to thank all participants in this study, especially Rosa and Santiago for sharing their story and home with me. Many thanks, too, to Carmen Alvarado and the Casa del Migrante for facilitating the research. The original project was funded by the National Science Foundation (DDRI #0802801). Finally, I am grateful to Tanya Golash-Boza for the opportunity to explore this particular migration story with a new lens.

References

Acosta, A., S. López, and D. Villamar. 2004. "Ecuador: Oportunidades y amenazas económicas de la emigración." In *Migraciones: Un juego con cartas marcadas*, ed. F. Hidalgo, 259–301. Quito: Ediciones Abya-Yala.

Carriére, J. 2001. "Neoliberalism, Economic Crisis and Popular Mobilization in Ecuador." In *Miraculous Metamorphoses: The Neoliberalization of Latin American Populism*, ed. J. Demmers, A. E. Fernández Jilberto, and B. Hogenboom, 132–49. New York: Zed Books.

Coleman, M. 2007. "A Geopolitics of Engagement: Neoliberalism, the War on Terrorism, and the Reconfiguration of US Immigration Enforcement." *Geopolitics* 12 (4): 607–34.

Conlon, D. and N. Hiemstra. 2014. "Examining the Everyday Micro-Economies of Immigrant Detention in the United States. *Geographica Helvetica* 69: 335–44.

Golash-Boza, T. 2009. "A Confluence of Interests in Immigration Enforcement: How Politicians, the Media and Corporations Profit from Immigration Policies Destined to Fail." *Sociology Compass* 3 (2): 283–94.

Hiemstra, N. 2012. "Geopolitical Reverberations of US Migrant Detention and Deportation: the View from Ecuador." *Geopolitics* 17 (2): 293–311.

Hiemstra, N. 2013. "'You Don't Even Know Where You Are': Chaotic Geographies of U.S. Migrant Detention and Deportation." In *Carceral Spaces: Mobility and Agency in Imprisonment and Migrant Detention*, ed. D. Moran, N. Gill and D. Conlon, 57–75. Farnham, Surrey: Ashgate.

Hiemstra, N. 2014. "Performing Homeland Security Within the US Immigrant Detention System." *Environment and Planning D: Society and Space* 32: 571–88.

Hiemstra, N., and D. Conlon. 2016. "Captive Consumers and Coerced Labourers: Intimate Economies and the Expanding US Detention Regime. In *Intimate Economies of Immigration Detention: Critical Perspectives*, Ed. D. Conlon and N. Hiemstra, 123–139. New York, NY: Routledge.

Jokisch, B. D. 1997. "From Labor Circulation to International Migration: The Case of South-Central Ecuador." *Yearbook, Conference of Latin Americanist Geographers* Austin: University of Texas Press.

———. 2001. "Desde Nueva York a Madrid: Tendencias en la migración ecuatoriana." *Ecuador Debate* 54: 59–83.

Jokisch, B., and D. Kyle. 2008. "Ecuadorian International Migration." In *The Ecuador Reader*, ed. C. de la Torre and S. Striffler, 350–58. Durham, NC: Duke University Press.

Jokisch, B. and J. Pribilsky. 2002. "The Panic to Leave: Economic Crisis and the 'New Emigration' from Ecuador." *International Migration* 40 (4): 75-101.

Kyle, D. 2000. *Transnational Peasants: Migrations, Networks, and Ethnicity in Andean Ecuador*. Baltimore: Johns Hopkins University Press.

Kyle, D., and Z. Liang. 2001. "Migration Merchants: Human Smuggling from Ecuador and China to the United States." In *Controlling a New Migration World*, ed. V. Guiraudon and C. Joppke, 200–21. New York: Routledge.

Meissner, D., D. M. Kerwin, M. Chishti, and C. Bergeron. 2013. "Immigration Enforcement in the United States: Rise of a Formidable Machinery." Washington, DC: Migration Policy Institute.

Ramírez, J., and S. Álvarez. 2009. "'Cruzando Fronteras': Una aproximación etnográfica a la migración clandestina ecuatoriana en tránsito hacia Estados Unidos." *Confluenze* 1 (1): 89–113.

Stoll, D. 2013. *El Norte Or Bust! How Migration Fever and Microcredit Produced a Financial Crash in a Latin American Town*. Lanham, MD: Rowman and Littlefield.

Thompson, G., and S. Ochoa. 2004. "By a Back Door to the US: A Migrant's Grim Sea Voyage." *New York Times*, June 13, 1.

US ICE. 2010. "Immigration Enforcement Actions 2009." https://www.dhs.gov/xlibrary/assets/statistics/publications/enforcement_ar_2009.pdf

US ICE. 2015. *ICE Immigration Removal Operations Report: Fiscal Year 2015*. https://www.ice.gov/sites/default/files/documents/Report/2016/fy2015removalStats.pdf

21

Barred *Por Vida*:
María Inez's Battle to Find Health and Well-Being[1]

San Juanita García

San Juanita García received her PhD in Sociology from Texas A&M University. Currently she is a postdoctoral fellow in the National Research Service Award Mental Health Services Research Training Program at the Sheps Center for Health Services Research at the University of North Carolina–Chapel Hill. This T32 training grant is jointly sponsored by the Department of Psychiatry and Behavioral Sciences at Duke University Medical Center. She will be joining the Department of Sociology as an Assistant Professor at the University of California, Riverside beginning July 2017. Her research interests are immigration, racial and ethnic relations, intersectionality, medical sociology, sociology of mental health, and Latino/a/x sociology. Her research has been funded by the Ford Foundation and the American Sociological Association Minority Fellowship Program.

Immigration is a highly contested topic that continues to take center stage, as evidenced by the current political and anti-immigrant climate. The new United States presidential administration has promised to increase enforcement efforts, including further construction of "the wall" between the US-Mexico border. The lives of approximately 11.1 million undocumented immigrants living in the United States (Passel and Cohn 2016), are being confronted by an even more precarious and uncertain future under this new administration. While the record-breaking number of deportations took place under former President Obama's administration, which led to him being dubbed the "Deporter in Chief" by some of his critics, the mass deportation apparatus is indeed anticipated to worsen under the new administration. In June of 2012, Obama introduced the Deferred Action for Childhood Arrivals (DACA), providing deportation relief and temporary work authorization for eligible undocumented young adults. Two years later in November of 2014, President Obama announced Deferred Action for Parents of Americans and Lawful Permanent Residents (DAPA) and an extension of DACA, aimed at widening access and protecting more undocumented immigrants from deportation while also providing temporary work permits. Yet DAPA and the extension of DACA were blocked but the previous DACA policy continues to exist.

However, with the new presidential administration having taken office in January 20, 2017, and which campaigned with promises of building "the wall," eradicating the DACA program, and of amplifying the deportation regime, the climate for all undocumented immigrants remains even more uncertain, anxiety and stress-provoking. While the entire undocumented immigrant population is at risk of deportation, previous policies have led to a further stratification of undocumented statuses. For example, undocumented immigrants currently living in the United States make up several statuses such as those that may have been previously deported, detained, and barred from entering the United States, and are currently residing in the United States. There is also a growing demographic among the undocumented, namely the aging undocumented population. This leads me to ask the questions of: What does it mean to grow old as an undocumented immigrant? And how is this experience further complicated for those undocumented immigrants that have been deported and banned from living in the United States?

This chapter tells the story of María Inez, a fifty-five-year-old woman with concerns of growing old in the United States without any way to legalize her immigration status. I had the privilege of meeting María Inez in December 2013 while conducting a research project examining how Mexican-origin women in Houston, Texas, experience illegality and its mental health impacts. I was introduced to María Inez by one of her daughters, Linda. María Inez was born in 1969 in a small *rancho* near Mexico City. Her four daughters (aged 33, 32, 31, and 24), and her son, 28, were all born in Mexico and now reside near each other in Houston.

"I'll never be able to legalize my status; I'll be forever undocumented," she explained with despair in her voice. Now facing a lifetime bar to legal residence in the United States because of her incarceration and subsequent deportation in 2007, María Inez faces a "legal dead end" (Menjívar 2012). Her story is one fraught with concerns of growing old as "forever undocumented," the consequences on her mental and physical health including the challenges she faces navigating the health care system, and the sacrifices she endures as she fights the nostalgia and longing to return to Mexico in order to remain united with her family in Houston, Texas.

"I don't know. I don't know what I feel." Speaking in Spanish, María Inez paused as tears ran down her face and her voice trembled. "If I go back to México, to leave my family here . . . but I don't feel comfortable living here either. I don't know, it's because this country is very foreign for me and I frequently want to leave and [sigh] I think about it again, since we don't have papers it's very difficult for us." María Inez described her discomfort with life in the United States. She has lived in the United States for over ten years and continues to long for Mexico. What keeps her in the United States are her children, grandchildren, and husband, Jesús, who all live in Houston, Texas. "If it weren't for them, I'd be in México," she told me. They mean the world to her and, although she is not too optimistic about adjusting to the United States anytime soon, she remains. It is a sacrifice she is willing to make to be with her family. Nevertheless, she feels excluded as an older undocumented immigrant woman who has been banned from legally living in the United States.

María Inez described her childhood as "difficult, because I had to work a lot to survive." She reminisced how her mom would send her off with a basket full of candies to sell in the streets of Mexico City when she was six years old. "My mom bought me a basket. Every time I see baskets here, they fascinate me. I fall in love with them because from there I helped my family. Look, she bought me a very pretty little basket like this [hand gesturing the size of the basket to me], with different kinds of candy, 'Look you are going to sell them and bring me back 5 pesos,' and I brought back 10, [Changing her tone of voice to portray her mom] 'And how did you do it?' I didn't know how to count, didn't know how to read, but God enlightened me." Life at home was economically rough but María Inez is proud that from a young age she learned the value of hard work. Although she did not have formal schooling, she learned quickly how to make an honest living in the streets of Mexico City.

María Inez met her husband, Jesús, in Mexico City, and they later moved to a *rancho* in the state of Guanajuato, where Jesús was born. They, along with their children, all lived in one room with only one small stove in it. Her children also worked at young ages helping María Inez clean, cook, and sell food. Before coming to the United States, María Inez worked laundering clothes and washing, cleaning, and preparing hot dog carts. Her husband, who also did not have formal schooling or training and did not know how to read or write, worked tirelessly from 6 am to 11 or 12 at night. He made very little money, too little to feed the family properly, so he decided to migrate to the United States. He left in 1990, when María Inez was three months pregnant with her youngest daughter. Jesús made it to the United States and was able to find a job with an American family as a handyman. To this day, he works for the same family, but now for the children of his previous boss, who has passed away. For years, Jesús traveled back and forth between Mexico and the United States. When their youngest child was nine and the oldest was eighteen, he asked the family to join him in the United States. Jesús first brought three of his daughters in 2000. María Inez, their son, and their youngest daughter followed in 2001.

After arriving in the United States, María Inez supplemented her husband's income by selling snow cones, fried pork rinds, fruit cups, and corn from a cart she drove around the neighborhood. During this time, María Inez began to have periods of heavy bleeding, more than her usual menstruation. It was happening two or three times a month. Her uncertainty about how to navigate the US health care system, where to find services, coupled with her worries about her health condition, created fear, confusion, and humiliation. This was compounded by her undocumented status, lack of financial resources, and potential language barrier concerns. Although an executive order was passed in 2000 called "Improving Access to Services for Persons with Limited English Proficiency," which requires language assistance for limited English proficient patients in health care settings (Chen et al. 2007), not all health care facilities meet this requirement and María Inez feared she would be unable to communicate her symptoms. This uncertainty led her to return to Mexico in 2002.

Once in Mexico, she quickly sought medical attention. The doctors found three tumors in her uterus and performed a hysterectomy. She rested for several months in Mexico and paid a *coyote* to bring her back to Houston a year later, in 2003. Two years later, she and Jesús returned to Mexico after her father-in-law passed away in 2005. Shortly after the funeral and burial, María Inez and Jesús traveled back to Houston. A year later, María Inez crossed the border once again, this time because her mother was gravely ill. In 2007, when attempting to return to Houston, María Inez faced a devastating event.

After María Inez's last visit to Mexico in 2007, she attempted to re-enter the United States and was stopped by Border Patrol agents. She was detained for one week. Later, she made another attempt and was again stopped by Border Patrol agents. This time she showed them someone else's identification, hoping to pass for a US citizen, but was put into a detention center for one month. "It's wrong, it's because they incarcerate you and it's bad, they shackle you like a criminal. . . . Wanting to be with my family is not a crime," she told me. Yet she was charged with and convicted of a felony—tampering with a government record—and placed in a detention center in south Texas. With her conviction came a lifetime bar of re-entry to the United States. She described what happened upon her subsequent deportation:

> They took away $130, my gold ring, my credentials, and everything, and when I got out they said I didn't have anything. . . . When I got on the bus, the driver said, "Who can loan this woman a jacket to cover these letters that she has on her back because when we get to the border, they will mess her up? . . . "Why?" I said, "I didn't do anything wrong, it is not a crime to come, y'all put me in prison because y'all think it is a crime but it is not." Then he said, "No ma'am, why didn't they return your clothes? That's prison clothes."

A young man on the bus loaned her a jacket so she could hide the orange prison uniform she was wearing. Once she made it to her home in Mexico she said she burned the ugly clothes and shoes.

For many years María Inez had made several trips to Mexico, despite the danger and cost. She was the only one in her family who did so.

Mexican migration was historically circular and temporary, but a shift in US immigration policies in the 1980s and 1990s led many undocumented migrants to settle in the United States (Massey and Pren 2012) rather than risk newly difficult border crossings. Even María Inez stopped her circular migration after her 2007 arrest and deportation. During the 1990s the United States began to see a shift in the criminalization of immigration. This criminalization can be traced back to immigration policies that have produced the "illegal" migrant but have also closed off avenues for some migrants to adjust their immigration statuses. One specific law that has facilitated this phenomenon is the 1996 Illegal Immigration Reform and Immigration Responsibility Act (IIRAIRA). This law took away judicial discretion, required mandatory detention for noncitizens, and criminalized illegal entry and re-entry. Indeed, this law transformed some immigration violations into crimes. All this resulted in the mandatory deportations of those convicted of aggravated felonies, regardless of extenuating circumstances, years in the United States, or their family ties to the United States. Legal permanent residents who have committed crimes years ago were also made deportable under this law (Menjívar 2012).

When we spoke in 2013, María Inez had been in the United States for over five consecutive years and has no plans to return to Mexico, although she yearns to go back. The journey has gotten even more difficult, and she is afraid that as she ages, the trip back to the United States will be exponentially harder. Furthermore, her intense fear of being caught again at the border, detained, and imprisoned, coupled with the increased costs associated with the hiring of *coyotes*, has halted her circular migration.

María Inez lives in what Heidy Sarabia (2012) describes as perpetual illegality defined by "the lack of laws to allow Mexican undocumented migrants to adjust their status, the criminalization of extralegal crossing, and the increased judicial processing of undocumented migrants" (Sarabia 2012, 57). The aftermath of María Inez's detention and deportation has created a constant state of anxiety and stress she continues to face daily. She voiced her concerns that she will never be able to legalize her immigration status numerous times throughout our interview. "I tell my daughters, I will not be able to fix, I'll never be able to fix [my papers]. . . . The day that I go is the day I'll never return," she said. María Inez, and millions of others who have been deported from the United States and banned from living in the United States legally, will remain in the shadows and unable to adjust their statuses. They live the consequences associated with perpetual illegality. In fact, María Inez's mere presence of being in the United States makes her a criminal in the eyes of the law. She is now a member of a group I call "forever undocumented," which includes immigrants living in the United States despite being banned. What differentiates María Inez from her daughters who are also undocumented is that María Inez has been banned from being in the United States and there are no current policies being discussed which alleviate the situations of those that live in perpetual illegality. While María Inez's daughters remain hopeful that they will be able to legalize their statuses, María Inez has no hope or dream of doing so.

By focusing on immigration laws, we can also examine the bumpy road some face toward one day legalizing their status. This road can be full of challenges and may be extremely lengthy or even nonexistent for those that have been banned to legally live in the United States for life. Indeed, this road may have detours, while others may face legal dead ends making them "forever undocumented." The results of this legal violence translate into feelings of exclusion and suffering, and can pose negative mental health impacts on undocumented immigrants, their families, and loved ones. María Inez's story illustrates how policies that criminalize immigrants create negative consequences for undocumented migrants like María Inez and her family. By sharing María Inez's story, I highlight how she survives and combats living as a forever undocumented migrant. I show how legal violence impacts María Inez and focus specifically on the stress associated with her forever undocumented status coupled with her fears about growing old as an undocumented immigrant.

Menjívar and Abrego (2012) build on concepts of structural and symbolic violence to conceptualize what they call legal violence. They have described how legal violence manifests itself in the lives of Central American immigrants and highlight how immigration laws are used to criminalize populations. They argue that the nexus of law and crime has been used to normalize the troubling effects that laws have on immigrants of color. Legal violence highlights the mechanisms and processes that immigrants experience today as a result of laws and immigration policies that have criminalized immigrants. Legal violence also captures the social suffering that punitive laws create for immigrants, their families, and loved ones.

The conflation of immigration and criminal law has resulted in practices that produce legal violence. Legal violence is also perpetuated as race-neutral. Indeed, a legal violence framework demonstrates how the criminalization of immigrants also creates a discourse surrounding immigration policies that claim to be color-blind. By focusing on how these laws are enacted, we can see how racial profiling plays out, leading to discrimination and disproportionate numbers of immigrants of color being deported (Golash-Boza and Hondagneu Sotelo 2013). María Inez's lived experiences are impacted by laws and immigration policies that have become increasingly punitive.

María Inez joins an increasing number of immigrants who are growing old as undocumented. "I tell my husband that I feel bad [being] in this country. It is not what one expects. . . . I would like to just cry and cry because it is a very drastic change for me, but for my daughters that arrived when they were young, I don't think so. So for one that is older [living in this country] is really hard." From the estimated 11.5 million undocumented immigrants residing in the United States in 2011, .5 million of this population were fifty-five and older (Hoefer, Rytina, and Baker 2012). Although this number may seem trivial compared to the total undocumented population, we also know that undocumented immigrants are living in the United States for longer periods consecutively (Krogstad, Passel, and Cohn 2016). Thus this number is anticipated to only increase if a path towards legalization remains non-existent. María Inez joins a growing population of older undocumented immigrants who are excluded from social welfare programs like Social Security, Medicare, food stamps, housing, or any other social programs that are available to senior citizens (Angel and Angel 2015).

"Not having papers affects everything. Look, we are here paying taxes and when I won't be able to work, who will help me when I'm older? We are here working and working and in the end, what? I don't like it here, I don't like the doctors, the people, but I stay to be with my family," María Inez described with dread. For María Inez, the situation of growing old as an undocumented immigrant is intensified by her forever undocumented status. This plays out in her life through her experiences with the health care system, the challenges she faces as she ages and as her health deteriorates, and the negative impact on her mental health.

María Inez is convinced she is ill but each time she visits the neighborhood clinic, paying the costs out of pocket, she is turned away and told she is fine. This infuriates her because she continues to feel sick and does not know how to navigate the health care system especially as a poor undocumented aging immigrant that does not speak English. She described this in more detail:

> I go to the doctor and they do lab tests and I don't have anything, I don't have anything. And I'm sick, I'm sick. . . . They charge me a lot, about 120, 130, 170 dollars, nearly every other eight days. But I go to the doctor and I don't have anything, and they draw blood and I don't have anything. They do an ultrasound of my kidneys and the specialist, well she only speaks English, and I did not understand anything, and she was indicating the little crosses which showed my kidneys. In the clinic, I didn't have anything and well it makes me angry. . . . and I tell my husband, what am I doing here? They are going to let me die. . . . Even when I die, I will be upset.

María Inez, like other undocumented immigrants, confronts a myriad of barriers in obtaining health care services. A recent study conducted by Karen Hacker and colleagues (2015), using a systematic approach to examine the literature published in the last ten years, found undocumented immigrants face barriers via policies, the health system, and at the individual level. At the policy level, both laws and policies dictate the access, availability, and service usage for the undocumented population (Chavez 2012; Edward 2014; Rhodes et al. 2015). Indeed one way to exclude a group from obtaining health services is by not providing them health insurance (Sommers 2013; Wallace et al. 2013). Undocumented immigrants are a vulnerable group that is impacted by their exclusion of insurance programs that are not made available to them (Derose, Escarce, and Lurie 2007; Sommers 2013). These laws and policies, in fact, bar access to health care services (Derose et al. 2007; Sommers 2013). The Affordable Care Act (ACA) also excludes undocumented immigrants from obtaining public insurance or any type of private coverage available through the health insurance exchanges it established (Sommers 2013; Wallace et al. 2013; Zuckerman, Waidmann, and Lawton 2011).

At the health system level, the focus was on the bureaucratic confusion, capacity, and discriminatory practices that unfold in health care systems (Chanlder et al. 2012; Derose et al. 2007; Wallace et al. 2013). At the individual level, undocumented immigrants may face a fear of deportation, lack of financial resources, communication barriers—not only based on limited English proficiency but also cultural discomfort with the ways in which dominant groups communicate (Chandler et al. 2012; Chavez 2012; Ponce, Hays, and Cunningham 2006)—shame in seeking services and/or concerns about being stigmatized for seeking services (Chandler et al. 2012; Hilfinger, McEwen, and Clark 2015), and little knowledge about how to navigate the health care system (Bustamante et al. 2012).

For María Inez, this is coupled with her distrust of doctors. Doctors that she believes do not have her best interest at heart. In one of the clinic visits, she described how she was turned away from asking a nutritionist questions because she is not diabetic, although she has been told she is pre-diabetic, and actually did not know the doctor was a nutritionist. She juxtaposed her US health care experiences with the health care system in Mexico, which she views favorably. Although María Inez described many strategies to avoid getting sick, and when sick she described a litany of health care strategies including: trying home remedies, phoning family and friends in Mexico to describe her symptoms and getting advice on which medicines to take, or obtaining under-the-counter Mexican medicines. After exhausting her list of strategies, and still not feeling better, she would finally convince herself to visit the neighborhood clinic.

However, formal mental health care for María Inez is nonexistent. Even though she described experiencing depressive episodes in the United States, she cannot afford therapy and prioritizes her physical health over her mental health. She also fears that if she sought mental health care, she would be turned away, as she was by the nutritionist. During our interview, I had María Inez answer some questions that have been used by mental health providers, researchers, and clinicians to capture depressive symptoms. The set of questions, known as the Center for Epidemiological

Studies Depression Scale (CES-D), is easily administered, has high validity and reliability, is easily accessible to the public, and is the most commonly used measure for depression. Answers are assigned point values and the total scores range from 0–60, with higher scores indicating more depressive symptoms. Previous studies have shown that a score of 25 or higher indicates a major depressive disorder (Haringsma et al. 2004). María Inez scored a total of 54 on the CES-D scale. However, her mental health remains untreated.

Today, María Inez works as a babysitter for her grandchildren, recycles metal, and decorates eggs to sell for the Easter holiday. She is trying to save as much money as possible and dreams of returning to Mexico one day. She knows that the longer she lives in the United States, the older she will become and thus her health care needs will continue to increase. She also knows that she will remain excluded because she will be forever undocumented. Yet, she stays hopeful that immigration reform, with a path toward citizenship for the millions of undocumented immigrants currently residing in the United States, including her children, will take place in her lifetime. She hopes that her children will one day have an opportunity to legalize their statuses so that she can return to Mexico and so that they can travel to visit her. "I tell my daughters that the day I'm really old and sick I am going to go back to México and die in my land. . . . I tell them, México is everything for me."

María Inez's experience is not unique. Her story captures the dismal reality of a growing aging undocumented population that lives as forever undocumented in perpetual illegality. Given that she has been banned from living in the United States, she endures additional risks even as she attempts to obtain health care. Her story is suggestive of the need for more research to examine the cumulative inequities that undocumented immigrants face as they grow old in a social milieu that continues to push them toward living in the shadows. María Inez's story also shows the human costs of current immigration policies—the tenuous situation as María Inez ages, her difficulty in obtaining health care, and her deteriorating mental health.

María Inez's story, and the stories of those in this book that have been deported and are now living in their countries of birth like Juan Carlos Guevara, Paloma, Ezequiel, Santiago, those introduced to us by Jill Anderson, and those like Sergio who live in the United States after previously being deported, are not being discussed in the current US political debates. The reality is that the United States continues to ignore those that have been processed by the government, marked as "criminal aliens," deported (including those living in the United States and in their native countries), and banned from entering the United States. Consequently, the numbers of those that fall into the category of "forever undocumented" will only increase, further stratifying the undocumented population and pushing some deeper into the margins. Moreover, if immigration and health care debates do not provide viable solutions for the undocumented population, the gap of those that are aging while undocumented will consequently be widened. The stories shared in this book also demonstrate the human suffering associated with living undocumented, the aftermath of deportations, and the broader impacts this has beyond the individual, extending into the lives of family members and loved ones of the undocumented, all which are indicative of deep-rooted problems that desperately need reform.

Acknowledgements:

I thank María Inez and her family for sharing their life experiences with me. I am grateful for the funding I received to undertake this research including the Ford Foundation, the American Sociological Association Minority Fellowship Program, and the Race and Ethnic Studies Institute at Texas A&M University. I'm also grateful to the NRSA Mental Health Postdoctoral Fellowship for providing the space to write this chapter. Finally, I am thankful to Heidy Sarabia, Lorena Murga, Eugenia Conde, and Will Hall for reading and commenting on this chapter.

Notes

1. This research was supported by the National Research Service Award Postdoctoral Traineeship from the National Institute of Mental Health sponsored by Cecil G. Sheps Center for Health Services Research, University of North Carolina at Chapel Hill, and the Department of Psychiatry and Behavioral Sciences, Duke University School of Medicine, Grant No: T32 MH019117

References

Angel, Ronald J., and Jacqueline L. Angel. 2015. *Latinos in an Aging World: Social, Psychological, and Economic Perspectives.* New York, NY: Routledge Press.

Bustamante, Arturo Vargas, Hai Fang, Jeremiah Garza, Olivia Carter-Pokras, Steven P. Wallace, John A. Rizzo, and Alexander N. Ortega. 2012. "Variations in Healthcare Access and Utilization among Mexican Immigrants: The Role of Documentation Status." *Journal of Immigrant and Minority Health* 14 (1): 146–55.

Chandler, Juliet T. Ruth E. Malone, Lisa M. Thompson, and Roberta S. Rehm. 2012. "'*No me ponían mucha importancia*': Care-Seeking Experiences of Undocumented Mexican Immigrant Women with Chronic Illness." *Advances in Nursing Science* 35 (2): E24–E36.

Chavez, Leo R. 2012. "Undocumented Immigrants and Their Use of Medical Services in Orange County, California." *Social Science & Medicine* 74 (6): 887–93.

Chen, Alice Hm, Mara K. Youdelman, and Jamie Brooks. 2007. "The Legal Framework for Language Access in Healthcare Settings: Title VI and Beyond." *Journal of General Internal Medicine* 22 (2): 362–67.

Derose, Kathryn Pitkin, José J. Escarce, and Nicole Lurie. 2007. "Immigrants and Health Care: Sources of Vulnerability." *Health Affairs* 26 (5): 1258–68.

Edward, Jean. 2014. "Undocumented Immigrants and Access to Health Care: Making a Case for Policy Reform." *Policy, Politics, & Nursing Practice* 15 (1–2): 5–14.

Golash-Boza, Tanya. 2015. *Deported: Immigrant Policing, Disposable Labor, and Global Capitalism.* New York: New York University Press.

Golash-Boza, Tanya and Pierrette Hondagneu-Sotelo. 2013. "Latino Immigrant Men and the Deportation Crisis: A Gendered Racial Removal Program." *Latino Studies* 11 (3): 271–92.

Hacker, Karen, Maria Anies, Barbara L. Folb, and Leah Zallman. 2015. "Barriers to Health Care for Undocumented Immigrants: A Literature Review." *Risk Management and Healthcare Policy* 8: 175–83.

Haringsma, Rimke, G. I. Engels, Aartjan T. F. Beekman, and Philip Spinhoven. 2004. "The Criterion Validity of the Center for Epidemiological Studies Depression Scale (CES-D) in a Sample of Self-Referred Elders with Depressive Symptomatology." *International Journal of Geriatric Psychiatry* 19 (6): 558–63.

Hoefer, Michael, Nancy Rytina, and Bryan Baker. 2012. "Estimates of the Unauthorized Immigrant Population Residing in the United States: January 2011." *Population Estimates, Office of Immigration Statistics, Department of Homeland Security.*

Hilfinger Messias, D. K., Marylyn M. McEwen, and Lauren Clark. 2015. "The Impact and Implications of Undocumented Immigration on Individual and Collective Health in the United States." *Nursing Outlook* 63 (1): 86–94.

Massey, Douglas S. and Karen A. Pren. 2012. "Unintended Consequences of US Immigration Policy: Explaining the Post-1965 Surge from Latin America." *Population and Development Review* 38 (1): 1–29.

Menjívar, Cecilia. 2014. "The "Poli-Migra": Multilayered Legislation, Enforcement Practices, and What We Can Learn About and From Today's Approaches." *American Behavioral Scientist* 58 (13): 1805–19.

———. 2012. "U.S. Immigration Law, Immigrant Illegality, and Immigration Reform." In *Agenda for Social Justice: Solutions 2012*, ed. Glenn W. Muschert, Kathleen Ferraro, Brian V. Klocke, Robert Perrucci and Jon Shefner, 63–71. Knoxville, TN: Society for the Study of Social Problems.

Menjívar, Cecilia and Leisy J. Abrego. 2012. "Legal Violence: Immigration Law and the Lives of Central American Immigrants." *American Journal of Sociology* 117 (5): 1380–421.

Passel, Jeffrey, and D. Cohn. 2016. "Overall Number of U.S. Unauthorized Immigrants Holds Steady Since 2009." *Pew Hispanic Center*, Washington, DC.

Ponce, Ninez A., Ron D. Hays, and William E. Cunningham. 2006. "Linguistic Disparities in Health Care Access and Health Status among Older Adults." *Journal of General Internal Medicine* 21 (7): 786–91.

Rhodes, Scott D., Lilli Mann, Florence M. Simán, Eunyoung Song, Jorge Alonzo, Mario Downs, Emma Lawlor, Omar Martinez, Christina J. Sun, Mary Claire O'Brien, Beth A. Reboussin, and Mark A. Hall. 2015. "The Impact of Local Immigration Enforcement Policies on the Health of Immigrant Hispanics/Latinos in the United States." *American Journal of Public Health* 105 (2): 329–37.

Sarabia, Heidy. 2012. "Perpetual Illegality: Results of Border Enforcement and Policies for Mexican Undocumented Migrants in the United States." *Analyses of Social Issues and Public Policy* 12 (1): 49–67.

Sommers, Benjamin D. 2013. "Stuck Between Health and Immigration Reform: Care for Undocumented Immigrants." *New England Journal of Medicine* 369 (7): 593–95.

Wallace, Steven P., Michael Rodriguez, Imelda Padilla-Frausto, Armando Arredondo, and Emanuel Orozco. 2013. "Improving Access to Health Care for Undocumented Immigrants in the United States." *Salud Pública de México* 5 (Suppl 4): S508–S514.

Zuckerman, Stephen, Timothy A. Waidmann, and Emily Lawton. 2011. "Undocumented Immigrants, Left Out of Health Reform, Likely to Continue to Grow as Share of the Uninsured." *Health Affairs* 30 (10): 1997–2004.

22

Sergio Rodriguez's Dream Deferred: Illegality, Deportation, and the Long-Term Impacts of Lives in Limbo[1]

Roberto G. Gonzales

Roberto G. Gonzales is assistant professor of Education at Harvard University Graduate School of Education and author of Lives in Limbo: Undocumented and Coming of Age in America (University of California Press, 2016).

ROBERTO: What does being American mean to you?

SERGIO: Being part of this culture. You know, I was raised here, what can I say? If I go to Mexico I can't speak straight Spanish, you know, they would kick me out. I mean, what am I gonna do? If I get deported one way or another I would have to come back here because this is my home. I can't go over there. If I go over there everyone will tease me. I feel home over here, but they still don't accept me.

In 2003 I first interviewed Sergio Rodriguez, a young man who had moved to Los Angeles from Mexico as toddler. He told me that he was conflicted about his identity, largely because he felt rejected by the home he knew, and feared rejection by the home of his birth. He was proud to be Mexican. He did not identify as Mexican-American or the pan-ethnic term, Latino, used to group together related ethnic groups from Latin America. He loved all things Mexican—music, food, art, sports teams. He told me that he almost got a very large Aztec calendar tattooed on his back.

But he felt a strange ambivalence. His only memories of Mexico were from childhood. Because he could not travel there, he could only patch together images of his homeland through family stories and television. He told me, "I grew up here, but I can't [travel to] see where I was born. I wish I could, but I can't. I'm not from here, but I don't know there." Sergio worried that he would not fit in.

Sergio also yearned for a day he could call himself an American citizen. But even though he had spent nearly all of his life in the United States he was not an American citizen. He lacked a Social Security number, the nine digits that would affirm his status as an American.

What does it mean to have lived most of one's life in the United States but, nevertheless, be deportable? Between 2003 and 2015 I followed a group of undocumented young adults who had migrated to Los Angeles as children and who had grown up in communities throughout the metropolitan area. These young people are part of a group academics like me refer to as the 1.5 generation, because they fit somewhere between the immigrant first and the American-born second generation, but are more commonly known as "Dreamers." The median age at migration of the 150 young adults I followed in Los Angeles was six. Because they migrate as children they receive most of their schooling in the United States. Their early years are defined by the same experiences and similar processes of socialization as their US-citizen classmates. However, as they grow older, they share more in common with their parents, whose legal limitations serve as bright boundaries that elucidate their outsiderness. In a sense, they straddle two worlds. They have varying memories of and connections to their countries of birth, however, for many of them growing up in the United States, "their roots are on the wrong side of their lives."[2]

Stories of Dreamers' academic achievements and of their lack of responsibility for their situations, having been brought across the border by their parents, have drawn attention and sympathy to their plight. These narratives have carefully located the policy problem in the areas of access to postsecondary education and high-skilled jobs. In an era when returns on education have become increasingly high, these young people fall significantly behind their native-born and citizen peers. This level of blocked access represents one of the biggest civil rights issues of our time.

However, exclusion from higher education and employment is only part of the Dreamers' story. Many of these young people grow up in impoverished households where at least one of their parents is also undocumented. The sting of legal exclusions during adolescence and the stigma of being different from peers at a critical phase of life are debilitating and spirit-crushing. And the ever-present threat of deportation frames everyday lives with fear and anxiety. Many of the young people I met either did not identify with or were not associated with the Dreamer label. Moreover, they struggled to make adolescent and adult transitions amid shifting legal realities and an intensified enforcement regime.

Sergio was eighteen years old when I met him; he was attending a continuation school housed in a community center in Southern California where I was conducting preliminary research for what would become a twelve-year study. Sergio was outgoing and popular among the students at the center. His boyish grin and youthful demeanor belied the "troublemaker" label that dogged him throughout his high school years. But the supportive environment fostered by his teachers and the staff at the community center provided the assurance that he belonged. In 2002, Sergio, was making steady progress toward his high school diploma, he was the community center's go-to technology assistant, and he was well-liked by fellow students and staff alike. He was often at the center from dawn till dusk, an enthusiastic participant in many of the center's programs. Few had doubts about his level of motivation. That summer I had several conversations with Sergio. Ultimately, I kept up with him for more than twelve years.

Sergio had moved to California with his mom and his older brother when he was three years old. The early years were especially difficult for his family, as his mom struggled to make ends meet on her meager wages as a seamstress. She took on extra work to earn more money, but the extra hours translated to less time with her two sons. Even with the added work, she barely had enough money to meet all of her expenses. Sergio's family bounced around, making their home in other people's living rooms, dining rooms, and even in another family's garage. Eventually Sergio's mom remarried and her family enjoyed greater financial security as a result. Nevertheless, Sergio worried. His stepfather was a good provider, and was seldom out of work for significant periods of time. But without much formal education his job options were limited to low-wage labor sectors.

Growing up, Sergio lived in nine different homes. He seldom saw his stepfather and his mom was often tired when he came home from school. Moving around so much limited Sergio's ability to form lasting friendships. But he enjoyed playing handball on the school's courts and he liked to tell jokes. This was his currency on the school playground.

Around his sixteenth birthday life began to change for him. His friends were starting to drive and to take jobs after school. Naturally, Sergio wanted to follow suit. However, when he went to take the written exam for his driver's permit his world was turned upside down. He was told at the Department of Motor Vehicles that he needed a Social Security number in order to apply. So he went home and asked his mom. That was when she told him that he didn't have one, that he did not have legal status. "That really sucked," he told me, "it really messed me up."

For the first time in Sergio's young life, he was being told that he could not join friends because of his immigration status. It was unsettling, debilitating. He began to think about the other ways his status would affect his life. Frustration and despair colored all of his interactions. He told me that he could no longer see his future and that he felt there was little point in trying.

He started acting out in school and began ditching classes. Sergio was unwilling to disclose his secret to teachers or to other school personnel. He was afraid of what they might do if they knew that he was undocumented. But he was also bothered that nobody reached out to him. He told me, "I just felt like nobody there cared about me. I was a troublemaker, and that's all they wanted to see. Nobody knew me." After an accumulation of truancies and altercations with other students, Sergio was expelled. He had not even finished his sophomore year.

The 1982 Supreme Court decision in *Plyler v. Doe* all but guarantees undocumented children access to public K–12 schools. But it does not guarantee them a good education. The vast majority of undocumented children live in poverty. Increasingly, they are in resource-challenged communities and attend overcrowded, de facto segregated schools, with high student-to-counselor ratios, that are unable to provide all of their students the resources they need to be successful. In California, students face grave challenges. Low-income schools are marked by high teacher turnover and a relatively high proportion of teachers lack proper qualifications. As of 2013–14, eight of California's ten largest school districts, six of which are in the Los Angeles Metropolitan Area, were majority-minority. The Los Angeles Unified School District has an 89.6 percent minority student population, with more than 75 percent of their students receiving free or reduced lunches. California ranks thirty-second in the nation in high school completion and graduation rates are especially low in the Los Angeles area; thirty-five Los Angeles County high schools are counted among the lowest-performing schools in the state and only two-thirds of Los Angeles Unified School District students graduate from high school. These conditions are particularly disadvantageous for low-income, immigrant, and Latino students like Sergio.

Sergio was not the typical "Dreamer." His walls weren't covered with awards and other evidence of academic achievement. He wasn't even in the top half of his class. He wasn't involved in extracurricular activities at his school or in his community. Very few reporters or politicians highlight stories like Sergio's, stories that reflect more ordinary pathways, but they are not uncommon, given the number of undocumented youth living in poverty.

In Sergio's large high school classes, he had no one he felt he could turn to. There was no teacher or coach who had taken him under their wings. Sergio had no one he felt he could turn to, to confide in. He had not developed trusting relationships with teachers or counselors at his school. His immigration problems went unnoticed. But leaving school meant exiting a world that was legally permissible and entering one that was increasingly defined by his inability to do mundane things like drive, work, and vote.

Several years before I met Sergio, his mom had remarried. Her husband was a lawful permanent resident and in 2000 took steps to sponsor his new family for an adjustment of their immigration status. This was an exciting possibility for Sergio. However, there was no timeline. The then-Immigration and Nationality Service (INS) faced a tremendous backlog and there were many stories in the community of long waits. In 2003 Sergio told me, "Supposedly, I'm waiting for their approval, but you know, now everyone has told me once the approval comes, you have to wait six months [to be] approved so I can get a work permit. I don't know what to do. I've been waiting for three years."

The waiting put Sergio in a state of limbo. He faced a difficult decision: Should he put his life on hold while he waited or try to move forward, perhaps by pursuing a job or driving without a license, knowing that in doing so he risked arrest, detention, and deportation? He chose to take the safe route in hope of someday being able to work and drive without worry. During the years Sergio was going to continuation school, he worked only occasionally, taking temporary jobs in catering or helping at parties for a day or weekend. He avoided all forms of ongoing employment and, whenever he needed to get somewhere, he walked or asked friends for rides. He told me that he didn't want to jeopardize his chances by getting caught.

> The thing is that I've been offered job(s), but the thing is that it messes me up. There's ways around it but let's say okay, there's a job I've been offered, if I get it, I have to buy fake papers, if I get caught with fake papers, that's a federal offense so I'll be screwed, and I mean, I'm closer than I've ever been on getting my papers. I don't want to mess it up with something like that so I can't get it later on.

But the wait turned out to be much longer than Sergio had thought, and time did not bring positive change. By 2004, he was becoming noticeably frustrated with the wait. He began falling behind in his studies and the staff started to worry about his declining motivation. He told me, "When you don't have papers you're not really motivated . . . you can't go anywhere."

Between 2004 and 2006, Sergio's life changed significantly. He turned twenty-one and aged-out of eligibility to be sponsored by his stepfather. To make matters worse, his family discovered that the person they had hired as an attorney to help them with their immigration case was merely a notary public, representing himself as qualified to offer legal advice and services concerning immigration. This confusion is due in part to the meaning, in Spanish of the title, *notario publico*. While a notary public in the United States is only authorized to witness the signature of forms, in many Latin American countries the title refers to a person who has received the equivalent of a law degree and who is licensed to represent others before the government. In this case, Sergio's family had paid large amounts of money to a person who was not qualified to handle their case.

Over the years this gentleman had asked them for thousands of dollars to process various forms. In the end, while they were waiting for news about their immigration case, he was pocketing their hard-earned money. No documents were ever filed, and they lost valuable time.

They later learned that he had victimized many members of their community.

Meanwhile, Sergio met a young woman and they had a child together. The new family was no longer living under their parents' roofs and Sergio felt compelled to assume greater financial responsibility. He could no longer linger in limbo. He took a full-time job at a factory thirty minutes away from his apartment. Despite his diminished hopes of becoming a citizen, Sergio knew that working was risky. He had little choice, but there were ways for him to be less visible, less likely to get ensnared in the immigration dragnet. He met a coworker who lived near him and offered him money for gas if they could carpool to work. However, Sergio's coworker was not squeaky clean.

One evening after work, as Sergio was riding home with his coworker, local police pulled them over. The tattoos covering his coworker's bald head were a flashing sign to police of potential criminality. As the officer began questioning the two young men he noticed drug paraphernalia in a cup holder in plain sight. He asked them to get out of the car. Searching the car, the police found a homemade explosive device. Sergio was unaware of the contents of the car. It didn't matter. He was charged as an accomplice to a federal crime and ordered to serve a three-year prison term.

In 2009, after he finished his prison time, Sergio was deported to Tijuana. At age twenty-five, he found himself in a country he had not visited since he left as a young boy. The nostalgia he conveyed in our 2003 interview for a homeland he never really knew was being directly challenged. He had to start over from scratch.

This unfortunate development brings to light an important paradox for young people, like Sergio: They can make strong claims to social or cultural citizenship based on their longtime presence in the United States and attachments to people, places, and institutions, but they can also be stopped, detained, and removed from the country. This fragile sense of belonging strongly underscores the salience of the law in framing their lives.

Sergio spent two and a half years in Tijuana. He was homeless off and on and took odd jobs to make ends meet. He eventually met an older woman who rented him a room in her apartment above a loud bar. He later told me that these were the toughest years of his life. His experience in Mexico was a tough dose of reality—far from the nostalgic views he had once held. He became very depressed, but in the process realized he was much more resilient than he had imagined.

Sergio returned to Los Angeles in 2012. He was vague about the details of his return, and he was now even more cautious of authorities. He told me that he was doing his best to stay "under the radar." He found work in an assembly plant a couple miles away from his home. He walks to work. As a person deported on criminal grounds, if Sergio were apprehended by ICE he could face a mandatory ten-to-fifteen-year prison sentence. Avoiding arrest and deportation was even more important now that he had two children. Ten years prior he clung onto the hope that his stepfather could assist him in attaining a pathway to legal status. However, following his arrest and deportation, Sergio now has no viable pathway to legalization.

Back in 2004, before his arrest, Sergio told me:

> I can't do anything that could help me. I'm stuck. That's the point, I'm stuck. I mean, with citizenship I could get a good job, I could finish my education in a good college. If you don't have papers you can't do anything. You can't move into a new area, into a good area. You can't buy a house. You can't buy a car. You can't do anything. That's what's holding me back, that's what's holding a lot of people back.

Over the years, Sergio's world has become increasingly small, narrowly circumscribed by legal limitations and his deportability.

There are more than two million young people like Sergio who have grown up in the United States but whose lives are marked by exclusion, fear of deportation, and a fragile sense of belonging. I began this work in the wake of the introduction of the federal DREAM Act (Development, Relief, and Education for Alien Minors) in 2001. At the time, there was a general recognition by Congress that the circumstances of children were different from those of their parents or other adults. In 2016, fifteen years later, Congress has yet to pass legislation that could assist them. Instead, the years have been very cruel to many of them. Time has slowed their progress and dampened their spirits. Their legal circumstances have dramatically circumscribed their everyday lives within the United States. And, for young people like Sergio who join an estimated half million others who have returned to Mexico, current deportation policies have not only sown anxiety and fear, they have (re)severed their roots.

Notes

1. Parts of Sergio's story appears in Roberto G. Gonzales, *Lives in Limbo: Undocumented and Coming of Age in America*, Oakland: University of California Press, 2016; and Roberto G. Gonzales, "Learning to Be Illegal: Undocumented Youth and Shifting Legal Contexts in the Transition to Adulthood," *American Sociological Review* 76, no. 4 (2011): 602–19.
2. Zúñiga, Victor. 2012 "Comment" following "'Awakening to a Nightmare': Abjectivity and Illegality in the Lives of Undocumented 1.5 Generation Latino Immigrants in the United States," by Roberto G. Gonzales and Leo R. Chavez, *Current Anthropology* 53 (3): 255–81.

Epilogue

The stories in this book make it clear that immigration law enforcement has long been traumatic for immigrants. The election of Donald Trump has exacerbated the fear of deportation in immigrant communities, and the effects of these fears extend far beyond the immigrants themselves. As Trump has transformed his campaign promises into draconian executive orders, this fear has intensified. It is also becoming increasingly clear that the intention of Trump's rhetoric and actions is primarily to create fear, which makes immigrants and their families even more vulnerable.

Once in office, Trump wasted no time before implementing fear tactics. In the run-up to the presidential election, candidate Trump had argued that the United States should prevent Muslims from entering the United States.[1] Shortly after taking office, Trump signed an executive order called *Protecting the Nation from Foreign Terrorist Entry into the United States*,[2] which temporarily banned the admission to the United States of people from seven majority-Muslim countries: Iraq, Syria, Iran, Libya, Somalia, Sudan, and Yemen. The ban was implemented with flights from these countries in mid-air, which caused chaos and widespread fear. The fact that the ban was implemented with so little thought and so much fanfare is a clear sign that a major goal of this Executive Order was to create terror in these communities. There was a huge outcry on social media and thousands flocked to airports to protest the ban. Several states and individual plaintiffs sued the federal government on the grounds that the ban was not constitutional. On February 3, 2017, a district judge in Washington state suspended the ban nationwide with a temporary restraining order. Although the ban was lifted, the fear that any immigrant or visitor from those seven countries could be denied entry to the United States at any time persists.

While campaigning, Trump promised to repeal Obama's executive orders, including Deferred Action for Childhood Arrivals (DACA). As of this writing in February 2017, DACA remains in effect. Some immigrant youth such as Rafael (Martinez, this volume) have been able to legalize because of loopholes created by DACA, and are now relatively safe from deportation due to their permanent legal status. However, most DACA recipients have not been able to legalize and remain in legal limbo. If DACA is repealed, they will go back to being undocumented and may be at a higher risk for deportation because of information they gave to the government to acquire DACA. Fears were heightened among DACAmented youth when, on February 14, 2017, a young man with DACA, Daniel Ramirez Medina, was detained during an ICE home raid. ICE agents claimed they detained him due to his tattoo, which reads "La Paz BCS," the name of the capital of Baja California Sur (BCS), the state in Mexico where Ramirez Medina was born ("la paz" is also Spanish for "peace"). ICE agents determined the tattoo to be gang-related despite Ramirez Medina's claims to the contrary and his lack of a criminal background.[3] Although it is not clear this was a lawful detention, his arrest sent a strong message to DACAmented youth that they are not safe during a Trump presidency.

On the campaign trail, Trump criticized Obama for not deporting enough criminals. Shortly after taking office, on January 25, 2017, Trump issued an executive order called *Enhancing Public Safety in the Interior of the United States*,[4] which includes a priority system that is different from that promulgated by Obama. Whereas Obama prioritized immigrants who had been *convicted* of crimes, Trump's order includes immigrants who have only been *charged* with a criminal offense or even who *may* have committed a crime but not yet been charged—giving immigration enforcement officers broad leeway to deport people like Daniel Ramirez Medina who have no criminal record. Whereas during Obama's second term, immigrants without a criminal record were relatively safe from deportation, this is no longer the case under Trump as the deportation dragnet has broadened significantly.

Notably, Trump has broadened the number of people to be targeted for deportation, yet it is not clear how many people will actually be deported during his presidency. In the run-up to the election, Trump also promised to create a deportation force that would dramatically increase the number of deportees. Historically, deportations have increased (or decreased) incrementally, as the executive branch needs time to build capacity for deportations. The plan of the Trump administration is to triple the number of ICE agents. This tripling will not only require considerable congressional appropriations, it also will take years to hire, train, and deploy 10,000 ICE agents. Moreover, it is not clear how much of an effect the tripling of ICE agents would have. Direct ICE arrests of undocumented people through home or worksite raids are a highly inefficient way to deport people. In 2016, ICE agents took 65,332 people into custody, but the vast majority of these people were first apprehended by police officers, and then handed over to ICE agents. Only 20 percent of these people—about 13,000—were directly arrested by ICE agents in home or worksite raids.[5] It is not clear that an increase in the number of ICE agents will significantly increase the number of arrests made after an apprehension by local law enforcement. An increase here depends on the willingness of localities to cooperate, and there are some signs that local police are not thrilled with the prospect of enforcing immigration laws.[6]

A significant increase in ICE deportations would also require a substantial expansion of immigration judges as well as immigration detention centers. There is currently a tremendous backlog in immigration courts. As of January 2017, there was a backlog of half a million cases. The current average wait time for an immigration hearing is thus two years.[7] Under current laws, in order to deport a person who lives in the United States, there needs to be some sort of court process. Unless Congress changes these laws or appropriates a lot more money for immigration judges, Trump will not be able to increase the number of deportations much beyond the current historic highs. Immigration detention is also currently at full capacity. Congress could appropriate additional funds to house detainees. The quickest way to do that would be to take advantage of the available bed space in private prisons. This could increase capacity from about 40,000 to perhaps as much as 60,000 detention beds. However, any capacity beyond that would likely have to be built. Building prisons is costly and it is unclear how much political will there is to build additional bed space for immigrants. With these limitations in mind, it is clear that prospects for undocumented migrants and their families will not improve under a Trump presidency. With a Republican-dominated Congress, any hopes for comprehensive immigration reform will have to wait. Nevertheless, we can expect for immigrants and immigrant rights activists to continue to organize and demand justice for immigrants in the United States. The passage of DACA was due in large part to pressure from grassroots organizers. Since the introduction of the DREAM Act in Congress in 2001, organizations such as United We Dream, National Day Laborer Organizing Network, and the Immigrant Youth Justice League have pushed for the passage of the DREAM Act as well as comprehensive immigration reform. In 2006, these and other organizations led massive marches in major cities around the country demanding an end to the criminalization of immigrants. This movement has gained renewed energy with the election of Donald Trump and his implementation of anti-immigrant executive orders and policies. The youth organizers who lead this movement call themselves "undocumented and unafraid," a slogan that is more important now than ever.

Notes

1. Reuters. "Donald Trump Calls for Complete Ban on Muslims Entering the US – Video." *The Guardian*. Guardian News and Media, 07 Dec. 2015. Web. 21 Feb. 2017. <https://www.theguardian.com/us-news/video/2015/dec/08/donald-trump-calls-for-complete-ban-on-muslims-entering-the-us-video>.
2. Trump, Donald J. "EXECUTIVE ORDER: PROTECTING THE NATION FROM FOREIGN TERRORIST ENTRY INTO THE UNITED STATES." *The White House*. The United States Government, 30 Jan. 2017. Web. 21 Feb. 2017. <https://www.whitehouse.gov/the-press-office/2017/01/27/executive-order-protecting-nation-foreign-terrorist-entry-united-states>.
3. Shapiro, Nina. "Do Feds Have Evidence That Detained Dreamer Is a Gang Member beyond Tattoo?" *The Seattle Times*. The Seattle Times Company,

16 Feb. 2017. Web. 21 Feb. 2017. <http://www.seattletimes.com/seattle-news/feds-says-detained-dreamer-is-gang-member-lawyer-denies-it/>.

4. Trump, Donald J. "Executive Order: Enhancing Public Safety in the Interior of the United States." *The White House*. The United States Government, 25 Jan. 2017. Web. 21 Feb. 2017. <https://www.whitehouse.gov/the-press-office/2017/01/25/presidential-executive-order-enhancing-public-safety-interior-united>.
5. TRAC Immigration. "ICE Immigration Raids: A Primer." *Transactional Records Access Clearinghouse (TRAC) - Comprehensive, Independent, and Nonpartisan Information on Federal Enforcement, Staffing and Funding*. N.p., 13 Feb. 2017. Web. 21 Feb. 2017. <http://trac.syr.edu/immigration/reports/459/>.
6. Calfas, Jennifer. "LAPD Chief: My Officers Won't Comply with Trump's Immigration Ban."*TheHill*. N.p., 29 Jan. 2017. Web. 21 Feb. 2017. <http://thehill.com/blogs/blog-briefing-room/news/316761-lapd-chef-my-officers-wont-comply-with-trumps-immigration-ban>.
7. "Immigration Court Backlog Tool" TRACImmigration. Accessed November 10, 2016 from http://trac.syr.edu/phptools/immigration/court_backlog/